Pastor John Corbly

and his neighbors in

Greene Township.

Don Corbly

Cover art by author

ISBN 978-0-557-95264-9

Printed and published in the United States of America.

Also by this author available at Lulu.com
and other major internet book sellers.

Mesquite Roots

Pastor John Corbly

The Last Colonials

Letterf, Journalf, and Diarief of ye Colonial America

In memory of our parents,
Earl and Fay Corbly

For my children, their descendants, and other readers.

Contents

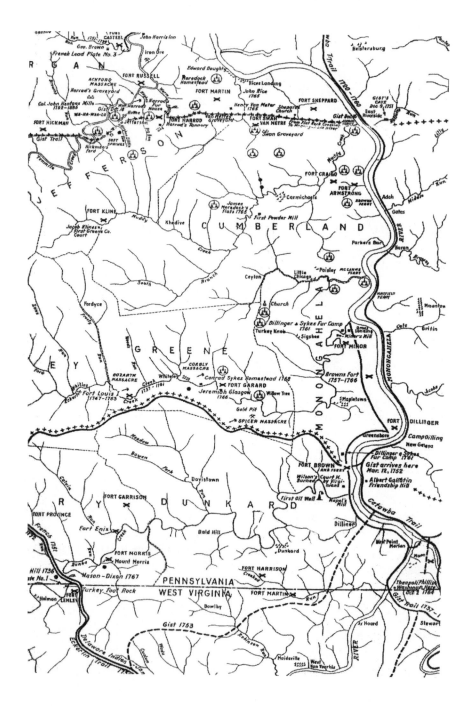

Archealogical map of southern Washington County, Virginia. The center portion became Greene Township, Greene County, Pennsylvania, in 1796.

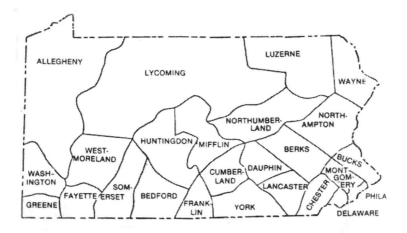

1796 map of Pennsylvania counties. Year when Greene County
was organized out of Washington County.

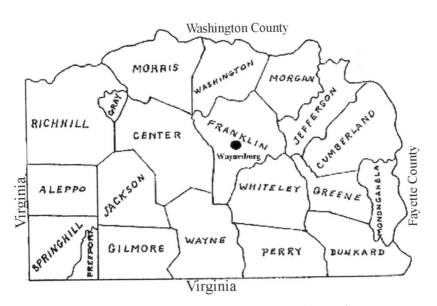

1796 Greene County Townships. County seat at Waynesburg.

Jefferson Township

Cumberland
Township

Whiteley Township

Monongahela Township

Dunkard Township

1796 platt of Greene Township, Greene County, Pennsylvania.

PART ONE

GREENE TOWNSHIP

The western boundaries of the Colonies of Virginia and Pennsylvania, as established by their Charters, were not spelled out concisely and led to decades of hostility between them. The Charter of Virginia predated that of Pennsylvania by 72 years, giving the Governor of Virginia a previous right of ownership of the disputed land.

In 1606 James I, (1566-1625), established by charter the Virginia Company of London and the Virginia Company of Plymouth. The Virginia Company of London was given permission to plant a colony 100 miles square between latitude 34°N and latitude 41°N in North America. The Virginia Company of Plymouth was chartered to found a colony between latitude 38°N and latitude 45°N. The overlapping area was open to settlement by either company, except that neither Company was permitted to establish a colony within 100 miles of the other. By 1609 the Plymouth Company had become inactive and the London Company became the only holder of a charter. The King's Governor of the Colony of Virginia believed that its chartered land extended westward to the Pacific Ocean and included all land north of the Ohio River.

King Charles II, (1660-1685), signed the Charter of Pennsylvania on March 4, 1681. It was awarded to William Penn in repayment of the King's debt to Penn's father, Admiral Penn, and included the land between the 39th and 42nd degrees of north latitude and from the Delaware River westward for five degrees of longitude.

The Governors of the Colonies of Virginia and Pennsylvania bitterly contested ownership of the disputed lands until their arguments were set aside during the Revolutionary War. After the War, the dispute over land ownership was finally put to rest by the completion of the Mason and Dixon Line in 1784 which established surveyed boundaries for the first time. That stopped the overt hostilities that had occurred between Virginia and Pennsylvania, but straightening out the legal ownership of individual tracts of land did not begin until 1785.

During its first hundred years the Colony of Virginia existed as a group of parishes governed by a succession of Proprietary Governors; the first was Edward Maria Wingfield in 1607. By 1712 Virginia was still divided into 49 parishes. In 1734 St. George's Parish was renamed Spotsylvania and St. Mark's Parish was renamed Orange. Spotsylvania County was divided and from it was formed Orange County which comprised the whole of the Colony of western Virginia.

In the 1720s increasing numbers of emigrants were settling in Orange County, Virginia, and it became apparent that new counties needed to be formed to absorb the influx. In 1738 two Shenandoah Valley counties were carved out of Orange; Frederick and Augusta Counties, the latter "to extend to the utmost limits of Virginia." That meant that Augusta County was to extend westward and include British territory all the way to the Pacific Ocean and north of the Ohio River.

The Colony of Virginia formed Augusta County in 1738, but its government was not organized until 1745. It was the parent county, in whole or in part, of Bath, Botetourt, Frederick, Rockbridge, and Rockingham Counties. For the first seven years of Augusta County's existence, settlers had to conduct their business in present day Staunton, the county seat.

Belatedly, to establish authority over its western land holdings, the Province of Pennsylvania created Westmoreland County by an Act of Assembly in 1773. It covered all of what was broadly known as southwestern Pennsylvania, but it was restricted in fact by Virginia's seizure and governance of a large portion of the disputed territory. The land west of the Allegheny Mountains and north of the Ohio River became known as the "Pittsylvania Country."

In 1776 the Colony of Virginia formed the Counties of Monongalia, Ohio, and Yohogania (the latter was abolished in 1786) out of the District of West Augusta (the western part of Augusta County, an area which held its court at Fort Duquesne in present day Pittsburg). Monongalia County was situated north of Augusta County and east of Ohio County. Its courthouse was near New Geneva in present day Fayette County, Pennsylvania.

In 1778 the part of Augusta County west of the Ohio River was formed into Illinois County (which was abolished in 1784). The northeastern part of the remainder of Augusta County became Rockingham County and the southwestern part was combined with part of Botetourt County to form Rockbridge County. The northern part of Augusta County was combined with part of Hardy County to become Pendleton County.

It was not until 1780 that Virginia agreed to accept the results of the future joint survey by Mason and Dixon which was to extend the southern boundary line of Pennsylvania to a distance of five degrees of longitude west of the Delaware River. In 1781 the Pennsylvania legislature formed out of Westmoreland County a separate county known as Washington County which included parts of present day Greene, Fayette, and Washington Counties. Westmoreland County included all of Pennsylvania west of the Monongahela River and south of the Ohio

River. Virginia and Pennsylvania accepted the Mason and Dixon Line in 1784 which finally defined the borders of Maryland, Virginia, and Pennsylvania

In 1790 Augusta County assumed its present dimensions when its remaining western part was combined with parts of Botetourt County and Greenbrier County to form Bath County.

Present day Greene County, Pennsylvania, was formed in 1796 from Washington County and included the original Washington County townships of Greene, Cumberland, Morgan, Donegal, Franklin, and Richhill. In subsequent years these additional townships were formed in Greene County:

i. In 1798 Whiteley and Dunkard Townships were formed from Greene Township.
ii. In 1798 Morris and Jackson townships were formed from Richhill Township.
iii. In 1807 Wayne Township was formed.
iv. In 1817 Aleppo Township was formed from Springhill Township.
v. In 1822 and 1842 Monongahela and Perry Townships were formed from Greene Township.
vi. In 1820 Center Township was formed from Franklin and Morris Townships.
vii. In 1838 Washington Township was formed from Morgan Township.
viii. In 1839 Jackson Township was formed from Richhill Township.
ix. In 1857 Gilmore Township was formed from Richhill Township.
x. In 1860 Springhill was formed from Aleppo and Gilmore Townships.

LAND OWNERSHIP

Acquiring land was the 18th century settler's primary concern. Land was needed to grow crops for his family. In the eastern colonies along the seaboard, land speculators held most of the vacant land and demanded higher prices as the available land became scarcer. Not able to afford the inflated prices, the cash-poor tenant settlers and immigrants traveled across the Allegheny Mountains to the western "uncivilized lands" where land was available for the taking.

The "tomahawk grant" was part of American folklore. The settler blazed a perimeter of trees that surrounded his newly chosen tract of wilderness land. A right to tomahawked land was only as good as the owner's enforcement of ownership, oftentimes over the barrel of a musket, or, if he could afford it, a rifle. As settlements were developed contiguous boundary lines became established and adhered to by succeeding generations. The settler who elected to build his cabin and farm in an unsettled area was on his own. If he could not enforce his claim satisfactorily, he was obliged to forfeit it to the stronger adversary. It was not until a land office became available that he was able to legalize his claim by obtaining a deed. He entered his claim description and got an official authorization or warrant to have the tract surveyed. The survey provided a legal description that the government used to grant title to that specific tract of land. That title was the first-title deed, usually called a grant or patent.

At first, surveys relied on local features to describe boundaries of land using "metes and bounds." The distances in the first patents or deeds were measured in poles, rods, and perches. Because the surveyor used compass bearings nearly all tracts were "indiscriminate" surveys, meaning that the surveys were not part of a larger survey grid. Natural or man-made features tended to disappear over the years and the property owner, in the company of local officials, neighbors, and sometimes a surveyor, might retrace the property bounds and repair or replace survey points that were disappearing or had been lost from memory. This walking and remarking of the boundaries was called "processioning."

Early Virginia surveys often merely specified a distance along a riverbank and projected a geometric boundary into the woods which was determined to contain a certain number of acres. Descriptive bounds of "up the meanders of the creek" had to be approximated based on the existing boundaries of established tracts of settled land.

The first land recorder's office was established in western Pennsylvania in 1785, a year after the acceptance of the Mason and Dixon survey by Virginia and Pennsylvania. Prior to that time, land titles could be obtained only through the Camp Cat Fish Corte, a court established by the Governor of Virginia in an Indian fishing camp which later became the town of Washington, Pennsylvania. The first land transaction case heard at the new Camp Cat Fish Corte was entered for redress at the June term of Corte in 1772.

Legal titles began to replace tomahawk rights, corn grants, and squatter's land claims, although these were often settled by purchase instead of going through the court. Sometimes a claimant found another person squatting on the land he had bought. Rather than fight or sue, he would perhaps trade a rifle or greatcoat to the squatter and thus take full possession. Rather than pay the high prices demanded by Pennsylvania settlers who held land without a legal title, many settlers found it more profitable to buy unimproved land in Kentucky, Virginia, and Ohio.

Land was cheap and had little value for trading purposes. Records show that many settlers sold their tomahawked land for a rifle. A soldier at Fort Pitt gave his army coat for a tract of land.

The average settler in Pittsylvania Country was cash poor and generally trade was done by the barter system. They were careful not to obligate themselves monetarily if they could not repay a debt. A debtor who could not meet his obligation when due went to jail and the creditor had to pay the debtor's jail boarding cost.

During the Revolutionary War the Council of Safety at Philadelphia, where the War was prosecuted, adopted the method of awarding "Donation Land" to veterans because the colonies could not afford to pay its soldiers adequately during wartime. Pennsylvania granted Donation Land to each of the soldiers who served to the end of the war in the Pennsylvania Line. These lands in certain western counties remained free from taxation as long as the soldier lived there and retained ownership.

In addition, certain veterans were eligible for "Depreciation Land." A large tract of land was appropriated by the Act of Assembly of March 12, 1783, for the redemption of depreciation certificates issued in lieu of pay (no merchant would accept the Continental Dollars) to soldiers during the Revolutionary War. The Council of Safety in Philadelphia had little money to pay monthly wages to soldiers during the war, but they did have vast amounts of land west of the Allegheny Mountains. The depreciation certificates were issued in certain amounts of pounds sterling that were redeemed after the war for equivalent amounts of land.

> Pres. Reed to Gov. Geo. Clinton
> Philad. April 12th, 1780
> Sir,
> Your Favour of the 11th March has been duly received & in Answer thereto beg Leave to inform your Excell That the Provision made for the Pennsylvania Troops in Addition to the Pay & Allowance of Congress are as follows. To the Officers, One Uniform suit, consisting of a Coat, Waistcoat 2 Pair Breeches, 8 Shirts, 3 pair of Stockings, 3 pair of Shoes & 3 Stocks annually during their being in actual Service. To every Officer & Private during such Service certain enumerated Articles of Stores consisting of Rum, Sugar, Tea, Coffee & Soap, in the follow Proportions viz. For each Ration Week, one Pint of Rum at the Rate of 5s. Gall. 1 lb

Sugar at the Rate of 1s. 1 oz of Tea at 12s. 1lb Tobacco at 9d. 1 lb hard Soap at 6d.

By a Law of the State the half Pay given by Congress for 7 Years is extended to life under certain Limitations & Restrictions. And at the last Sessions the House of Assembly voted Land in the following Proportions, viz.

Rank	Acres
A Major General	2,000
A Brigadier General	1,500
A Colonel	1,000
A Surgeon	600
A Major	600
A Chaplain	600
A Captain	500
A Lieutenant	400
A Ensign	300
A Sergeant	250
A Private	200

These lands to be free from Taxes while in the Hands of the immediate Grantee. The Widow or Children of every Officer or Soldier falling in Battle is entitled to the Land the Husband or Father would have had if he had lived. The Provision for disabled Soldiers is a Pension ordered by the Orphan's Court of the County payable by the County Treasurer not exceeding half Pay & Rations. The Provision for Widows & Orphans is under the same Direction but the Court has a discretional Power as to the Amount of the Pension or Annuity.

Thus, I have endeavoured to give your Excell'y a compendious View of our System it doubtless admits of many Amendments, but hitherto it has proved satisfactory to the Army. In the hasty Removal from this City on the Invasion of the Enemy, the whole of our laws passed to that Period were left so as to fall into the Enemy's Hands.

It is in Contemplation to print a new edition as soon as that is done or if any of the Missing Copies can be procured I shall immediately forward a complete Sett. I esteem myself happy in this & every other Occasion, to express the Respect & Esteem with which I am Your Excell'y Most Obed. & very Hbble Sen. Directed, His Excell'y George Clinton Esq, Govr. of the State of New York.

Grants to Revolutionary War veterans followed a similar process as for sales to individuals except that the veteran's donated lands were surveyed before the applications were made. That meant that their patents could be applied for when the applications were made. Virginia donated land for services in the French and Indian War, Dunmore's War, and the Revolutionary War and set aside a large area of land for that purpose on the western bank of the Scioto River north of the Ohio River. Pennsylvania set aside donated land, but none within the present borders of Washington, Greene, or Fayette Counties. The land granted by Pennsylvania lay in the northwestern counties of the State.

Much of the land patented after about 1788 was considered valueless and was abandoned by the first purchasers, causing it to revert to the State. Some land overlooked in earlier surveys was only patented when it became valuable for the coal that was found underneath the surface. Late patents were secured for the coal, gas, and oil leasing for the small overlooked triangles of land or worthless streambeds, rocky hillsides, or swamplands. In these instances a legend was sometimes found in some surveys "by virtue of a Virginia Certificate."

In Pennsylvania the allotted lands were usually farm-size tracts that went directly to individuals. There were some very large grants in Virginia. Two of the largest were 92,000 acres to Benjamin Borden and 118,000 acres to William Beverley, both in 1739 in the upper Shenandoah Valley, both part of the total of 539,000 acres granted in 1740 to eight individuals or partnerships.

Conveyances and sales of land were a matter of record and important to ownership. Good deeds came only from the Colonial authorities after the land dispute between Pennsylvania and Virginia was settled. The state land records offices became more standardized and patents or deeds were readily enforceable and transferable.

Virginia and southwestern Pennsylvania originally claimed the same land and issued their own patents. Many pioneers purchased their land in the Washington County area from the Colony of Virginia. In 1786 the land claimed by Virginia was finally ceded to Pennsylvania. As part of the deal, the Commonwealth of Pennsylvania honored the claims of those holding land under Virginia Certificates. The lands were resurveyed so that patents could be issued to the owners. Very often, because of the length of time between when the Virginia Certificate was issued and when Pennsylvania issued the patent, two different people appeared on the records. The Washington County land warrant maps noted each tract if its warrant was under a Virginia Certificate.

The process of acquiring land from the provincial government in the early days of Pennsylvania was known as the application process. There were several ways to acquire first title to lands, but usually they followed the four steps of petition, warrant, survey/plat, and grant/patent.

1. The petition was a request to acquire land. The petitioner approached the appropriate officials—the colony's council or the land office clerk—and presented a satisfactory reason for getting land, such as paying the purchase price, or it being promised land for military service, or bringing an emigrant into the colony and thus becoming eligible for the headright land bounty (especially used in the South and West), or being able to produce a government order for a specified amount of land.

2. The warrant certified the right to a specific acreage and authorized an official surveyor to survey it, assuming there were no prior or conflicting claims.

3. The plat, or survey, was the surveyor's drawing of the legal description so that the land was identifiable. It was his certification that everything was in order so far as the warrant, approved acreage, and legal description were concerned.

4. The patent/grant was the government's or proprietor's passing of title to the patentee/grantee. This was the first-title deed and the true beginning of private ownership of the land.

The application process was not rigidly followed by everyone, however. The time when the land was to be paid for often changed. As a result, some settlers never paid for their land or completed the transaction to acquire a patent. A settler who lived on the land was usually adequate proof against claims from later buyers.

The government or proprietor made the patent a permanent official record. The plats were sometimes recorded in volumes and the surveyor's loose copy was sometimes also kept. Some land offices kept permanent warrant records; others did not. The petition was rarely recorded because the warrant was the formal statement of an authorized petition, though petitioner information was occasionally included in council minutes—especially for colonial headrights.

In certain times those persons who brought himself or another person to the colonies entitled the importer to a "headright" of land. Virginia granted 50 acres per importation, but sailors abused it every time they sailed to Virginia by claiming their 50 acres and then selling their claims. In the case of indentured servants, their 50 acres went to the person who paid the servant's passage. Those headrights could be bought and sold, so the person claiming 200 acres for importing four persons was not necessarily the person who actually paid the passage costs. Thus, if Mark Randle claimed 450 acres for transporting nine persons including Mary

Randle, it is possible Mark merely bought headrights to nine persons and never saw or knew Mary. It is also possible that Mary paid her own passage and sold her headright rather than claim the land. Furthermore the nine persons need not have come on the same ship nor arrived in the same year.

Farms were known as plantations and family needs were made or raised on the place. Flax and wool spinning and other tasks were done at home and other home industries were developed for profit. Tanneries were set up in several communities and flour and saw mills used all the available waterpower furnished by Ten Mile Creek and other creeks in Pittsylvania County. One flourmill at Carmichaels Town shipped as many as 120 barrels of flour to New Orleans each season. The account of one such expedition in 1793 showed that even after building the flatboat to convey the flour, buying barrels from local cooperages, paying inspection fees and dues as well as the employment of five or six men, the interested parties made more than $800 on the venture.

Rifles and guns manufactured across the Monongahela River from the present town of Crucible, which lay just above Carmichaels Town, were sold for £5 each. They had an exchange value of about $3 for each English pound sterling.

Woolen mills were built at nearby Clarksville and iron was smelted there. Felt hats were made at Waynesburg before 1800. Coopers were kept busy supplying an average of 70 whiskey still houses with barrels. Salt, paper, powder, and indigo for dying cloth were the principal items brought in from the outside.

Besides farming for a living, each man had some trade in order to earn a few pounds or dollars to buy his family's needs at a trading post. There was some market for the surplus products he raised. During the Revolutionary War, Fort Pitt supplied stores for the troops quartered at that place and after the war a Captain Craig made frequent supply trips to Fort Pitt for the army.

Boat builders on several streams entering the Monongahela River included John Minor at Whiteley Creek, John Armstrong at Muddy Creek, another at the mouth of Ten Mile Creek, and one at Rice's Landing. Coal was mined at nearby Jefferson

MILITARY SERVICE AND TAXES

During the Revolutionary War men could enlist for a month at a time. Such short tours of duty made it extremely difficult for a unit commander to develop an effective unit with the necessary esprit de corps. Part-time soldiers found employment in a military unit a convenient way to supplement their income during the off-season on their farms. When it was planting or harvesting time, the farmer-soldiers deserted their units leaving only a cadre of regular officers and sergeants. Desertion in those days did not carry the stigma that it does today.

The Federal Effective Supply Tax was first levied in 1779 under the "Act for Funding and Redeeming the Bills of Credit of the United States of America and for Providing Means to Bring the Present War to a Satisfactory Conclusion." This tax did not set well with many settlers. It was not too much earlier that they had joined with other disgruntled colonials in opposing the taxes imposed by the British Crown to pay for the expenses of the British Army imposed upon them. The imposition of taxes was one of the Intolerable Acts that had led to their war again Great Britain.

Those settlers on the northern and western frontiers of Pennsylvania during 1776 to 1784 who had been driven from their lands by the Indians were exonerated from paying interest on their purchase of new land. Those people were listed in each county's taxation book as "Persons Exonerated on the Frontiers of Washington County for having been distressed by the Incursions and Depredation of the Indians." Such persons had to prove by the oath of a credible person that in the course of the Revolutionary War the claimant was actually driven from his land by the Indians.

WESTSYLVANIA

The settlers in far western Pennsylvania, beyond the Allegheny Mountains, believed that they had long been ignored by the legislature in Philadelphia in their pleas for protection against the Indians. They did not receive the same benefits of government that the eastern Pennsylvanians enjoyed. The only solution, as they saw it, was to develop a new state of Westsylvania out of the lands west of the Alleghenies known as Pittsylvania Country.

In the summer of 1776 settlers in the region proclaimed their independence from Pennsylvania and Virginia by petitioning the Second Continental Congress to recognize Westsylvania as the fourteenth state. In "The Memorial of the Inhabitants of the Country West of the Allegheny Mountains," the petitioners said that the dispute between Pennsylvania and Virginia would "in all Probability terminate in a Civil War." They informed the Congress that "Land Speculators" were unlawfully encroaching on Native American land which would produce "a bloody, ruinous and destructive War with the Indians."

Hoping to create order out of this chaos, the petitioners asked that:

The Said Country be constituted, declared, & acknowledged a separate, distinct, and independent Province & Government by the Title and under the name of the Province & Government of Westsylvania, be empowered and enabled to form such Laws & Regulations & such a System of Polity & Government as is best adapted & most agreeable to the peculiar Necessities, local Circumstances & Situation thereof & its inhabitants invested with every other power, Right, Privilege & Immunity, vested, or to be vested in the other American Colonies, be considered as a Sister Colony & the fourteenth Province of the American Confederacy.

Despite their plea to the government in Philadelphia, the new state was never created. The Congress stopped this and future similar efforts by declaring them "treasonous."

MIGRATION TRAILS TO FORT PITT AND GARARD'S FORT

The two major destinations for the migrants who traveled west of the Monongahela River, which flowed along the western foothills of the Allegheny Mountains, were Fort Pitt in the north and Garard's Fort in the south.

The northern migration trail from Lancaster, Pennsylvania, to Fort Pitt went across the Allegheny Mountains and passed through present day Harrisburg, Carlisle, Bedford, and Greensburg. It was referred to as Nemacolin's Path, named for the Delaware Indian who had guided Colonel Thomas Cresap when he blazed a path from Cumberland, Maryland, to one of the trading posts of the Ohio Company of Virginia which was located at present day Brownsville, Pennsylvania. Major George Washington later widened part of the trail to accommodate his supply wagons; that section of road became known as Washington's Road. Later, during the French and Indian War, British General Braddock widened Washington's Road westward from Fort Necessity, the site of Major Washington's defeat which occurred in present day Fayette, Pennsylvania.

In the late 1740s William Trent, an English fur trader, built a trading post at the junction of the Allegheny and Monongahela Rivers which formed the Ohio River. French soldiers from Quebec launched an expedition to that site to establish a fort to unite French Canada with French Louisiana via the Ohio River. Outnumbered, the Virginians vacated Trent's Fort. The French rebuilt it and named it Fort Duquesne.

Virginia Governor Dinwiddie sent Major Geprge Washington to warn the French to withdraw and then rebuild the fort which was to be named Fort Prince George. By that time, the French were well entrenched at the Forks of the Ohio River and Fort Prince George never materialized.

France's seizure of land that the English and their Virginia colonists claimed eventually led to the French and Indian War (1756-1763). In 1755 English General Edward Braddock led an unsuccessful expedition to recapture Fort Duquesne.

In 1758 the French burned Fort Duquesne before fleeing from the advancing British troops led by General John Forbes. The English rebuilt the fort and named it Fort Pitt in honor of William Pitt, the English Prime Minister during the French and Indian War, who had determined that the only way that England could defeat France in Europe was first to conquer the French in the New World. The fort served as an important trading post with the Ohio Country Indians for the British and the American colonies. The fort was garrisoned with British soldiers who actively protected migrants moving into that part of what was then the Colony of Virginia.

In 1774 upon the commencement of the Revolutionary War, the Governor of Virginia, Lord Dunmore, seized Fort Pitt and renamed it after himself. When the colonists began to gain the upper hand against the British Army, Lord Dunmore fled to the safety of a British man-of-war off the coast of Virginia. The American militia regained the fort which was again named Fort Pitt. As late as 1794 during the Whiskey Insurrection the settlement that had grown around Fort Pitt had less than 500 souls. According to Judge Breckinridge, who was a participating member of the Whiskey Insurrection, the settlement of Pittsburgh could hardly field a force of 200 armed men.

The major southern migration trail led from Winchester, Virginia, across the Allegheny Mountains and passed through present day Hancock, Cumberland, Cresaptown, and Morgantown, Pennsylvania. Much of that trail was blazed by Christopher Gist, the guide and explorer for the Ohio Company. When it neared the Monongahela River it became known as the Warrior Trail which passed through Garard's Fort.

In 1766 Reverend John Garard, his sons, and several other men of the Mill Creek Regular Baptist Church near Winchester, in then Berkeley County, Virginia (present day Gerrardstown, West Virginia), migrated to White Clay Creek in then Augusta County, Virginia. They led the way westward for the fleeing Virginia Baptists who were being persecuted for not adhering to the Anglican Church mandated by King Henry VIII.

George Morris, one of their neighbors in Winchester, had explored that part of Augusta County in 1764 and spent several weeks on White Clay Creek which was situated at its confluence with Dunkards Creek, both branches off the Monongahela River. His account of the land he had discovered caused the migration to the future site of Garard's Fort.

The main route, the one most commonly taken to the west bank of the Monongahela River in southwestern Pennsylvania, followed the Potomac River north to Frederick, Maryland, and then west to Hagerstown (then Fort Cumberland, Maryland). From there travelers turned northwest into Pennsylvania on Braddock's Road and on past Fort Necessity and Uniontown to arrive at present day Brownsville on the Monongahela River. Then they went up-river to Ten Mile Creek or down-river to White Clay Creek. Virtually all of the westward bound migrants were intent on settling west of the Monongahela River. Very few desired to inhabit that land immediately west of foothills of the Alleghenies. It was not as well watered and drained as the land west of the big river.

The Garard party undoubtedly followed the shorter road that Christopher Gist had blazed in 1753 for the Ohio Company. It followed an old Indian route from the mouth of Will's Creek to the mouth of Red Stone Creek on the Monongahela River. When they arrived at White Clay Creek, John Garard and his followers chose land to their liking and tomahawked their claims. Jonah Garard, one of John's sons, claimed the land where they built a 100-feet-square fort with a strong palisade near the creek just north of the Warrior Trail. Once their protection from the Indians was secured, they lived in the fort while they built a log church which was also to be used as a school. A cemetery was laid out just a few rods from the fort. They cleared and made claims to land, built cabins, and began to till the land to plant the seeds they had brought with them.

In building the fort, long, straight logs were split in halves and placed upright in a trench along the outer boundary. The logs of the outer row were placed close together with the flat side pointed outward. These palisades stood 15 feet above ground and four or five feet below the surface. An inner row of half-logs were placed upright against the outer row with the split side pointing toward the center of the fort. The entrance was through a large, heavy gate that swung on heavy, strong, wooden hinges held by large wooden pegs in a casement of heavy logs. There were no windows, only several small lookout holes and small portholes through which they fired on an approaching enemy. The woods around the fort were cleared to an extreme rifle shot distance from the fort. All brush and felled trees were burned. Nothing was left that an enemy could hide behind.

The fort was later enlarged to 200-feet-square that housed up to 100 families as the community's population increased. Only a few rocks that lined the entrance of the secret escape tunnel remain today, just yards from Whiteley Creek. The Indians murdered many settlers within the settlement, but the fort itself was never successfully attacked due to its superior construction. No records of the fort exist today, but it was reportedly the oldest fort in present day Greene County.

The fear that the marauding Indians would ransack and burn vacated farmhouses was always present and there was no alternative to seeking safety in the fort. There were too many instances of Indians murdering defenseless families throughout the valleys to take the chance of remaining in their cabins.

Even with all these precautions taken, there was always tragedy to be visited upon some hapless family. There were no organized militia units provided by Virginia or Pennsylvania for the settlers in these far reaches of the frontier. Every family's safety depended upon the father's long gun and quick help from their neighbors.

The population of Garard's Fort at that time was not recorded for history. The earliest count of settlers was in 1771 when 30 Baptists became the founding members of the Goshen Baptist Church. There were another known dozen settlers at Garard's Fort at that time, so the population of the settlement may have been as many as 50 people when the church was established. It was the largest settlement south of Fort Pitt and west of the Monongahela River, and was the destination of those migrants who did not want to live in the "heavily populated" Fort Pitt settlement.

Ten Mile Creek attracted many settlers and soon a moderate-size community was formed which served as the spawning catalyst for other settlements. The swift waters of the broad creek supported grain and saw mills. Coopers and whiskey stills were prevalent throughout the area and making wooden barrels for the distillers and the flour and gristmills became a cottage industry. Just across the creek at the present day town of Crucible respectable long guns were manufactured for five pounds each. Woolen mills were set up at Clarksville and a small amount of iron was smelted there as well. Waynesburg became known as the place to buy good felt hats and fur coats. Boat builders were common along the Monongahela River John Rice Jr at Rice's Landing. (This Rice was the son of John Rice Sr, John Corbly's close neighbor on the Cacapon River who had cared for his children.) Nearly every man, in addition to farming, had a trade by which he could arn a few pounds.

PART TWO

The earliest settlers of Greene Township are listed here in the order of the dates when their land warrants were issued.

There were earlier men who "squatted" on a piece of land while they hunted or trapped animals for furs. Those men were transients; not settlers. They were followed by settlers who built their cabins and cleared enough land to grow a few crops to add to their diet of wild game from the forests. They tomahawked the land they settled on and were joined by other settlers. Each settler picked out the piece of land that he or, in some instances, she desired which resulted in oddly shaped plats when they were later surveyed.

The Indian threat was always their main concern. Each cabin was a fort, but there was safety in numbers. They selected small hills or promontories on which to build a palisaded fort which they could flee to in numbers when the Indians came. Some chose to live in the forts and go forth to farm their blazed land. A settlement was formed of groups of contiguous farms or "plantations."

These pioneer settlers usually respected the tomahawk marks of their neighbors. There was no other way of identifying their claims until 1785 when the first land offices were developed. The completion of the Mason and Dixon survey furnished, for the first time, surveyed boundaries between Virginia and Pennsylvania. Each boundary was marked at one-mile intervals. Individual land claims could finally be surveyed using a milepost marker as a beginning point.

The settlers were eager to have their land become legal and rushed to the land offices where claims were awarded warrants on a first-come, first-served basis. On the basis of the warrant, the land was then surveyed and finally a patent was issued to the land claimant. Besides his musket or, later, a rifle, the settler's prime possession was his land. His patent made his land as secure as was possible. It became easier to sell since the buyer could see exactly where the undisputed boundaries were.

The earliest settlers chose the prime pieces of forested land near running water and their tomahawked boundaries meandered accordingly, following the best terrain for its levelness or drainage, resulting in a hodge-podge of irregular shaped tracts. Tracts of land along the creeks or rivers were always the first to be chosen.

Soon, these lands were occupied until all that was left in a given area was the wasteland that nobody wanted. Those spots were too hilly, too uneven to plow, or were not well drained during the rainy season. Eventually they were acquired mainly for their mineral right

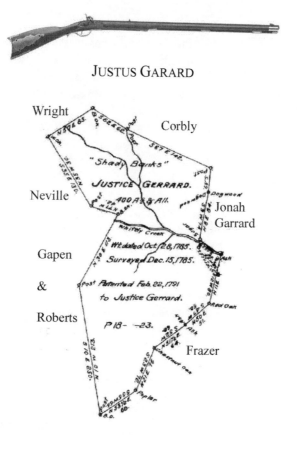

JUSTUS GARARD

The children of Reverend John Garard (1720-1787) and Mehetable Haugen (1746-1768) were:[1]

    i. Sarah (1740-1815), born in Fredrick County, Virginia, died in Green County, Ohio. She married James Buckles in 1760 in Gerrardstown, Berkeley County, Virginia.

    ii. William (abt 1743-).

    iii. John (abt 1744-1782), born in Fredrick County, Virginia, died in Elizabethtown, Hardin County, Kentucky.

    iv. Mehetable (abt 1745-1768), born and died in Berkeley County, Virginia.

    v. David (abt 1748-1821), born in Berkeley County, Virginia, died in Gerrardstown, Berkeley County, Virginia.

vi. Jonah (1750-1782), born in Gerrardstown, Berkeley County, Virginia, died in Washington County, Pennsylvania.

vii. Isaac (1751-1795), born in Virginia.

viii. Nathaniel (1752-1832), born in Berkeley County, Virginia, died in Staunton Township, Miami County, Ohio.

ix. Justus Garard (1755-1828), born in Gerrardstown, Berkeley County, Virginia, died at Garard's Fort.

x. Abner (1759-1819), born in Montgomery County, Ohio.

xi. Jonathan (1763-1837), born in Berkeley County, Virginia, died in Washington, Anderson Township, Ohio.

In 1773 John Corbly and his first wife Abigail Kirk's (1727-1768) 13-year-old daughter, Rachel (1760-1842), married Justus Garard. Justus owned a 400-acre farm which abutted the south boundary of John's farm making it quite easy for Rachel to visit her stepmother, Elizabeth Tyler Corbly, and siblings. Justus and Rachel Corbly Garard's log cabin was probably built in 1769; later another log cabin was added to it. The log home burned to the ground about 1925.[2]

In October 1785 Justus received a warrant for 400 acres of land in Washington County that he called Shady Banks. It was situated immediately west of his brother Jonah Garard's farm. He had it surveyed December 15, 1785, patented on February 22, 1791, and recorded in the Washington County Patent Book P18, page 23.

He was included in the List of Persons Exonerated in 1789 for being distressed by the Incursions and Depredations of the Indians on the frontiers of Washington County.

On June 30, 1785, the Goshen Baptist Church at Garard's Fort received Henry Jackson and his wife; Justus Garard and his wife Rachel, and Sarah Clark by baptism. On February 1790 the Goshen Baptist Church parishioners met at Muddy Creek "according to app't and proceeded to business. The Church appointed Ross Crosley, Joseph Frazer, Justus Garard, and Jonathan Morris to examine into a complaint made against Ely Mundle for bad conduct and singing vulgar songs and to cite him to come to the next monthly meeting where they are to make a report...."

On March 27, 1790, the Goshen Baptist Church "met according to app't and proceeded to business. App'd Justus Garard to cite Ely Mundle to come to next monthly meeting." On June 19, 1794, the church "met at Muddy Creek and appt'd John McIntosh to cite Andrew Mundle to attend next meeting, appt'd Justus Garard to cite Bro Jno Miller."[3]

In the 1790 census for Greene Township Justus was listed as the head of a household with three males under the age of 16 and four females.

The Greene County Tax Book for 1797 made by Joseph Willford, Assessor, assisted by Elias Stone and Stephen Gapen, assessed Justus Garard for 175 acres of land at $200, 30 cleared acres of land at $30, one cabin at $1, one barn at $2, one horse at $15, and six cows at $36. In 1798 his assessment was for 175 acres of land at $210, 30 acres of cleared land at $24, one house at $6, one barn at $6, and six cows at $36.

In the 1800 census for Greene Township, Justus Garard was listed as the head of family with his wife and two males between 16 and 26 years of age, four males under 10 years of age, two females between 10 and 16 years of age, and one female under 10 years of age.

Justus Garard voted in Greene Township at the house of John Campbell on October 14, 1806.[4]

On August 22, 1807, the Church "met according to appointment after addressing the throne of grace and proceeded to business:

1) Received minutes of the Philadelphia Baptist Association for 1806 the circular letter compound upon the subject of gospel missions by Brother Rogers is esteemed very excellent.

2) A letter prepared by Brother Hersey to our next Association was read and approved. Brother Hersey, Abner Mundle, Levi Harrod, Justus Garard, William Brown were appointed Messengers to Association."[5]

[1]Fordyce, Nannie L. *The Life and Times of Reverend John Corbly.* 1953. (2nd ed., Leola Wright Murphy. Mayhill Pub. Co., Knightstown, IN, , 1970).

[2] Corbly, Don. *Pastor John Corbly.* (Lulu Press, Raleigh, North Carolina, 2008) 114.

[3] Corbly, Appendix F, page 273.

[4] http://www.cornerstonegenealogy.com/greene_county_voter _lists_1801.htm

[5] Corbly, 273.

WILLIAM MINOR

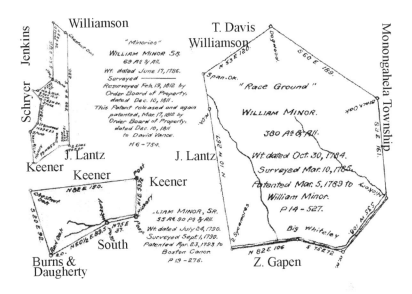

The first member of the Minor family to come to America was Thomas Minor (1608-) who was born in England. In 1629 he arrived on the ship Arabella and settled first in Massachusetts and then Connecticut. In 1634 he married Frances Palmer. Some of his siblings may have been born at Hightstown, New Jersey. One of their sons, Stephen (-1751), married Athaliah Updike (1705-). Estate records at Winchester, Virginia, show that Stephen Minor died in Frederick County, Virginia. His widow, Athaliah, administered his estate which had little value. Not much more is known about her except that there was an Athaliah Minor baptized at Goshen Baptist Church at Garard's Fort on April 28, 1787.[6] Stephen Minor and Athaliah Updike's children were:

i. Abia, the father of John P., who married Huldah McClelland. John and Huldah's daughter, Rebecca, the fourth of nine children, married Joseph Gregg of Greene County, Pennsylvania.

ii. Samuel.

iii. William (1735-1804) died in Greene County, Pennsylvania. He married Frances Ellen Phillips and was buried in the Old Cemetery on the Hill at Greensboro, Greene County, Pennsylvania. There was a memorial stone in the Garard's Fort Cemetery which read, "In Memory Of / Cols. John & William Minor / Soldiers in the Revolutionary War / Among the First Settlers in This / Section of Pennsylvania." William and Frances Ellen Phillips' children were:

1. Stephen (1760-1815), born in Greene County, Pennsylvania, died in Natchez, Adams County, Mississippi. He married Martha Ellis.

2. William Jr (1766-), married Ellenor Phillips (1765-), daughter of Theophylus Phillips.

3. John (1768-bef 1802), died in Cincinnati, Ohio.

4. Theophilus (1770-), married Ellenor Phillips (1765-) in 1802, the previous wife of his brother, William Jr.

5. Philip (1772-), married Anne Baird (1760-) about 1780.

6. Frances (1774-), married (1)...Dye (1760-) about 1782. She then married (2) Andrew Mundell in 1785.

7. Joseph (1775-).

8. Samuel (1777-1859), was born in Greene County, Pennsylvania, and died in Monongalia County, Virginia. He married (1) Susannah Clegg (1777-1818) in 1794 in Monongalia County, Virginia, the daughter of Alexander Clegg and Margaret Farmer. He then married (2) Permelia "Millie" Lancaster (1790-) about 1815. As a young man, Samuel settled on Dunkard Creek about two miles east of Blacksville where he lived until his death. His first wife, Susan Clegg, was captured by Indians along with her father and taken to a western Indian town. There were children born to Samuel and Susannah. After her death Samuel married Millie Lancaster and they became the parents of 11 children. He was buried in Monongalia County, Virginia.

9. Noah (1779-1865), born in Shirley, Tyler County, Virginia, married (1) Sarah Elizabeth South (1779-) about 1799. He then married (2) Mary Menks (1790-) about 1815. The children of Noah Minor and Sarah Elizabeth South were Otho, Samuel, Elizabeth, Nancy, Sarah, and Rebecca.

iv. John (1737-1834), born in Winchester, Loudon County, Virginia, in 1747 married (1) Christina Williams who died in childbirth in 1772. He then married on February 22, 1776, (2) Cassandra Williams, cousin of his first wife. She became the mother of 12 children and died March 3, 1799. He married (3)

Jane (Wilson) Hawkins. Two children were born by the third marriage. He is buried in the Greensboro Cemetery in Greene County, Pennsylvania.

William Minor (1735-1804) was a soldier in the French and Indian War during 1755-1763. In 1760 he was sent with his Militia Company to Loudoun, Virginia, to help garrison Fort Pitt. In 1764 he returned to West Augusta County, present day Monongalia County, and established his home on Dunkard Creek just west of present day Blacksville.[7]

In 1764 William's brother, John Minor from Virginia, chose land on Whiteley Creek a half mile west of Mapletown and tomahawked his claim. He also marked land for William and a contiguous plantation for his kin, Zachariah Gapen. The land he selected was not far off the Indian Trail mentioned by Christopher Gist in his journal in 1752 as the one which followed Dunkard Creek to its source near the forks of Wheeling Creek. This route was used by the Wetzels, Bonnetts, Waggoners, and others to settle near the Ohio River on Wheeling, Fishing, and Grave Creeks. It was also a favorite road used by the Indians to infiltrate into the settlements to perpetrate the many massacres in the Whiteley Creek Valley.[8] The following year a train of migrants consisting of John and William Minor and Zachariah Gapen with their families set out for Big Whiteley Creek from the Conecocheague Valley between Chambersburg and Frederick in present day West Virginia.

Most of the settlers on the Whiteley Creeks had a strong allegiance to Virginia even though many were not native Virginians; the Minors and Gapens were from New Jersey. They settled for a time in the Upper Shenandoah Valley and were soon followed to the Big Whiteley Creek area by their former neighbors Garard, Sutton, VanMeter, and other members of a Baptist group, some of whom tarried for a time in Fayette County. Thus, in 1773, the Goshen Baptist Church was established at Garard's Fort to supply the civilizing influence needed on this frontier

William Minor built a fort on Big Whiteley Creek which became the principal place of safety during Indian raids in the Whiteley Creek Valley.[9] It was the main stockade where the Tories imprisoned during the Revolutionary War were confined until they could be taken to Fort Pitt or Williamsburg, Virginia, for trial. They were led to Williamsburg where they took the oath of allegiance, were pardoned, and then returned home.

Josiah Prickett's pension application from Clermont County, Ohio, submitted on August 1, 1832, (National Archives, Pa.-W-5584), confirmed that in 1782 Captain William Minor, on the authority of Colonel Williamson of Cross Creek, hired Sergeant Henry Sykes, John Guthery, John Knotts, Stephen Gapen, Jeremiah Williams, William Hanna, and others to work as Indian spies on Big Whiteley Creek. On one occasion William Hanna was killed, Amos Morris was wounded, and Richard Hall narrowly escaped from the Indians. Richard Hall killed the Indian who killed Hanna and three days later the Indian's body was brought into Garard's Fort.

The spies had been on a tour of duty for six months and were discharged. They had no other officers at Garard's Fort at that time except Captain William Minor.[10]

In Philadelphia on March 21, 1783, an order was drawn on the Treasurer in favor of Mr. Matthew Ritchie for £25 to be paid by him to Alexander Wright and William Minor. That was the reward allowed by the Council for two Indian scalps taken in the County of Washington.

> The Council, taking into consideration the proclamation of the 22d day of April 1780 offering a reward for Indian scalps, and the reasons upon which the same was founded no longer continuing, Resolved, That the same be made null and void, anything therein contained to the contrary notwithstanding. Ordered. That the foregoing resolution be sent to the Lieutenants of the county of Washington. There is due to Alexander Wright, and William Minor, each, the Sum of twelve pounds, ten shillings, specie, amounting to twenty-five pounds, agreeable to a proclamation of Council, for two Indian scalps taken per within Certificates. By Order of the Comptoller General's Office, March 21, 1783.[11]

William Minor bought 380 acres called Race Ground on a warrant dated October 30, 1784. It was surveyed on March 10, 1785, patented on March 5, 1789, and recorded in the Washington County Patent Book P14, page 527.

He next bought 69 acres called Minories on a warrant dated June 17, 1786. It was resurveyed on February 19, 1812, by order of the Board of Property dated December 10, 1811. That patent was released and was again patented on March 17, 1812, by the Board dated December 10, 1811, to David Vance. It was recorded in the Greene County Patent Book H6, page 754.

In 1789 William Minor and his brother, John Minor, Esquire, were included on the List of Persons Exonerated on the Frontiers of Washington County for being distressed by the Incursions and Depredations of the Indians.

William Minor bought 55 acres and 90 perches called Bunker's Hill on a warrant dated July 24, 1790. It was surveyed September 1, 1790, patented on April 23, 1793, to Sebastian Keener and recorded in the Washington County Patent Book P19, page 276. He bought four additional tracts of land in Washington County from 1784 to 1790 for a total of 590 acres.[12]

In the 1790 Greene Township Census William Minor was listed as head of a household with two sons under the age of 16 years, two females, and five slaves.

The Minor family tradition says that John Minor one day purchased a slave girl as a present for his brother William's wife who was a fat woman and therefore not able to handily do chores and general house work. He told the slave master that he wanted a woman without relatives, because his conscience would not consent to separating a family. The terms were agreed upon and the money paid, but when the girl was about to leave the slave ship she gave a hideous and plaintive shriek. It was only then that John learned that she had a husband. Minor absolutely refused to take the girl and demanded his money back, but the slave dealer proposed to sell him the man also. Finally, a bargain was struck and with "Ratcliff" for himself and "Sal" for his sister-in-law, he set off for home. Ratcliff and Sal produced a number of young slaves. By law they belonged to William Minor, the owner of the mother. But, by an understanding between the brothers, John retained the males and William the females. Ratcliff and Sal had but one son, George, who was the last slave in Greene County and one of the last two slaves in the state. Several daughters were born, however, and it was said that as each of William Minor's daughters were married, one of old Sal's daughters was sold and the proceeds given to the bride as a "setting out."

Ratcliff choked to death by a sliver of bone in a piece of sausage he was eating. His widow Sal married one of Zachary Gapen's slaves, one Dick Sterling, a pompous negro once owned by Lord Sterling. They had a son, Dick, whom the Gapens claimed as their property, but he was replevined (recovered as personal property unlawfully taken) and recovered by William Minor. George lived with the John Minor family, a kind of privileged character, until he was very old. It was said that John Minor made a provision in his Will making it incumbent on his heirs to keep him, giving him the privilege of choosing with whom he should live. In his old and decrepit days, George, while in search of one of his two surviving sisters in his wanderings about Pittsburgh, met with his mother, Sal.[13]

During the early stages of the Whiskey Insurrection, Albert Gallatin, an important leader of the new Democratic-Republican Party and its chief spokesman on financial matters, opposed the entire program of the Secretary of the Treasury, Alexander Hamilton. He called a public meeting at his home, Friendship Hill, on the Monongahela River near present day Point Marion six miles southeast of Garard's Fort on June 17, 1791, to discuss Hamilton's new Federal excise tax on whiskey, the chief export of the southwestern Pennsylvania settlers. Several leading men in southwest Pennsylvania attended including Colonel John Minor, Captain William Minor, Jessie Hook, Zachary Morgan, George Teagarden, John Heaton, Thomas Hughes, Abram Hickman, Desoe Bennington, John Canon, Dorsey Pentecost, John Horn, and Pastor John Corbly.

In the 1798 Greene Township Assessors Book made by Joseph Willford and his assistants Elias Stone and Stephen Gapen, William Minor was assessed for 380 acres of land at $580, 80 acres of cleared land at $70, one cabin at $1, one barn at $6, four horses at $40, and 13 cows at $78, a total of $775. The following year he was assessed for 200 acres of land at $160, 55 acres of cleared land at $55, one house at $4, one cabin at $1, one barn at $6, two horses at $40, and seven cows at $42, a total of $308.

There was no record that William Minor applied for, or received, a pension based on Revolutionary War service, notwithstanding his years of service in the Washington County Militia at Garard's Fort. He filed his Will in the Greene County Will Book, Volume 1, page 45.

DAVID VANCE

The Vance families of Ireland came to America and settled in Chester County, Pennsylvania, on land that was unoccupied, but not legally theirs. The Quaker owners sued, forcing the Vances to move to the Shenandoah Valley in 1731.

Andrew, James, and David Vance Sr (1721-1767) first settled near Opequon Creek and later moved about 10 miles farther south and settled near Isaac Zane's Iron Works at Marlboro, about 12 miles from Winchester, Virginia.[14] He was later among the original settlers in Cross Creek Township, Washington County, Pennsylvania.[15]

David Vance Sr (1721-1767) married (1) Janet...about 1741 and (2) Ann...before 1767 in Virginia. David and Janet Vance's children were:

  i.   David Jr, the eldest, married Sarah Quimby (1757-1846) and they had David, Daniel, Ephraim, John, Elisha, Elijah, Elizabeth, Sarah, and Jane.
  ii. John.
  iii. Joseph Colville (1759-) married Sarah Wilson.
  iv. Mary married Andrew Greet.
  v.   Ann married Joseph Vance.
  vi. Martha married Solomon Vail.
  vii. Jannet (1763-1842) married Miles Wilson.

William Minor's 69 acres called Minories was patented by the Land

Board on March 17, 1812, to David Vance Sr. It was recorded in the Greene County Patent Book H6, page 754.

David Vance Sr had devised his Will on September 18, 1767, and filed it in the Greene County Will Book, Volume 1, page 299. On March 1, 1768, his Will was proven in Frederick County, Virginia. David Vance Jr and his brother, John, inherited their father's land after the death of his second wife, Ann. David Sr's Will required David Jr to have first selection of the land and was tasked to share half the expense of the building of his brother John's home, clearing of 20 acres of land, and planting an orchard for John. If David Jr failed to do this, he was to pay John £30 current Virginia money and give John Vance a plough and plough irons when he reached 21 years of age.[16]

[1] Leckey, Howard. *Tenmile Country and its Pioneer Families*. Rpt, (Closson Press, Apollo, PA. 2007) 628.
[2] *A History of Blacksville, West Virginia*. 2010. http://www.wvpics.com/blacksvillewvhistory.htm
[3] Hadden, James. *History of Uniontown: the County Seat of Fayette County, Pennsylvania, 1845-1923*. (New Werner Co., Akron, OH. 1913.) 232.
[4] Leckey, 243.
[5] Leckey, 631.
[6] Pennsylvania Archives, Series 1, Volume IX, page 772.
[7] Egle, William Henry. *Warrantees of Land in the Several Counties of the State of Pennsylvania, 1730-1898, Volume III*. (William S. Ray, State Printer of Pennsylvania, 1899).
[8] Evans, L. K. *Pioneer History of Greene County, Pennsylvania*. (Waynesburg, Republican Press, Waynesburg, PA, 1941) 62, 53.
[9] http://www.popenoe.com/Shenandoah.htm#Vance/Colville
[10] Creigh, Alfred. *History of Washington County from its first settlement to the present time...Rpt*. Washington, PA, 1870. (Nabu Press, Charleston, SC, 2010) 232.
[11] http://freepages.genealogy.rootsweb.ancestry.com /~kieffer/p758.ht.

JOHN CORBLY SR

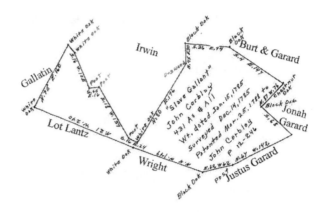

Reverend John Corbly Sr (1733-1803) was born in Ireland, emigrated to America in 1747, and died in Greene County, Pennsylvania (see *Pastor John Corbly*, his biography[1]). He was buried in the Garard's Fort Cemetery with Elizabeth and Nancy, his second and third wives.

Abigail Kirk (1727-1768) married John Corbly in 1752. She was buried on the family farm on the Great Cacapon River, Berkeley County, West Virginia. Their children were:

> i. Margaret (1758-1833) married George Morris (1745-1842), son of Joseph Morris. Both were buried in the Garard's Fort Cemetery.
>
> ii. Rachel (1760-1842) married Justus Garard (1755-1828) born in Virginia, the son of Reverend John Garard. Both were buried in the Garard's Fort Cemetery.
>
> iii. Priscilla (1762-1833) married in 1775 to William Knight (1751-1820). They were buried in the Staunton Cemetery near Troy, Ohio.
>
> iv. John Jr (1768-1814) married about 1791 to Elizabeth Fansler. She next married Mathias Corwin of Ohio.

His second wife, Elizabeth Tyler (1756-1782), died of wounds received in the Corbly Massacre. They married in 1773 at Redstone Fort, Pennsylvania. She was buried next to him in the Garard's Fort Cemetery. Their children were:

> v. Delilah Corbly (1774-1839) died in Miami County, Ohio. She married Levi Martin (1764-1835). They were buried in the Staunton Cemetery near Troy, Ohio.
>
> vi. Elizabeth (1775-1796)) scalped by the Indians in 1782, died just before she was to have married Isaiah Morris. She was buried in the Garard's Fort Cemetery.

vii. Isaiah (1776-1782), killed in the Corbly Massacre, was buried in the Garard's Fort Cemetery.

viii. Mary Catherine (1778-1782) killed in the Corbly Massacre, was buried in the Garard's Fort Cemetery.

ix. Nancy Ann (1782-1782) killed in the Corbly Massacre, was buried in the Garard's Fort Cemetery.

His third wife, Nancy Ann Lynn (1761-1826), married him in 1784 at Brownsville, Pennsylvania. She was buried next to him in the Garard's Fort Cemetery. Their children were:

x. Mary (1785-1864) married in 1800 to Jacob Myers 1780-1862). They were buried at Savannah, Georgia.

xi. Andrew Lynn (1787-1850) married in 1810 to Elizabeth Myers (1792-). He was buried in the Springhill Cemetery at Tyler County, West Virginia. She lived out her life with the family of their son, Joseph Myers Corbly, and was buried at Cedar Rapids, Linn County, Iowa.

xii. Pleasant (1789-1860) married Peter A. Myers Jr (1783-1830) in 1805. They lived at Garard's Fort and were buried in the Garard's Fort Cemetery.

xiii. Cassandra (1791-1869) married in 1810 to Joseph Gregg (1782-1868). They were buried in the Garard's Fort Cemetery.

xiv. Sarah (1793-1814) married in 1813 to John Wright (1792-1880). They were buried in the Garard's Fort Cemetery.

xv. Amelia (1796-1855) married in 1814 to Amos Wright (1795-1871). They were buried in the Garard's Fort Cemetery.

xvi. Nancy (1798-1803) died in an accident at home. She was buried in the Garard's Fort Cemetery.

xvii. William (1801-1875) married Rebecca Stephens (1800-1855) in 1823. He was buried in the Ludlow Cemetery in Illinois; she in McArthur, Vinton County, Ohio.

In 1761 John Corbly and his wife, Abigail, (dismissed from her Quaker Meeting because she had married John, "not a member of the Friends") joined Reverend John Garard's Mill Creek Baptist Church at present day Gerrardstown, West Virginia.

John applied to Lord Thomas Fairfax's designate for a land grant and on June 17, 1765, he was granted 52 acres of land situated on both sides of the Great Cacapon River which meandered through Berkeley County into Hampshire County, Virginia.[4]

Reverend John Corbly's zeal for the new Baptist religion got him into trouble with the Anglican Church and he was jailed in Culpepper, Virginia.[4] The charge entered in official records read:

> At a court held in Orange County of Thursday, 28th day of July 1768. This day Allan Wiley, John Corbly, Elijah Craig, and Thomas Chambers in Discharge of their Recognizance entered into before Rowland Thomas, Gent, of being charged as Vagrant and Itinerant Persons for Assemblying themselves unlawfully at Sundry times and places under the denominations of Anabaptists and for teaching and preaching Schismatik Doctrines. Whereupon the Court having examined the Witnesses and heard the counsel on both sides are of the opinion that the said Allan Wiley, John Corbly, Elijah Craig, and Thomas Chambers are guilty of a breach of good behaviour and Ordered that they enter into bond each in the sum of 50 pounds and two securities in the Sum of 25 pounds each to be of Good Behaviour until the 25th of October next and in case they .fail to enter into such Bond as aforesaid that each of them so failing shall be committed to Gaol until same shall be performed.

After Abigail died in 1768 he left his children in the safekeeping of his neighbor John Rice's family while he went to southwest Pennsylvania to continue his ministry away from the vindictive Anglicans in Virginia. When he returned for his children in April 1773, he sold his land to John Rice for five shillings and "the payment of one ear of Indian corn in and upon the First day of Christmas if the same be demanded." This was his gift to them in payment for his children's upkeep. The transaction was recorded in the Hampshire County Patent Book 3, page 137.

In 1768 John Corbly set out for the Western District of Augusta County with Reverends John, James, Isaac, and Benjamin Sutton and a small group of travelers in one of the many wagon trains departing from Winchester, Virginia. They camped temporarily on Simpson's Creek (at present Bridgeport, Pennsylvania) before pushing on farther south to Muddy Creek and Whiteley Creek.

John Corbly set up his temporary camp on Muddy Creek three miles north of Garard's Fort. No records have been found to indicate that he acquired land at this time on Muddy Creek. Within a month he was appointed the supply minister to Redstone Old Fort, 19 miles north at present day Brownfield. Work was just beginning on building a Meeting House in Garard's Fort.

The first record of John Corbly's arrival at Garard's Fort was his letter sent to the Augusta Town Court which was two miles west of present day Washington in April 1769, in which he stated that the first bridge in that settlement, built on Big Whiteley Creek at the site of Garard's Fort by Conrad Sykes and Jeremiah Glasgow in the winter of 1767, was burned by the Cayuga-Huron Indians. He was listed that year on the Augusta County tax roll with an assessment of ten shillings.

The Cat Fish Camp Corte, the first judicial court established in western Virginia (or Pennsylvania, according to which state the settler claimed allegiance), recorded those settlers in its jurisdiction in June 1772 who owed poll taxes. The only one among them who was found in 1796 in the newly constituted Greene Township, Greene County, was John Corbly who was taxed ten shillings.

In 1772 John Corbly and Conrad Sykes agreed upon terms and on April 10, 1772, John bought Sykes' claim. It was the first land transaction case heard at the new Cat Fish Camp Corte and was entered for redress at the June term of the Corte in 1772:[4]

> Sale claim to be made in a witness contract by and between Conrad Sykes and one 'Parson' John Corbly, No. II Peace Agreement: An agreement made by Conrad Sykes and one Parson John Corbly on April 10th, 1772, the said Conrad Sykes did trade his tomahawked rights to his 274 acres of land on the North Shore of White Clay Creek—with all his rights—his good will and peace of life to the said John Corbly for the sum of 36 pounds and six live goats. All his own free property from Stanton, State of VA. The said parties ask confirmation of this agreement by the Camp Cat Fish Corte. The Corte made each state under oath their agreement and on payment of 10 shillings made Ord that this first land title made by Ord of this Corte be set in the Cort records—payment being made this 14th day of Jun 1772. The same is in Book III. Jacob Horn, Justie.

John lived on that claim until his death in 1803. After Nancy Ann Lynn Corbly's death in 1826 the farm was inherited by their youngest child, William, who sold it in 1837 and moved to Athens County, Ohio.

In 1772 Pastor John Corbly assisted Reverend James Sutton in organizing the North Ten Mile Baptist Church which was located on a ridge two miles north of Ten Mile village and 24 miles north of Garard's Fort.[4] The church was constituted in the Bane settlement in Amwell Township at the house of Enoch Enochs. The earliest record of a church meeting there was December 1, 1773. Reverend James Sutton was the pastor for the first seven years. The minutes of 1781 read, "At our meeting June 16, 1781, we gave our Ministering Brother, John Corbly, an invitation to attend with us statedly in the administration of the word and the ordinances of the Gospel." John Corbly served as pastor to this church from 1781 to 1783. This early Baptist church associated with John Corbly passed into history as did other churches he organized including the Great Bethel, Ten Mile, Turkey Foot, Pike Run, and Yough churches.

John helped organize the Peters Creek Church in Allegheny County. It was organized November 10, 1773, at Library about 12 miles south of Pittsburgh

The Goshen Baptist Meetinghouse (Church) was constituted by Reverends Isaac Sutton and Daniel Fristoe on November 7, 1773, with a membership of 30 people.[4] Reverend James Sutton was the pastor of the church until 1775 when John Corbly was received by letter from the Mill Creek Baptist Church and was ordained a Reverend on June 10th of that year. He pastored the church for 28 years until his death in 1803. The Peter's Creek Church, first called Church of the Yough, was organized on November 10, 1773, and was the oldest Baptist church in Allegheny County, Pennsylvania. The Pike Run Baptist Church, long since extinct, was located northeast of Washington, Pennsylvania

The Indian uprising in 1774 known as Dunmore's War slowed the progress of any church organization. To escape the Indians, settlers near the Goshen Baptist Church fled to Garard's Fort for safety. No worship services or business meetings were recorded in the minutes of the Goshen Baptist Church from April 10, 1774, until May 12, 1775. During that time John Corbly preached to local gatherings of settlers in the scattered frontier settlements. The North Ten Mile congregation, including Pastor James Sutton and most of the other inhabitants west of the Monongahela River, took refuge in Morris' Fort at the foot of Laurel Mountain until peace was made with the Indians.

In 1774 John Corbly, then a 41-year-old Baptist preacher, was elected to be the leader of 20 scouts to pursue the Indians who had killed their neighbors, Cephas Conwell and Isaac Brown. John sent his wife, Betsey, and their children to Garard's Fort for safety while he was gone. On August 8 John and his scouts tracked and killed three of the Indians on the south bank of Muddy Creek. They buried the bodies and then tracked more Indians to the trail crossing at the mouth of Muddy Creek on the Monongahela River, not far from John's Muddy Creek Baptist Church. There they discovered three Indians cutting up a sheep. They crept up in a semicircle until they were about 100 paces away. Twelve rangers saw them clearly, killed all three, and then buried them. They saw no more Indians and thought their actions would bring an end to the Indian raids west of the river, but it was not to be.

John Gwathmey wrote, "A list of Revolutionary War Soldiers was posted at Augusta Town (three miles southwest of present day Washington, Pennsylvania) by Samuel McCullough." On November 10, 1775, by order of Colonel John Canon, as set forth by the Colony of Virginia, the list included Pastor John Corbly in the Virginia Militia.[4]

John Corbly organized the Muddy Creek Baptist Church on Jacob VanMeter's plantation as a branch church of the Whiteley Creek Goshen Baptist Church. The extra church was needed for the people from the Fort Jackson and Ruff Creek areas. He preached twice a month at each church. The Muddy Creek Baptist Church has long been extinct. The Goshen Baptist Church still flourishes.

John Corbly was instrumental in assisting in the organization of churches, but he could not establish a church until he was ordained a minister in 1775.

On June 14, 1775, Isaac Sutton and John Corbly organized the Turkeyfoot Church with 32 members and the Sandy Creek Glades Church with nine members, both organized under one constitution. Turkeyfoot Church was located near the present towns of Confluence and Ursina in Somerset County, Pennsylvania, at the junction of three mountain streams—hence the name Turkeyfoot. Because so many of its members came from New Jersey it was also known as the Jersey Church.

On November 5, 1775, John Corbly established the Forks of Cheat Baptist Church where he served as supply pastor from 1775 until 1788.[4] The meetinghouse, located on a high hill near the confluence of the Cheat and the Monongahela Rivers, was built of "Square Loggs of 28 feet in length, 28 feet in breadth, and 12 loggs high." This church remains the oldest continually active church in West Virginia west of the Allegheny Mountains. The church is located near Stewartstown, West Virginia. On July 30, 2010, the Forks of Cheat Church celebrated its 235th anniversary.

According to E. B. Iams, the historian of Washington, Pennsylvania, John Corbly either established or helped to establish the Patterson Creek Baptist Church in 1775.[4]

The Redstone Baptist Association records state that the Cross Creek Baptist Church in present day Brooke County, West Virginia, 60 miles northwest of Garard's Fort, was organized by Pastor John Corbly and his close friend and neighbor, Pastor William Wood, in 1776.

In 1776 John Corbly preached in the Bates Fork Baptist Church which was established when two cousins, Mrs. James Riley, wife of a fur-trader, and Mrs. Jeremiah Ruff held services in their homes in what became present day Sycamore, Pennsylvania.

Pastor John Corbly, generally recognized as the founder of the Redstone Baptist Association, was elected its moderator at its first meeting and William Wood was elected its clerk. Fourteen messengers representing their churches met at the Goshen Baptist Church at Garard's Fort on October 7, 1776, to inaugurate this new Association and establish its rules.

When the District of West Augusta was divided into the three counties of Ohio, Youghiogheny, and Monongalia in October 1776 John Corbly was appointed a Justice of the Peace in Monongalia County by Governor Patrick Henry.[4]

John Corbly was one of the 84 men from the Ten Mile Country who signed the petition opposing the formation of Transylvania.[4]

The Petition of the inhabitants, and some of the intendesettlers, of that part of North America now denominated TRANSYLVANIA, humbly sheweth: Whereas some of your petitioners became adventurers in that country from the advantageous reports of their friends who first explored it; and others since, allured by the specious show of the easy terms on which the land was to be purchased from those who style themselves proprietors, have, at a great expense and many hardships, settled there. But your petitioners have been greatly alarmed at the late conduct of those gentlemen, in advancing the price of the purchase money. At the same time they have increased the fees of entry and surveying to a most exorbitant rate. And your petitioners have been more justly alarmed at such unaccountable and arbitrary proceedings, as they have lately learned that the said lands were included in the cession or grant of all that tract which lies on the south side of the river Ohio. We humbly expect and implore to be taken under the protection of the honorable Convention of the Colony of Virginia, of which we cannot help thinking ourselves a part, and request your kind interposition in our behalf.

Reverend John Corbly was listed as a Chaplain in the roster of Revolutionary War soldiers posted in Augusta Town on April 16, 1776, by C. Horn as directed by Colonel John Canon and David Morgan, Esquire.[4]

A list of Revolutionary War Soldiers posted at Augusta Town included John Corbly under the command of Captain George Hill by order of

Colonel John Canon as set forth by the State of Virginia.

He was included in the Roll of 1777 as a Patriot of the Home Guard Service Militia in the area that is present day Greene County.

When Colonel Morgan Morgan organized the Virginia Rifle Corps the troops elected Captain John Corbly to serve in the Officers' Home Guard element of that Corps. Throughout the Revolutionary War, Pastor John Corbly was a volunteer in several militia units commanded at various times by Colonel Canon, Captain Andrew Heath, and Lieutenant James Yeates, all of Virginia. In addition, he was a member of the Garard's Fort militia for many years following that war when fighting Indians in southwest Pennsylvania.

There was a major Tory uprising in 1777 in the Garard's Fort area. John Corbly, John Minor, and William Crawford, the Justices of the Court, were threatened with their lives but stood firm against the Tory sentiment. It came about when the demoralized and beaten Continental Army retreated from Quebec leaving Ticonderoga to the British.

In 1777 Pastor John Corbly was elected by the settlers in the newly-created County of Monongalia (it had been formed out of Augusta County) to be their representative in the General Assembly in Williamsburg, Virginia, during that year and next. There was a difference of opinion whether ministers of the Gospel could serve in either house of the General Assembly or Privy Council; this question being asked by Thomas Jefferson. John had already served in the House of Delegates of Virginia from May 5 to June 28, 1776, but was excluded from the October 22, 1777, to January 24, 1778, session. He was the first person to be denied the right to serve in the Virginia General Assembly solely because he was a minister, a conflict that was not settled for the next 30 years. A clause in the state's new Constitution was added to preclude ministers of the Gospel from being admitted as delegates to the Virginia Assembly.

In 1778 Virginia Governor Patrick Henry sent General George Rogers Clark to conquer the Northwest Territory and select and establish a settlement on the Ohio River. He was further tasked to recover some settlers who had been captured during an earlier raid on Fort Ruddell and Martin's Fort and taken to Detroit and some Indian villages on the Ohio River. Several members of the Goshen Baptist Church decided to join the settlement at the Falls. Pastor Corbly accompanied the advance party on their journey. Upon their arrival at the Falls these men and the families already there selected William Harrod, Richard Chenowith, Edward Bulger, James Patton, Henry French, Marsharn Brashers, and Samuel Moore to lay out a town. Probably by prior arrangement, they employed John Corbly to devise a plan of the town and make a surveyed plat of it. On April 14, 1779, John Corbly surveyed and platted the town of Louisville, Kentucky, then a Province of Virginia, on the east bank of the Ohio River. He made the first map of the future town site and then returned to Garard's Fort. This map can be seen in the County Clerk Court records in Louisville, Kentucky.[4]

Captain William Harrod led a Company in George Roger Clark's Expedition to Kaskaskia in 1778 and was at Chillicothe with a Company in 1779.[4] Private John Corbly served in his company at the Battle of the Falls of the Ohio (Louisville). The muster roll of his Company in 1780 found in Collins' History of Kentucky, Volume 1, page 12, contains some additions and makes room for known casualties of previous campaigns. John Swan Jr was second in command at Kaskaskia but was missing from the 1780 list because he was killed that year while traveling to Kentucky.

Throughout the Revolutionary War years Captain Harrod's company stood guard in the Garard's Fort settlement. Captain Harrod had been a soldier of the French and Indian War and had been a Captain under Lord Dunmore. His company's muster roll in 1780 included John Corbly as one of 92 Privates.[4] This service by John Corbly was in addition to being a member of Captain George Morris's company of militia.

GENERAL POTTER TO PRESIDENT REED, 1779.[4]

Penns Valley, May 19th,

1779.

D' Sir,

I Received a letter from Col. Hunter with your Compliments and two papers. He Informs me that a great number of the Inhabitants of that part of the County have left the County since the last stroake the savedges gave us, and many more are agoing. I have Just Heard that they have dun great dammage in Westmoreland County, and last week there was some Indians seen at or near Franks town. I think they are allways on some part of our frontier. In my letter of the third Instant I Informed you of Capt. Corbley's coming to this place, he left this last sabath, with ten of his Horse, leving his Lieut and seven hors. He is gone to Buffler Valley; in a few days I expect the Lieut, to go off after him. Then we will have left us in this Valley one Lieut, and 15 men, in three forts, as a guard, and on the fourth of June there time will be expired, then, it is more than probable, we, in this Valley, will have to fley untill the armey goes out, if there is not some Militia ordered us. I can't help being surprised that there .has been no Militia sent to that part of Bedford County that Joynes us; neither to Franks town, nor Standing stone, except that small company of Buchanan's Battalion, that would not go to Fort Roberdeau. I am Informed that the people about Franks town are fleying from there Habitations. That small company of 30 men has encurredged the people of standing Stoan Valley to stand as yet, altho' it is too few men for that place.

Sir, I would not be understood as dictating to you, but I think the Back parts of Cumberland should be ordered to guard there one frontier, and the people would do it much freer than march to a distance, leaving there famleys in daneger. It may be said that Cumberland County has no frontier, I acknowledge it, if County lines is ment for a guard, but if inhabitance is ment they may be said to be fruntier settlers, for there is no Inhabitance Northerly of the back parts of them but Penn's Valley and standing stoan Valley, and they are in forts, and if not assisted with Guards will be obliged to leve them; for my one part I am sorry I have not mov'd off one year ago.

I am well Convinced that you do every thing in your power for the back Inhabitance. It is imposable for you to know the situation of every part of the Country, and if you did it is Imposoble to defend against such an Enemy. I am, Dear Sir,

With the greatest Esteem,

Your Excellencey's most obed't Humble Servant,

JAS. POTTER.

P. S. This Valley is at too great a distance from sunsberey to be supleyed with the standing Armey, and they have enuff to do nearer the town.

J. P.

Directed,

On public service. To His Excellencey, Joseph Reed, President of the state of Pennsylvania, Philadelphia.

In 1780 the Shirtee congregation requested that the Redstone Baptist Association constitute a Baptist Church in their community. The Association resolved that Elders William Wood and John Corbly attend there the Saturday before the fourth Sabbath in October and comply with their request. The Shirtee membership (Chartiers Township, pronounced

"Shirtee" by the locals) was 12 people.

In the 1800 United States Census John Corbly was listed as "residing in Greene County, Pennsylvania. Rev. John Corbly, head of family, two males aged between 10 and 16 (Andrew and unknown), one male aged over 45 (himself), four females aged under 10 (Cassandra, Sarah, Amelia, and Nancy), one female aged between 10 and 16 (Pleasant)."

The 1781 Effective Supply Tax Rates of Greene Township, Washington County, assessed John Corbly $4 for 100 acres of land, two horses, and two cattle.[4] John Corbly was included in the 1784 Assessment Rolls for Greene Township, Washington County, Pennsylvania.[4]

On July 8, 1785, John wrote to his friend Reverend William Rogers, Pastor of the First Baptist Church of Philadelphia, describing the well-publicized but often misstated tragedy of the Corbly Massacre:[4]

> On the second Sabbath in May, in the year 1782, being my appointment at one of my meeting-houses, about a mile from my dwelling-house, I set out with my dear wife and five children for public worship. Not suspecting any danger, I walked behind 200 yards, with my bible in my hand, meditating. As I was thus employed, all on a sudden, I was greatly alarmed with the frightful shrieks of my dear family before me. I immediately ran with all the speed I could, vainly hunting a club as 1 ran, till I got within 40 yards of them; my poor wife seeing me, cried to me to make my escape; an Indian ran up to shoot me; I then fled, and by so doing out-ran him. My wife had a suckling child in her arms; this little infant they killed and scalped. They then struck my wife several times, but not getting her down, the Indian who aimed to shoot me, ran to her, shot her through the body, and scalped her; my little boy, an only son, about six years old, they sunk the hatchet into his brain, and thus dispatched him, A daughter, besides the infant, they also killed and scalped. My eldest daughter, who is yet alive, was hid in a tree, about 20 yards from the place where the rest were killed, and saw the whole proceedings. She, seeing the Indians all go off, as she thought, ,'got up, and deliberately crept out from the hollow trunk; but one of them espying her, ran hastily up, knocked her down and scalped her; also her only surviving sister, on whose head they did not leave more than an inch round, either of flesh or skin, besides taking a piece of her skull. She, and the before-mentioned one, are still miraculously

preserved, though, as you must think, I have had, and still have, a great deal of trouble and expense with them, besides anxiety about them, insomuch that I am, as to worldly circumstances, almost ruined, I am yet in hopes of seeing them cured; they still, blessed be God, retain their senses, notwithstanding the painful operations they have already and must yet pass through.

John Corbly's farm was located one mile north of Garard's Fort and about 10 miles north of Mt. Morris, Pennsylvania, where the Pennsylvania boundary survey of 1767 was abandoned. He lived on his farm from 1773 until a temporary boundary line was run in 1779 without knowing whether he would be living under the jurisdiction of Virginia or Pennsylvania. The temporary boundary line was not made permanent until the Mason and Dixon survey of 1784 after which he received a Pennsylvania warrant for his land which was recorded in the records of Washington County, Pennsylvania, Land Survey, Book I, page 294, which read, "Warrant dated, January 15, 1785, for survey of 431 acres for John Corbly, survey completed December 14, 1785."

His land patent was not granted until March 25, 1788. His 431-acre farm was warranted on January 15, 1785, from his original claim. The recorder labeled it Slave Gallant, a degradation of Slieve Gallion as he named it after a mountain near his birthplace in Ireland. It was surveyed December 14, 1785, patented March 25, 1788, and recorded in the Washington County Patent Book P12, page 246.

In 1786 John Corbly established the Mount Hermon Baptist Church near Amity, Pennsylvania, 24 miles north of Garard's Fort in the home of Jesse Bane.

A charter was granted September 24, 1787, for an Academy at Washington, Pennsylvania, for which a donation of 5,000 acres of land helped establish the first school of higher education in Pittsylvania Country. Pastor John Corbly was one of the original Trustees. Reverend Thaddeus Dodd was the headmaster. There being no funds to erect a building, the upper rooms of the Court House were hired for the purpose.[4]

Reverend John Corbly was included on the 1789 list of persons exonerated on the frontiers of Washington County for being distressed by the incursions and depredations of the Indians.[4]

The 1790 Census record for Washington County, Pennsylvania, listed Reverend John Corbly as head of household with one male under 16 years of age and six females.

The first business meeting of the Maple Baptist Church, originated as the Baptist Church Enan, was held on March 19, 1791, in a log house located near the Monongahela River opposite the village of present day Belle Vernon in Fayette County. On November 1, 1800, John Corbly was one of the six men chosen to administer to the church's business.[4]

After the arrest in 1794 of the rebellious settlers in southwest Pennsylvania during the Whiskey Insurrection, 18 men were sent to Philadelphia for trial, including Pastor John Corbly. These prisoners left the Pittsburgh garrison on November 25 surrounded by 40 soldiers under the command of Ensign McCleary. They were paraded before a detachment of Major James Durham's troop of cavalry and were then placed in the center of these cavalry soldiers and started for Greensburg where they arrived November 27th. Two days later they were taken from the jail, paraded in mud and snow in the streets, and were formally delivered to Major Durham to proceed on their weary march to Philadelphia. Each prisoner marched between two soldiers of Light Troop, guards on horseback, who were ordered by "Blackbeard" (General Anthony M. White) to keep their swords "always drawn and if any attempt were made to escape, off with their heads."

They marched for 30 days in the most inclement season of the year. One of the prisoners, Captain Robert Porter, kept a diary:[4]

> On the 25th of December, paraded before the Black Horse Tavern (in Philadelphia). The prisoners, drawn up, rank and file, were given slips of white paper as cockades by the major, to be put in their hats to distinguish them from the rest of the crowd they were to be marched through; or as trophies of victory. The prisoners, after having been marched through the streets, in view of a great concourse of spectators, were lodged in the new jail. The Rev. John Corbly was admitted to bail March 4th. Captain Porter, when no evidence was presented, was acquitted by the jury after six-month's imprisonment on May 18, 1795, as were all of the other prisoners excepting John Mitchell, a weak-minded man, who robbed the mail near Greensburg for Bradford and others.

Greene County, Pennsylvania, was erected out of Washington County by a legislative act on February 9, 1796, and was originally composed of the townships of Cumberland, Franklin, Greene, Morgan, and RichHill.

Garard's Fort and John's land had been associated with several counties as a result of the Virginia-Pennsylvania boundary dispute. John's home no longer was in the Western District of Augusta County; Washington County; Westmoreland County; or Monongalia County.

Finally, John and Nancy's land, the bounds of which were confirmed by the Mason and Dixon survey, lay within Greene County where they re-remain to this day.

In 1796 they set out to build a much-needed new home. A few feet from their two-room cabin that he had bought many years earlier from Conrad Sykes, John laid out a foundation for a large, handsome two-story Federalist-style brick home. It was said by many at the time to be the grandest home in the Garard's Fort settlement. It was not a result of income he received as a preacher; during his ministry he did not receive any cash income until 1785. The income from the sale of land inherited by Nancy in her father's Will provided the cash.

In the 1797 Tax Book for Greene County made by Joseph Willford, Assessor, assisted by Elias Stone and Stephen Gapen, John Corbly was assessed for 250 acres of land at $150, 40 acres of cleared land at $40, one house at $5, one barn at $10, two horses at $30, five cows at $30, and one slave. In 1798 he was assessed for 250 acres of land at $300, 40 acres of cleared land at $40, one house at $5, one barn at $10, two horses at $20, five cows at $30, and one slave. In 1799 he was assessed for 300 acres land at $240, 50 acres of cleared land at $50, one house at $50, one barn at $10, two horses at $30, six cows at $36, and one slave. In 1800 he was assessed for 300 acres of land at $300, 50 acres of cleared land at $50, two houses at $10, one barn at $10, two horses at $30, six cows at $36, and one slave at $100.[4]

The slave, name unknown, was bequeathed to Nancy in her father's Will and lived out his life on the Corbly farm.

In the 1800 Census for Greene County John Corbly was listed as head of family with two males aged between 10-16 years of age, four females under ten 10 years of age, one female between 10-16 years of age, and one female between 26-45 years of age (his wife).

John Corbly was one of the voters residing in Greene Township, Greene County, who voted at the Annual Election held at the house of John Burley on October 13, 1801.

In 1801 John Corbly received a honorary commission from Governor Thomas McKean of Pennsylvania which read:

> Thomas McKean, Governor of said Commonwealth, to John Corbly of the County of Greene. Gentlemen, Greeting: Know that, reposing special trust and confidence in your patriotism and ability, I have nominated and appointed you, the said John Corbly, to be Coroner of the said County of Greene. (Court Records, Deed Book 1, page 497, Waynesburg, Pennsylvania).

He became the second coroner of Greene County, succeeding James Boone who held the first office from 1796 to 1801.

In 1801 Brothers Corbly and Luse were appointed to attend Short Creek Baptist Church on the second Lord's Day in November for the ordination of Brother Thomas Hersey.

In January 1802 William Wood, John's close friend and neighbor, died. They had attended the first meeting of the churches which were formed into the Redstone Baptist Association and frequently traveled together on their missions to the outlying settlements. On January 22 John Corbly and Jonathan Morris appraised the estate of Reverend William Wood, deceased, at a value of $376.35.

On Thursday, June 9, 1803, at the age of 70, John was at home preparing to attend the next Redstone Baptist Association's meeting when he suddenly expired with Nancy Ann at his side. His funeral ceremony was held on the following Sunday at the Goshen Baptist Church. By one account the service had to be conducted outside to accommodate the over-flow crowd. Reverend Edgar David Phillips, pastor of the Peter's Creek Baptist Church, based his funeral sermon on Revelations XIV, 13: *Blessed are the dead which die in the Lord from henceforth: Yea, saith the Spirit, that they may rest from their labours; and their works do follow them.*

John Corbly's Will was filed in 1803 by his executor, Nancy, in the Greene County, Pennsylvania, Recorder's Office in Registry 38, Book 58, page 1. His estate was filed in Registry 300, Book 541, page 1.

John Corbly was later mentioned in a court action on May 11, 1804, between his neighbor, John Lantz, and Matthew Hannon.[4]

...Deposition of Peter Myers heard on November 10, 1805: He was with Rev John Corbly and Corbly was about to purchase a tract of land from Matthew Hannon on Kellums Fork of Dunkard Creek. Hoover told Corbly that John Lantz claimed part of the land and Corbly went to George Shinn to ask who had a right to the disputed land, as Shinn was an old settler there. Shinn told Corbly that Hannon owned the land down the creek to the point below a "good shugger camp on the creek." Corbly told Shinn if the land did not extend below the sugar camp not to buy it from Hannon. Shinn replied, "You need not doubt it never did belong to Lantz's place....

In the 1810 United States Census, Nancy was listed as "head of the family along with one male aged under 10 years of age (William, 9), one female aged between 10-16 years of age (Amelia, 14), two females between 16-25 years of age (Sarah, 17, and Cassandra, 19), one female between 26-45 years of age (Mary or Pleasant may have been visiting), and one female over 45 years of age (Nancy, 49)." Nancy had her hands full raising these children for the next several years. The last one, William, did not marry until 20 years after John died. Nancy was then 61 years of age and lived but three more years before she died in 1826. After Nancy's death, William sold the family home at Garard's Fort and moved to Athens County, Ohio, in 1837.

[1] Corbly, Don. *Pastor John Corbly.* (Lulu Press, Raleigh, NC, 2008).

[2] Leckey, Howard. *Tenmile Country and its Pioneer Families.* Rpt, (Closson Press, Apollo, PA. 2007) 581.

[3] Order Book Orange County, Va., 1763-1769, page 514.

[4] Court Record, April 1772, Offis of Justie Jacob Horn, Westmoreland, Pennsylvania, page 80.

[5] Crumrine, Boyd. *History of Washington County, Pennsylvania with Biographical Sketches of Many of Its Pioneers and Prominent Men.* (Philadelphia: L. H. Leverts & Co., 1882).

[6] Payton, Jacob S. *Our fathers have told us: the story of the founding of Methodism in western Pennsylvania, 1884.* (Ruter Press, Cincinnati. 1938).

[7] Gwathmey, John H. Historical Register of Virginians in the Revolution, Vol. 1: Soldiers, Sailors, Marines, 1775-1783. (Genealogical PubliShinng Company. 2010).[8] Fordyce, Nannie L. The Life and Times of Reverend John Corbly.1953. 2nd ed., (Leola Wright Murphy. Knightstown, IN) 9.

[9] Iams, E. B. *Baptist Historian.* (Washington County, Pennsylvania.)

[10] Leckey 582.

[11] Collins, Lewis and Richard. *History of Kentucky, Vol II.* (Covington, Ky., 1878) 510-511.

[12] Evans L. K. *Pioneer History of Greene County. 1941.* Rpt. (Waynesburg: Greene County Historical Society, 2000 117.

[13] Scientific American Department. *The Encyclopedia Amer cana, Universal Ref. Library.* (Scientific American, 1904).

[14] Leckey, 25.

[15] Leckey, 582.

[16] Pennsylvania Archives, Series 1, Volume VII, 1779, pages 418, 419.

[17] Leckey, 736.

[18] Leckey, 135.

[19] Corbly, 154.

[20] Smith, Joseph. *History of Jefferson College: Including an Account of the Early log-cabin Schools... 1796-1868.* (J.T. Shryock, Pittsburgh 1857).

[21] http://listsearches.rootsweb.com/th/read/PAGREENE/1999-07/0931158294. Tax Lists 1787-1789.

JOHN LANTZ

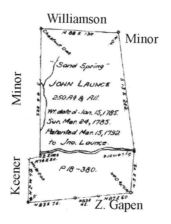

Williamson
Minor
Minor
Keener
Z. Gapen

John (1749-1817) and Andrew Lantz were descended from Hans George Lantz (-1778) who came from Germany about 1747 to Philadelphia. On October 20, 1747, Hans took the Oath of Allegiance to Great Britain. Nicholas Lantz came with them. Hans George Lantz went to Maryland where he lived for a time on the Monoquacy River and then moved to the Shenandoah Valley where he received a grant in Virginia of 470 acres from Lord Fairfax on October 6, 1766. He died there leaving a wife, Maria Margaretha Benderin, a daughter Margaretha, and sons George who settled in Barbour County, Virginia, John (1749-1817), Andrew, and Jacob who settled in Washington County, Pennsylvania.

John Lantz (1749-1817) was born on the Monoquacy River and died in Greene County, Pennsylvania. He married (1) Clara Fuschain in 1772 and (2) Barbara Waggoner.[1] His children with Clara Fuschain:

   i. John Jr (1773-1853) was born probably in the Shenandoah Valley. He was buried in the Lantz Cemetery in Greene County with his wife, Elizabeth Bonnett (1773-1873), who he married on March 26, 1795. They had 10 children.

   ii. Andrew (1755-1824) was born on the Monoquacy River in Maryland and died at his plantation on Whiteley Creek, Greene County, Pennsylvania.

   iii.Catherine (1777-) was left $20 in her fathers Will in 1817.

John Lantz's second marriage was about 1780 to (2) Barbara Waggoner (-1850), daughter of Wilhelm Waggoner and Agnessa. Barbara died in Wetzel, Virginia. His children with Barbara Waggoner:

   iv. Anna Maria "Mary" (1782-1833).

v. William (1784-1825).
vi. John George (1787-1818).
vii. Lewis (1789-).
viii. Jacob (1791-1858).
ix. Alexander (1793-1873).
x. Samuel (1797-1809).
xi. Elizabeth (1800-1884).

Many names in the original plat of Greene County, Pennsylvania, spelled phonetically by the County Surveyor in his field notes, were repeated by the plat maker. In the patents of land on Whiteley Creek, John's last name was spelled Launce. Andrew's name on the adjoining tract was spelled Lance.

After the Battle of Yorktown in 1781 John Lantz migrated westward and tarried for a time in Bedford County, Pennsylvania, where in 1782 he served a tour of duty in Captain Henry Rush's Company of the Bedford County Militia, his name appearing on the Muster Roll as John Lance.[2]

The 1781 Effective Supply Tax Book for Greene Township, Washington County, included John Lantz with 450 acres, five horses, five cattle, and one sheep valued at $111. Andrew Lantz had 50 acres, three horses, and one cow valued at $62. John and Andrew Lantz were on the 1784 Assessment Roll for Greene Township, Washington County, Pennsylvania.[3]

In 1782 he served as a Private in the Seventh Company of the Second Battalion of the Lancaster County Militia, according to the Pennsylvania State Archives, Revolutionary War Military Abstract Card File.

On January 15, 1785, John Lantz was granted a warrant for 250 acres of land situated on Big Whiteley Creek called Sand Spring. The warrant was dated January 15, 1785, surveyed on March 24, 1785, patented on March 15, 1792, and recorded in the Washington County Patent Book P18, page 380.

In 1789 John was included in the Tax Lists of Persons Exonerated on the Frontiers of Washington County for being distressed by the Incursions and Depredations of the Indians.

He was listed in the 1790 Census of Greene Township, Washington County, as head of household with seven males under 16 years of age and three females.

On March 10, 1796, John had warranted to him 399 acres of land on Dunkard Creek. He moved his family to this tract and began buying adjacent tracts. When he died he owned 1,000 contiguous acres lying partly in Greene County and partly in Monongalia County, Virginia. He made his home in Greene County.

In the 1797 Greene Township, Greene County Tax Book, which was made by Joseph Willford, Assessor, assisted by Elias Stone and Stephen Gapen, John Lantz was assessed for 580 acres of land at $400, 60 acres of cleared land at $60, one cabin at $1, one barn at $10, four horses at $60, and three cows at $18. The following year he was assessed for 480 acres of land at $300, 60 acres of cleared land at $60, one cabin at $1, one barn at $6, four horses at $40, and seven cows at $42.

John Lantz was ordered into court in Monongalia County in 1815 upon the complaint of Matt Hannon concerning a tract of land. [4]

In the Monongalia Chancery Court in 1815 John Lantz was summoned to answer a Bill exhibited against him by Matt Hannon on May 11, 1804. Hannon's complaint was that on April 25, 1781, Aaron Jenkins, assignee of Alex Clegg, obtained a certificate in right of settlement entered with the surveyor in May 1781. At that time the lines were fixed and marked, and said Jacob Hoover held his title only by virtue of a settlement made thereon before the lands were opened. On 28, 1784, he made a survey agreeable to the certificate, registered the survey, and obtained a patent (deed). He said he obtained a certificate for an additional 400 acres and Hoover was making his survey on this 400 acres, disregarding lines already marked, and had surveyed out 50 or more acres the better part of his 400 acres and has sold the same John Lantz. He said Hoover had taken out a title in the State of Pennsylvania and by virtue of said certificates, he holds more than he aught. He prayed the Court to summon Hoover and Lantz to be questioned in the matter.

Lantz's answer: According to the present boundaries one in Virginia on which the patent was issued for 128 acres, which was part of Hoover's settlement right, it appeared as running on the division line between the states to lie in Virginia. Hoover should have had on the Pennsylvania side 273 3/4 acres to make up 400 acres. Hoover states to lie in Virginia. Hoover held and obtained on the Pennsylvania side no more than 250 acres making a total of 376 1/4 acres held on the certificate for 400 acres. He said it appeared as if Hoover's claim is older than Hannon's or any of his preceding assignors. Hoover's certificate was obtained before Jenkins under whom Hannon claims. Hoover's survey was made first and his patent was issued first, Hoover did all by legal means without fraud. He said he did not know of any line agreements or markings and many older residents questioned denied any patent was issued first or any knowledge of agreed line. He said he held title by virtue of the following deed and denies all fraud and prayed the Court to dismiss this action with reasonable cost on April 1, 1805. Deed made by Jacob Hoover and Mary his wife, Fayette County, Pennsylvania, to John Lantz, Greene County, Pennsylvania dated August 13, 1798, for £50, 128 3/4 acres beginning at a black oak in the Pennsylvania line on north side of Dunkard Creek, being the same tract as granted to said Hoover on June 15, 1784, joining Nicholas Shinn, signed by Jacob Hoover and Mary (x) Hoover. Order to County Surveyor to survey the land in dispute and return to March 1811 Court and the Sheriff and a Justice attend the survey, 14 January 1811. Five copies of the survey made by Samuel Hanway, SMC, dated 24 October 1811. Hanway's plat shows an interference of 66 acres that Lantz overlaps Hoover's 400 acres. Copy of certificate dated 25 April 1781 to Aaron Jenkins, assignee of Alexander Clegg, for 400 acres on Keller's Fork of Dunkard Creek joining lands of Philip Doddridge, to include his settlement made 1773, signed by Commissioners John Duvall, James Neal, and William Haymond.

Deposition of George Shinn, Greene County, Pennsylvania, before Justice John McFee: He purchased an improvement commenced on John Lamtz's plantation, where he now lives, from Richard Harrison about 1773. In 1774 he sold the same to Jacob Hoover. About 13 years later, Hoover sold the same to John Lantz. Shinn said he knew nothing about the lines, signed by George (x) Shinn, no date.

Deposition of Peter Myers heard on 10 November 1805: He was with Rev John Corbly and Corbly was about to purchase a tract of land from Matthew Hannon on Kellum's Fork of Dunkard Creek. Hoover told Corbly that John Lantz claimed part of the land and Corbly went to George Shinn to ask who had a right to the disputed land as Shinn was an old settler there. Shinn told Corbly that Hannon owned the land down the creek to the point of a rise below a "noted good shugger camp on the creek." Corbly told Shinn that if the land did not extend below the sugar camp on the creek," he would not buy it from Hannon. Shinn replied, "You need not doubt it never did belong to Lantz's place." He heard Shinn say "since the suit is brought, that John Lantz keep back part the pay from Hoover's heirs to compensate him if Matthew Hannon gains the land. I also was informed by Shinn that Hoover was his father-in-law and that by the late death of Hoover, Shinn becomes...in the suit Lantz's favor against Matthew Hannon."

Deposition of Alexander Clegg heard before Justice Samuel Minor on 7 October 1805: He said John Merrial first improved the disputed land and he, Clegg, bought the land from Merrial. Sometime later Hoover informed him that he had the land surveyed and went further up the creek than he had a right to hold and that Hoover never claimed above the forks of the creek. He said Merrial harvested corn from the land after Dunmore's War.

Deposition of George Snider heard before Justice Samuel Minor on 3 March 1807: He said he made an improvement on the left fork of Dunker Creek between the survey now claimed by John Corbly's heirs and John Lantz now in dispute, part in each claim, as they now show the lines. The improvement was made in 1771 or 1772 and he said he gave up his right of improvement to John Merrial.

Deposition of Stephen Stiles heard before Justice William Jobes on 15 March 1808: About seven years ago he and George Shinn were traveling along the path up Kellum's Fork of Dunkard Creek when they came to a spot at a steep bank of the creek where there was once a cabin built by old James Piles below a "noted good sugger camp" now claimed by Matthew Hannon. They stopped and Shinn pointed and showed him where he sold to his father-in-law Hoover the land at that time was vacant to Doddridge's line.

Deposition of William Stiles heard at same time: He and George Shinn were going down the creek from Doddridge's place. As they neared the place called Beavers Dam, Shinn showed him the line between Doddridge and Hannon and a little distance on Hannon's line on a point of the ridge below a "noted good suggar camp" now claimed by Hannon about four or five rods below a cabin foundation built where stood a large red oak tree. Shinn pointed and said this is where Hannon's place comes to end. He said, "I have gone square across the creek about nine years ago."

Deposition of John Knight heard at the same time: About ten years ago he and George Shinn were going up the creek and stopped at a large red oak. He asked Shinn how far Hoover's land came up the creek. Shinn said there wasn't any definite line, but that this is the spot.

The Suit brought March 11, 1804, ended June 14, 1815 term. Bill was dismissed and decree for defendants for costs.

John Lantz was included in the Greene County Will Testators Book PA30, page 175. His estate was probated in Greene County on April 5, 1817. His Will, recorded in the Greene County Will Book 1, page 175, showed that he also owned land in Ohio which went to his son, Andrew Lantz (1755-1824), who was married to Barbara Lemley. John Lantz was buried in the Lantz Cemetery on Miracle Run just east of Brave, Greene County, Pennsylvania.

The Will of John Lantz, January 1817, probated March 27, 1817, in part, named his children:[5]

2nd Secondly I give and bequeath to my beloved wife Barbara full liberty of the dividing house and her bed & bedding and such household furniture sufficient for her. My son Alexander is to provide her a full and sufficient living of the place where 1 now live in during her life and a good cow.

3rd To beloved son John $50.00 to be paid by my son Jacob out of his legacy.

4th To beloved son Andrew - 100 acres of land laying on the waters of Duck Creek state of Ohio.

5th To my beloved daughter Catherine $20.00 out of my estate.

To my beloved daughter Mary Stiles, $50.00 two years after my decease, to be paid by my son Alexander,

6th To my beloved son William, $10.00 three years after my decease, to be paid by my son Alexander,

To my beloved son George - the sum of $10.00 to bo paid three years after my decease, to be paid by my son Alexander,

To my beloved son Lewis the sum of $1.00, to bo paid by my son Alexander.

7th To my beloved son Jacob, all the land that is of the North side of Haver's Run, but lie is to pay my son John the $50.00 (that is afore mentioned of my son John legacy.

8th I give to my beloved son Alexander all the land I possess in the following boundaries: from Haver's Run up this creek to where the state line crosses the Creek, to wilt, a straight line to his back line, with all the appurtenances thereto belonging, The Widows legacy excepted.

9th To my beloved daughter Elizabeth the whole of the land that I possess above my son Alexander's legacy (hat lies either in the stale of Pennsylvania or in the state of Virginia from Gilliams fork, and a black mare that I now possess and one cow and a bed and bedding.

Executors: sons Alexander and John Lantz Jr. April 1817, John Lantz Signed, Sealed and delivered in the presents of Stephen Archer.

[1] Leckey, Howard. *Tenmile Country and its Pioneer Families.* Rpt, (Closson Press, Apollo, PA. 2007) 635.
[2] Pennsylvania Archives, Series 5, Volume V, page 117.
[3] Pennsylvania Archives, Series 3, Volume XXII, page 699.
[4] Zinn, Melba Pender. *Monongalia County (West) Virginia Records of the District, Superior, and County Courts, Volume 9: 1813-1817,* (Heritage Books Inc. 2009).
[5] Wagoner, Crystal V. *John Wagoner (1751-1842) and Margaret Bonner Waggoner: Ancestors, Families, and Descendants,* (Heritage Books Inc. Bowie, MD, 2009) 51.

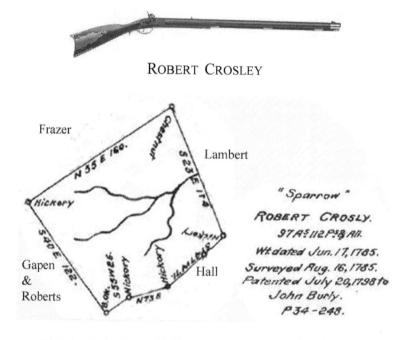

ROBERT CROSLEY

Robert Crosley Sr and his wife, Mary..., were dismissed from the Scotch Plains Baptist Church in Scotch Plains, New Jersey, in 1769 and traveled to the Mill Creek Baptist Church in Frederick County, Virginia. They were accompanied by Martha Frazer and Sarah Ross, the wife of their son, Ross (1755-1817).[1]

In 1772 Robert Crosley Sr bought 385 acres on Dillons Run on Back Creek in Berkeley County, Virginia, situated next to William Frost and David Ruble. He sold it in 1780 to Ebenezer Heaton of Berkeley County for 5 shillings; it was the drain land of Back Creek. Witnesses were Isaac Chenowith and Abraham and Thomas Roman. The transaction was recorded in Berkeley County Deed Book 5, pages 505-507. The next entry in the book was the release indenture by Robert Crosley and his wife, Mary, to Ebenezer Heaton.

A letter to Mr Joseph Gwyne, Collector of the Taxes of Cumberland Township, Washington County, for 1781 read, "You are hereby authorized and required to notify every person in your township what their taxes is either personally or in writing as expressed in your duplicate at least five days before the appeal which will be held at home of Henry VanMetre Esq, Friday 16th of May instant." Robert Crosley Sr was one of the persons taxed in 1781 in Cumberland Township.

Moses Lambert, who also lived near Garard's Fort, referred to Ross Crosley, the executor of his Will which was written on February 28, 1782, as "my trusty friend and brother" (possibly his brother-in-law) and mentioned Ross' land on Stope Run next to his father, Robert Crosley Sr.[2]

About this time Robert Crosley Sr signed the Petition for a New State of Westsylvania which was circulated in present day Fayette, Washington, and Greene Counties.

In 1783 Robert Crosley Sr was listed in the Greene Township Tax List with 300 acres of land assessed for $40. In that year he was also listed in the Cumberland Township Tax List with 260 acres, three horses, and four cows assessed at $140.[3]

In 1785 Robert Crosley Sr paid £1.80.3s.9d. to the Receiver General of the Commonwealth of Pennsylvania for 280 acres of land that he called The Cove on Muddy Creek in Washington County situated next to William Cree, William Villers, and David Dunkin. It was surveyed on October 22, 1786, patented on December 13, 1791, and recorded in the Washington County Patent Book P, page 305.

Between 1782 and 1791 Robert married Catherine...of Washington County, Pennsylvania, and there was no further mention was made of his first wife, Mary. Robert and Catherine granted to Henry Aibleberger 82 acres of the land called The Cove to William Cree in Cumberland Township. Witnesses were James Basinger and James Henderson. The transaction was recorded in December 1799 in the Greene County Patent Book P, page 311.

They soon moved farther west and in September 1783 Robert Crosley Sr was received in the Goshen Baptist Church at Garard's Fort. In 1792 he provided wine for the communion.

Robert bought 200 acres of land in Washington County which was surveyed on January 17, 1785.[4] In 1785 he received a warrant for 97 acres which he called Sparrow. He had it surveyed on August 16, 1785. He sold it to John Burley on a patent dated July 20, 1798, and recorded the transaction in the Greene County Patent Book P34, page 245.

He was included on the List of Persons Exonerated in 1789 for being distressed by the Incursions and Depredations of the Indians on the Frontiers of Washington County.

In 1793 Robert and Catherine Crosley of Washington County sold to Nathan Veach for £50 100 acres of land called The Cove on Muddy Creek in Cumberland Township. Witness was William Bonar.[5]

On June 3, 1803, Robert Crosley and his wife Catherine of Cumberland Township patented to Thomas Mendenhall 103 acres of land situated next to Jacob Hibbs, James Henderson, William Cree, and Nathan Veach. Witnesses were Jonathan Johnson and Jacob Hibbs. The transaction was recorded in the Greene County Patent Book, Volume 1, page 711.

In 1812 John Beezley's Will was witnessed by John Warren, Robert Crosley, and William Christy. It was probated in Williams County, Ohio, on January 18, 1813.

In June 1818 Joseph Crosley of Miami County and Robert Crosley of Hamilton County paid $50 as partial payment to William Crosley of Hamilton County for Section 33, Township 4, 2nd Fractional Range of Township in the Miami Purchase situated next to John Ferris. Signed by Joseph Crosley, Robert Croslely, Mary Crosley, and Rachel Crosley. Witnesses: Henry Whittaker, James Lyon, and Thomas Sayer.

On April 1822 Sarah Crosley paid $500 in partial payment to Robert Crosley of Hamilton County for the southeast corner of Section 33, Township 4, 2nd Fractional Range of Township in the Miami Purchase.

In 1830, in the deed of the Duck Creek Baptist Church, several people stated that they were interested in the John Corbly farm. They included Sarah, Joseph, Robert, and William Crosley, heirs to John and Martha Crosley. Others were Simon Crosley and his wife, heirs to Paul and Justice Corbly.[6]

[1] http://www.angelfire.com/my/crosleyconnect/html.

[2] http://www.angelfire.com/my/crosleyconnect/ross.html

[3] http://www.angelfire.com/my/crosleyconnect/master4.html

[4] Pennsylvania Land Office. *Warrantees of Land in the Several Counties of the State of Pennsylvania, 1730-1898.* (Nabu Press, Charleston, SC. Rpt 2010.)
[5] http://www.angelfire.com/my/crosleyconnect/master4.html
[6] http://www.angelfire.com/my/crosleyconnect/master3.html

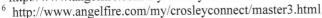

ZACHARIAH GAPEN

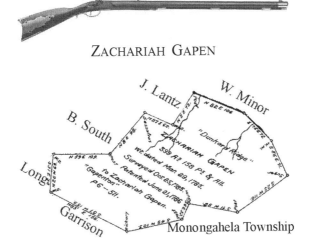

Monongahela Township

Zachariah Gapen (1733-1812) was born in New Jersey and died in Greene County, Pennsylvania. He married Ruth Tindall (1740-) and moved to Monocacy, Virginia, where their son, Stephen Gapen (1761-1838), was born.[1]

In 1764 John Minor traveled from Virginia to the Big Whiteley Creek area near the future Garard's Fort site to select land for himself, his brother William Minor, and for Zachariah Gapen. Most of the settlers on Whiteley Creek, though not native Virginians, were strong in their allegiance to Virginia. The Minors and the Gapens were originally from New Jersey and had settled for a time in the Conococheague Valley between Chambersburg and Frederick, Virginia. In the spring of 1766 a wagon train consisting of John Minor, Jeremiah Glassgow, William Minor, and Zachary Gapen with their families began their journey to southwestern Pennsylvania. They were soon followed to the Whiteley Creek area by their former neighbors the Garards, Suttons, and VanMeters, a Baptist group.[2]

Zachariah and his family lived on their selected tract which adjoined the lands of Colonel John and William Minor. They owned the land by the right of occupation, or "blazing," the marking of a land's boundaries by barking trees. It was not warranted to him until March 29, 1785, when surveyed land began to be recorded. He named it Dunkard Ridge (symbolic of his Dunkard Quakerism) and had it surveyed on October 25, 1785. It was patented to him as Gapenton on June 21, 1786, and was recorded in the Washington County Patent Book P6, page 511.

Zachariah's land was not far from the long-used Indian Trail mentioned in Christopher Gist's Journal on March 8, 1752, as "following Dunkard Creek to its source near the Forks of Wheeling Creek." That route was used by the Wetzells, Bonnetts, Waggoners and others to settle near the Ohio River on Wheeling, Fishing, and Grave Creeks. It was the favorite trail the Indians used to infiltrate into the Whiteley Creek area settlements to perpetrate their many massacres.

In the 1781 Effective Supply Tax Rate Book for Greene Township, Washington County, Zachariah Gapen was taxed $130 for 600 acres of land, two horses, 14 cows, and seven sheep.[3]

Zachariah Gapen was on the Assessment Roll for Greene Township, Washington County, in 1784 and belonged to the Westland Meeting of the Society of Friends (Quaker) in Washington County, Pennsylvania. His family and Jeremiah and John Long's families were neighbors. Sarah Gapen Long (1766-1850), a daughter of Zachariah Gapen and Ruth Tindall, married Noah Long and was named in Zachariah Gapen's Will of 1812 which was recorded in Greene County Will Book 1, page 99. It was probated on March 15, 1812. Further proof that she was a Gapen is in Slocum's biography of Noah Long, son of Jeremiah Long.[4]

Zachariah and his son, Stephen, signed as witnesses when John Long devised his Will. The Court record read, "On March 29, 1786, personally appeared before me Zachariah Gapen and Stephen Gapen after the attestation by law required say that they were personally present and heard and saw John Long sign and acknowledge the annexed Will and that they the said Gapens believe at the time of said Long's so doing that he was in his perfect reason. Affirmed before me the same day, Thomas Stokeley, Registrar. Signed, Zachariah Gapen and Stephen Gapen."[5]

Zachariah Gapen was included in the List of Persons Exonerated on the Frontiers of Washington County for being distressed by the Incursions and Depredations of the Indians according to the Washington County Tax Lists of 1787-1789.

Zachariah received a warrant dated March 30, 1796, for 407 acres called Lantzman in Whiteley Township. It was surveyed on March 29, 1802, patented on June 20, 1809, and recorded in the Greene County Patent Book H1, page 129.

In 1792 he was elected a Washington County Commissioner.[6]

In the 1797 Greene County Tax Book made by Joseph Willford and assisted by Elias Stone and Stephen Gapen, Zachariah Gapen Sr was assessed for 440 acres of land at $180, 60 acres of cleared land at $60, one house at $20, one barn at $2, two horses at $30, and three cows at $18. In 1799 he was assessed only for 150 acres of land at $120 and 25 cleared acres of land at $25. He was assessed in the 1809 Dunkard Township, Greene County Tax Book for 50 acres of land at $30 and one house at $4.

He was living in Dunkard Township when he filed his Will in the Greene County Will Book, Volume 1, page 99.

[1]Tippecanoe County Biographies. http://www.ingenweb.org/intippecanoe/ tbios.htm.

[2] Leckey, Howard. *Tenmile Country and its Pioneer Families.* Rpt, (Closson Press, Apollo, PA. 2007) 578.

[3] Pennsylvania Archives, Series 3, Volume XXII, page 699.

[4] Slocum, Charles Elihu. *History of the Maumee River basin from the earliest account to its organization into counties.* (Heritage Books Inc., Henry Company Ohio edition, Westminster, MD, 1997) Volume 9.

[5] http://monongahela.blogspot.com/2009/07/annie-eliza-long-warne-wife-of-theodore.html.

6   Creigh, Alfred. History of Washington County from its First Settlement to the Present Time...(Singerly, Printer, Harrisburg, PA, 1871) 259.

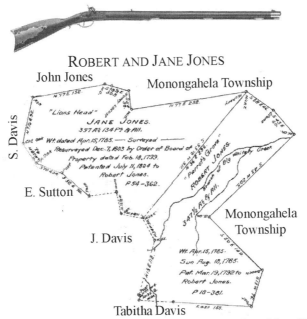

Reverend Morgan Jones, Parish of Llannon, Carmarthenshire, Wales, was the father (by his second wife) of: [1]

i. Samuel (1725-).
ii. Morgan Jr (1729-).
iii. John (1732-).
iv. Thomas (1735-).
v. Joseph (1737-).
vi. Benjamin (1740-).
vii. Robert (1743-1809) who was born in Duck Creek, Delaware, and settled about 1770 in Washington County near Fort Hudson (later Jenkins Fort) on Whiteley Creek near Garard's Fort. He and his wife, Jane Bolton (1763-1845), were among the founding members of the Goshen Baptist Church at Garard's Fort and were buried in the Garard's Fort Cemetery. Their children were.

> 1. Mary married Jesse Evans
> 2. Rachel married Lewis Evans
> 3. Rebecca married George Reynolds.
> 4. John married Mary J. Brice and had nine children: Robert, William, Benjamin, John, Rachel, Mary, Lydia, Louise, and Maria.

viii. Rachel (1747-).

Robert Jones served as a Private in Captain John Nice's Company in Colonel Samuel Atlee's Musket Battalion in the Pennsylvania Line and was reported missing "since August 27, 1776."[2]

The Deposition of "Margaret Lederman in 1777, of Yorktown:

...a widow, who being duly sworn on the Holy Evangelists of Almighty God, doth depose and say That on Sunday last in the forenoon a certain Robert Jones of Manchester Township, in the County of York, came to her house in Yorktown to inquire about a Load of hay, which as she understood her son had purchased of the said Jones at Thirty Shillings for which he was to pay him in work at the old price. She asked him what had become of his friend Rankin, & told him she had heard he was in Philadelphia, he asked her who told her so. She replied Mr. Peters. Jones then laughed and said if is so, it is true enough.

The Deponent is not certain whether he said Rankin came himself every week, but thinks something of the kind was mentioned, but is 'positive that the said Jones told her that the said Rankin came frequently out of Philadelphia as far as the rising sun, & that his family either saw him or had a Letter every week. That the said Jones then told her that the said Rankin would be here at York this winter, ort as soon as the Ice was fit to bear, & the Susquehannah frozen over the English would be here. That the said Rankin could travel from & into

Philadelphia, as far as to the rising sun easily for noboddy stops him. That by the said Jones's conversation she understood Rankin was to conduct the English to York that before the said Jones's departure, he desired the Deponent to keep the Matter secret, saying with much earnestness 'for God's sake dont tell that I told you of it, or else it will cost me my plantation,' but she on her Son's coming from Church, being much terrified with the apprehensions of the Enemy coming this way, told her son what had passed, with many other circumstances which she has now forgot, but from the whole of the said Jones's conversation she was so convinced that the Enemy would be here, that she was casting about for....

Board of War to President Wharton, 1777.
War Office, y^c 20 Decem', 1777-Sir,
In consequence of the Deposition of Mrs. Margaret Lederman, Yorktown, Copy whereof I have the honor of transmitting your Excellency, the Board concluded no time should be lost in securing the Person of Robert Jones, who it appears, directly or indirectly has had an intercourse with the Enemy. He is now under confinement, and the board beg leave to refer him over to the executive power of the State. His general character throughout the Neighbourhood is that of a Disaffected person, and it is greatly to be apprehended there are many others linked together that make a chain highly necessary to be broken & dispersed in the present situation of Affairs. This Jones not being so artful and cautious as the rest has inadvertently made public, what, he doubtless intended should for the present remain secret, indeed at his first examination he wholly denied the charge. I have the honor to be Your Excellencey's most ob' humble Serv. JOSEPH NOURSE, D. S. Directed His Excellency Th. Wharton, jun'r, Esq., President of the Council, State of Pennsylvania, Lancaster.[3]

Robert Jones served in the Westmoreland County Rangers on the Frontier during 1778-1783.

In 1782 Robert Jones signed the Petition for the new state of Westsylvania to be formed out of present day Fayette, Washington, and Greene Counties, Pennsylvania, and Ohio and Monongalia Counties, Virginia.[4] He was listed on the 1784 Assessment Roll for Greene Township, Washington County, Pennsylvania.

On September 17, 1784, he received $46.40/90 on Certificate No. 741128E for service in the First Pennsylvania Regiment of Foot in 1781. On the same date he received $80 on Certificate 74241A for service in the First Pennsylvania Regiment of Foot in 1782. On October 12, 1785, he received $80 on Certificate 75691L for service in the First Pennsylvania Regiment of Foot in 1780, $61.30/90 on Certificate 74016H for service in the First Pennsylvania Regiment of Foot in 1781, and $80 on Certificate 74332R for service in the First Pennsylvania Regiment of Foot in 1782. On June 13, 1787, he received $33.30/90 on Certificate 73841P for service in the First Pennsylvania Regiment of Foot in 1780.[5]

He and his wife secured warrants for tracts of land on April 15, 1785, Robert's tract being called Patriots Grove while Jane's tract was known as Lions Head. (The plat drafted in 1917 misspelled the name as Parrot's Grove.) Robert Jones bought the 347 acres of land on a warrant dated April 15, 1785. It was surveyed on August 18, 1785, patented on March 19, 1792, and recorded in the Washington County Patent Book P18, page381.

On a warrant also dated April 15, 1785, Jane bought 397 acres of land contiguous to Patriots Grove. It was resurveyed on December 7, 1803, patented on July 11, 1804, to Robert Jones, and recorded in the Greene County Patent Book P54, page 362.

Robert was a founding member of the Goshen Baptist Church and was mentioned often in the Goshen Baptist Church Minute Book.[6]

> i. October 29, 1785, the Church received John Guthrey, John Garard, Jane Jones, and Druzilley Knapp by baptism.
>
> ii. December 24, 1785, Bro Robert Jones and Brother Jonathan Morris chosen Deacons to assist Bro Moredock in the business of the church.
>
> iii. 10/6/1787, Bro Robert Jones appointed to cite Michael Hahn to out next monthly meeting to shew cause for his nonattendance likewise Received Sarah Brown same day for baptism.
>
> iv. April 1788, Met at Muddy Creek according to appt and proceeded to business viz Bro Robert Jones, Jo's Frazer, Elias Garard, Dan'l Clark, Jeremiah Gustin, David Price to meet at Brother Frazer on Wednesday next settle a matter betwixt Brother George Morris and Elijah Moore.
>
> v. July 26, 1788, Brother Robert Jones and Brother Joseph Martin chosen to raise hymns.
>
> vi. October 18, 1788, App'd Bro Lewis Williams, Bro Robert Jones, and Bro Guthery to go over the River and talk with Michael Hahn concerning his absenting himself from our society and make report to our next monthly meeting to all members.
>
> vii. April 18, 1789, The Church from the report of Robert

Jones, Jo's Frazer, Ross Crosley, Jeremiah Gustin concerning to Brother George Morris and Elijah Moore be laid under the censure of the Church.

vii. June 20, 1789, Appointed Brother Robert Jones to cite Brother Andrew Dye to come to our meeting for business.

viii. August 1, 1789, Sister Elizabeth Davis to decline communion til the Church inquire into the truth of her having another husband. On refusal the Church agrees to use their authority. Brother Jones and Brother James Moredock to acquaint her with the same.

ix. August 1789, App'd Bro John Corbly, Levi Harrod, James Moredock, Jonathan Morris, Azariah Davis, Charles Anderson, and bro Robert Jones Messengers to Association at Great Bethel and Bro David Price to prepare letter...Agreed to request Sister Elizabeth Davis to decline communion til the Church inquire into the truth of her having another husband. On refusal the Church agrees to use their authority. Bro Jones and Bro Moredock to acquaint her with same.

x. June 19. 1790, Bro Clark to cite Bro John Guthery and his wife to come to the next monthly to give reason for not attending at monthly meeting. Likewise Bro Robert Jones to cite Jonathan Mundle for the same.

xi. August 27, 1791, appointed Bros John Corbly, Robert Jones, Moredock, Chas Anderson, Azaraiah Davis, John Ross, Levi Harrod, Abner Mundle and Joseph Gibbins as messengers to ass'n at the Speers' meetinghouse.

Robert Jones bought 400 acres of land on April 1, 1785, and 150 acres on November 9, 1786, in Washington County.[7] Then he bought 363 acres of land in Whiteley Township on November 9, 1786, and called the tract Baptist. It was surveyed on 4, 1787, patented on March 16, 1792, and recorded in the Washington County Patent Book P18, page 380.

He was included on the List of Persons Exonerated in 1789 for being distressed by the Incursions and Depredations of the Indians on the Frontiers of Washington County.

He was listed in the 1790 Census of Greene Township, Washington County, as head of household with one male under 16 years of age and four females.

In the 1797 Greene County Tax Book made by Joseph Willford, Assessor, assisted by Elias Stone and Stephen Gapen, he was assessed for 1,200 acres of land at $1,380, 140 acres of cleared land at $140, one house at $5, and one barn at $5. In 1800 he was assessed for 580 acres of land at $580, 100 acres of cleared land at $100, one house at $10, one barn at $10, one horse at $20, and one cow at $6.

On April 6, 1794, he received 200 acres of Donation Land for service as a Private in the Second Pennsylvania Regiment during the Revolutionary War.[8] Jane was living in Whiteley Township when she filed her Will in the Greene County Will Book in Volume 1, page 297.

[1] Steiner, Christian; Meekins, Lynn; Carroll, David. *Men of mark in Maryland ...: biographies of leading men of the ..., Volume 3.* (Nabu Press, Charleston, SC, 2010).

[2] Pennsylvania Archives, Series 2, Vol. X, page 408, and Volume XV, page 407.

[3] Pennsylvania Archives, Revolutionary War, 1777, page 117.

[4] Continental Congress papers, No. 48, Folios 251-256, pages 89-96.

[5] Pennsylvania Archives, Revolutionary War Rolls, Claims.

[6] Corbly, Don. *Pastor John Corbly.* (Lulu Press, Raleigh, NC, 2008) 273.

[7] Egle, William Henry. *Provincial Papers: Warrantees of Land in the Several Counties of the State of Pennsylvania, 1730-1898.* (William Stanley Ray, State Printer, Pennsylvania, 1899).

[8] Pennsylvania Archives, Series 3, Volume VII, Chapter; Donation Lands granted Soldiers of the Pennsylvania Line.

JOHN AND DANIEL WHITMORE

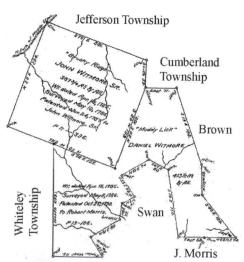

Francis Whitmore (1625-) was in Cambridge, Massachusetts, in 1649. He married Isabel Parke (1628-1665). His son, Samuel Whitmore (1658-

1724), was born in Cambridge, Middlesex County, and died in Lexington, Middlesex County, Massachusetts. Samuel married (1) Rebecca Gardner (1686-1709) and (2) Butterfield (-1730). Samuel and Rebecca Gardner had nine children including Francis, Samuel, Rebecca, Benjamin, Abigail, Sarah, Nathaniel, Mary, and John (1692-1759).

Samuel Whitmore (1658-1724), son of Francis, married (2) Mary Butterfield (1670-1730) of Middlesex County, Massachusetts, about 1714. Their child was John (1715-) who was born in Lexington, Middlesex County, Massachusetts. The descendancy from Samuel stops at this point. No records were found for the son John (1715-).[1]

John Whitmore (1692-1759), son of Samuel and Rebecca Gardner, was born in Cambridge, Lexington, Middlesex County, Massachusetts. He married (1) Lydia Cutter (1713-) in 1735 and then (2) Mary Burnell. John and Lydia Cutter's children were Mary (1735-) who married Joseph Healy; John (1737-); and Captain Samuel (1743-1808) who married Mary Whitney and had 12 children. Samuel bought a 30-acre lot in Gorham (then in Massachusetts) from Alexander Ross. He was a blacksmith, a selectman of Gorham, and town treasurer. In 1782 he was a member of the Committee of Correspondence, Inspection, and Safety of Gorham. He served in the Revolutionary war as Captain of a Company from Gorham that was part of the Third Cumberland County Regiment.

John Whitmore (1692-1759) next married (2) Mary Burnell in 1750. John and Mary Burnell's children were William (1752-1827) who married Amey Knight; Joseph (1755-1841) who married Abigail Babbidge; and Daniel (1758-1846) who married Anna S. Hill (1803-1820) in March 1782.

Daniel (1758-1846) was born in Baldwin and was a blacksmith. Anna was born in Buxton, a daughter of Jeremiah and Mary Hill. Daniel and Anna moved to Unity where they lived out their lives and were buried in the Village Cemetery in Unity, Waldo County, Maine. This Daniel bought 413 acres called Muddy Lick in Washington County on a warrant dated April 19, 1785. It was surveyed on May 11, 1786, patented October 25, 1792, to Robert Morris and recorded in the Washington County Patent Book P19, page 106. Daniel and Anna Hill had 10 children including Rebecca, Joseph, Simon, Mary, Hill (1794 -1820), George, Jesse, Anna (1803-1820), Daniel Jr, and Julia. Daniel Whitmore was listed in the 1788 Assessment Roll of unseated lands in Cumberland Township, Washington County, Pennsylvania.[2]

On April 19, 1785, John Whitmore Sr (1737-), son of John Whitmore (1692-1759) and Lydia Cutter, half-brother of Daniel (1758-1846), bought 387 acres called Brushy Ridge on a warrant in Washington County. It was surveyed May 10, 1786, patented November

24, 1787, and recorded in the Washington County Patent Book P11, page 396. A John Whitmore was a Private in April 1776 in Captain John Marshal's Company in Colonel Samuel Atlee's Second Musket Battalion of the Pennsylvania Line.[3]

There were several Whitmores during this time and many of their records stand alone without reference to parentage or other relationships. The most probable descendancy is from Francis Whitmore, the migrant from Cambridge, Massachusetts, in 1649 who married Isabel Parke (1628-). The fact that this John and Daniel bought their tracts on warrants issued the same day strongly indicates that they were closely related.

[1] http://freepages.genealogy.rootsweb.ancestry.com/~whitmore/folks/791.htm.
[2] Leckey, Howard. *Tenmile Country and its Pioneer Families.* Rpt, (Closson Press, Apollo, PA. 2007) 135.
[3] Pennsylvania Archives, Series 2, Volume X, pages 231, 234.

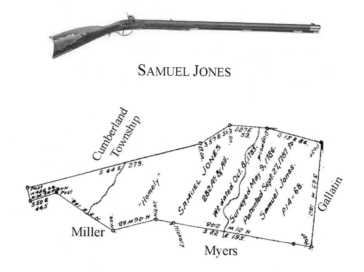

SAMUEL JONES

Samuel Jones (1742-1810) married Leah Thomas (1742-1793) in 1760 according to the J. H. Jones Bible. They were born in Hilltown, Bucks County, Pennsylvania. He married at about the age of 18 years. They raised a family of 13 children. His first daughter, Sarah, was stillborn and died September 15, 1762, in Bucks County. They apparently remained in Bucks County until about the start of the Revolutionary War. His name was on the list of taxables in that county in 1774.[1]

Samuel was a Second Lieutenant in Colonel Daniel Morgan's 15th Virginia Regiment in 1776 while his family was residing in Frederick County, Virginia. In 1777 he was the Regimental Paymaster and remained with that unit until January 1780 while it fought the battle of Saratoga and then departed to Valley Forge.[2]

Colonel Daniel Morgan was absent from Valley Forge during the spring of 1778 and in June First Lieutenant Samuel Jones was tried by Courts Martial for concealing and denying that he had in his possession a pair of mittens belonging to Captain Hull. He was also accused of gambling and behaving in a manner unbecoming an Officer and Gentleman. He reportedly used abusive language towards Captain Hull at the time of his arrest and tried to incense the officers against Hull. The court found him guilty of the charges and sentenced him to be discharged. General George Washington did not believe that Samuel was capable of having retained the gloves with a fraudulent intention, but it was clearly proved that he was guilty of the gambling. Therefore, he confirmed the sentence of discharge. When Colonel Daniel Morgan returned to Valley Forge records indicated his anger at finding that one of his men (Jones) had been "lashed." On June 11 General Washington received ample testimony of the general good character and behavior of Lieutenant Jones and being further satisfied by Generals Woodford, Scott, and other officers that Jones was not addicted to the vice of gaming, General Washington restored him to his rank and command in his regiment.

In January 1781 Samuel Jones retired from the military and by 1782 had moved his family to present day Washington County, Pennsylvania. On October 8, 1785, he bought 282 acres of land called Homely in that county, surveyed it on May 9, 1786, patented it on September 27, 1787, and recorded it in the Washington County Patent Book P14, page 68. They lived a mile from the village of Washington when Leah died. In 1799 he sold the remaining 29 acres of Leah's inherited land in Bucks County.

In 1806 he obtained six parcels of land in Ohio totaling 2,000 acres on Paint Creek near present day Chillicothe, Ross County, Ohio, and 1,000 acres on the Little Miami River in Greene County, Ohio.

According to DAR records he was buried in the Wooster Cemetery in Wooster, Wayne County, Ohio. The headstone inscription read:
Samuel Jones, b. 1742, d. 1810, Captain,
Virginia, married Leah Thomas.[3]

[1] Mathews, Edward. *The Thomas Family of Hilltown, Bucks County,* (Adams Apple Press, Perkasie, PA, 1993).

70

[2] Saffell, W. T. Robert. Index to Saffell's list of Virginia soldiers in the Revolution, 1866-1927, (Nabu Press, Charleston, SC, 2010) 266, 395.
[3] http://www.findagrave.com.

JOHN BRADFORD

Wood   Wright

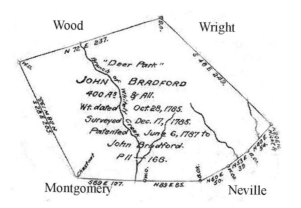

Montgomery   Neville

In 1719 John Bradford was a taxable in Rock Creek Hundred of Prince George's County, Maryland. His son, Robert Bradford (1730-1802), "the emigrant," was the pioneer ancestor of the Bradford family who settled in what is now Franklin Township, Greene County, at the head of Sugar Run where in 1785 he patented a tract of land called Pleasure.[1]

Robert Bradford was born in North Ireland and died in Franklin Township, Greene County, Pennsylvania. He married about 1753 Margaret…(1732-1806) who died in Greene County, Pennsylvania. Among their children were:

i. James (1753-1822) who was born in Northern Ireland and about 1784 married Barbara Yoho (1765-1816). She died in Whiteley Township, Greene County, Pennsylvania, and they were buried there in the Bradford Cemetery.

ii. John (1759-), born in Northern Ireland married Mary….[2]

John Bradford (1759-) answered the urgent call from the Council of Safety in Philadelphia for volunteers to enlist in General Washington's fledging Army. He enlisted as a Private in April 1777 in Colonel Moses Hazen's 25th Regiment of the Virginia Line. He served as a Private in

Captain Berry's Company in Colonel Abraham Bowman's 8th Virginia Regiment of Foot. For service in May and June 1777 he received £4 pay and £1.2s. pay for each month of July, August, and September. In August 1777 he reenlisted for three years.

He was a Corporal in Captain David Cady's Company in Colonel Samuel Chapman's Regiment of Foot in the Connecticut Militia in March 1799. He reenlisted in August 1779, was discharged in September, and was paid £3.3s. for 43 days of service. He next served in Captain Bacon's Company in Colonel Chester's Regiment of Foot in the Connecticut Militia for two months and was paid £4.6s.8d.

He served in Captain William Dyre's Company in Colonel Walbridge's Regiment of Foot of the Vermont Militia in October and November 1780 and was paid £1.13s.4d. He was a Private in Lieutenant Holmes' Company in Colonel Fletcher's Regiment of Foot in the Vermont Militia from December 1780 to April 1781 and was paid £5. He was also in Captain John Stark's Company during the Campaign of 1781 for which he received £3.12s. and for service from July to September 1781 he was paid £5.9s.4d.

The Effective Supply Tax of Cumberland Township, Washington County, in 1781 listed John Bradford living on one acre with one horse valued at $12 for tax purposes.[3]

After British General Cornwallis conceded defeat at Yorktown, thus ending the British domination over the colonies, John Bradford became a Private in William Crawford's Company of a Washington County Ranger Regiment in April 1781 to combat the Indians on the frontiers. At various times his neighbors, Ensigns Charles and William Swan, in what became Greene County, also served in the same company. John continued to serve in the Washington Militia through 1783.

In 1782 five Battalions of Militia were ordered organized from men living in present day Greene County. The First Battalion of Pennsylvania Militia was commanded by Lieutenant Colonel Henry Enochs of Clarksville and Major James Carmichael of Muddy Creek. John Bradford served as a Private in Captain Andrew Fourley's Company of that battalion which was recruited mainly from men in the Castile Run area near the town of Chartiers.[4]

In 1784 John Bradford was listed on the Assessment Roll of Cumberland Township, Washington County, Pennsylvania.

As a member of the Militia he was paid £1.8s. on November 9, 1784.

He petitioned for a new state of Westsylvania in 1782.[5]

He bought a 400-acre farm in 1784 that belonged to Sebastian "Boston" Keener. Keener's son, John, was killed on that land in that year by the Indian warrior Chief Logan who went on a murderous rampage of revenge to atone for the white man's killing of members of his family. The warrant was dated October 28, 1785, the land was surveyed on December 17, 1785, it was patented on June 6, 1787, and recorded in the Washington County Patent Book P11, page 168.

Keener's patent to John Bradford read "a certain Tract of Land called Deer Park Situated on a Branch of Whitely Creek in Washington County containing Four hundred Acres, John Bradford his Heirs and assigns forever free and clear of all Restrictions and Reservations as to Mines royalties, Quit Rents, or otherwise excepting and reserving only the fifth part of all Gold & Silver Ores for the use of this Commonwealth to be delivered at the Pits Mouth clear of all Charges." That grant was signed by Benjamin Franklin, a delegate to the convention which gave us the Constitution of the United States.

Mr Joseph Gwyne, Collector of Taxes in Cumberland Township, Washington County for 1788 assessed John Bradford $12 for one horse. The 1790 Census listed John Bradford in Cumberland Township, Washington County, as head of household with three males under 16 years of age and two females in the family.

In the Tax List for 1789 in Greene Township, Washington County, Pennsylvania, he was included as one of the Persons Exonerated on the Frontiers of Washington County for having been distressed by the Incursions and Depredations of the Indians.[6]

In 1792 John Bradford and his wife, Mary, sold part of Deer Park. In a Washington County Deed Book a deed was dated December 29, 1792, from John for 98.5 acres of land at a price of £20, it being a part of Deer Park. They sold that land to Joseph Price, his wife, Elizabeth, and Hannah Keener, Elizabeth's sister. In 1795 Joseph and Elizabeth Price and Hannah Keener sold it to Michael McCarty for £53.

The Tax Book for Greene County in 1797 was made by the Assessor, Joseph Willford, who was assisted by Elias Stone and Stephen Gapen. In it John Bradford had 200 acres of land assessed at $100. He had cleared 30 acres of it which was assessed at $30. His cabin was assessed at $1; his horse at $20; and his three cows at $18. In 1800 his land was assessed at $160; he farmed 25 acres of it which was assessed at $20. He acquired a second cabin which was assessed at $2, his horse at $15, and his three cows at $18.[7]

JOSEPH PRICE

The first mention of Joseph Price, one of the earliest settlers in present day Greene County, Pennsylvania, was when he bought part of John Bradford's Deer Park plantation in 1792 along with his wife,

Elizabeth,and her sister, Hannah. That is, that was the first mention he probably wanted anyone to know about.

He actually made his mark 18 years earlier according to the Provincial Council:

> Minutes of the Provincial Council, Philadelphia, April 22, 1774. Crawford, Esquire, and his Associates, Justices of Westmoreland County. The Governor laid before the Board the several Records of the Convictions of Joseph Price and …of this Province, the last Court of Oyer and Terminer held at Philadelphia for the County of Philadelphia in April Instant before William Allen, John Lawrence, and Thomas Willing, Esquires, Justices of the said Court… by which Records it appears that the said Criminals had all received Sentence of Death.
>
> …The Board duly considering the several Cases of the said Criminals, are of Opinion that Warrants should he issued for the Executions of Joseph Price and…on Saturday the thirtieth of this Instant. It is, therefore, Ordered that Warrants of Execution, Reprieve and Pardons, be forthwith made out accordingly. (the Governor approved leniency for the convicted prisoners and they were set free.)

Joseph Price married Elizabeth Keener, the granddaughter of Ulrich Keener. Elizabeth's father, John Keener (1746-1774), was one of Ulrich's grandsons by his son Sebastian. John Keener was born in Lancaster, Pennsylvania, and was killed by Chief Logan's scalping party on his father's (Sebastian) farm in Greene County, Pennsylvania. He was buried on the farm in Lantz Bottom on the Big Whiteley Creek.

John had married Hannah….and they had at least two daughters; Elizabeth who married Joseph Price, and Hannah (1790-1853) who married George Glendenning in 1814 in Preston County, Virginia. Hannah Keener was born at Whiteley Creek, Greene Township, Washington County, Pennsylvania, and died in Taylor County, Virginia.[8]

Joseph and Elizabeth Keener were probably married in Greene or Fayette County, Pennsylvania, since her family was in that area in the 1770s. They were listed in the Greene County, Pennsylvania, 1790 Census. By 1798 they had sons John, Jacob, William, and according to some accounts, another son named Henry.

Joseph Price was a joiner (carpenter) in 1776 when he enlisted in Captain Clark's Company of Militia of Ulster County, New York. The Company's Muster Roll identified him as five feet eight inches tall with a fair complexion, brown hair, and blue eyes. In July 1776 he enlisted as a Private in Captain McBride's Company in Colonel Hasbrouck's Regiment of New York Militia at the pay of £1.1s.4d. per month. He next enlisted as a Private in Captain Stout's Company in Colonel Maxwell's First Regiment of New Jersey Troops in 1776. Then he became a Corporal in Captain Graydon's Company in the Third Regiment of Light Foot of the Pennsylvania Line in September 1776.[9]

In 1776, just six weeks after the Declaration of Independence was announced to the general public, Joseph Price signed the petition to form a new state of Westsylvania. The petition was circulated in opposition to the lack of governance over the lands west of the Alleghenies by the Council of Safety seated in Philadelphia.[10]

The Revolutionary War just ended did not stop the continuous and increasingly deadly Indian attacks on the settlers. Joseph Price enlisted as a Private in Captain John Hugh's Company of Stockley Rangers in Lieutenant Colonel Henry Enoch's First Battalion of Washington County Militia and remained on call through 1783.

Joseph Price of Fayette County, Pennsylvania, received Donation Land of 150 acres in September 1834 for his service during the Revolutionary War.[11]

Joseph and Elizabeth moved to Greene County, Ohio, where he was appointed its first tax assessor. His final move was to Franklin County, Ohio, where, for service during the Revolutionary War, he drew a pension of $50 per year beginning March 4, 1834.[12]

[1] Leckey, Howard. *Tenmile Country and its Pioneer Families.* Rpt, (Closson Press, Apollo, PA. 2007) 383.

[2] http://freepages.genealogy.rootsweb.ancestry.com/~mysouthernfamily/myff/

[3] Pennsylvania Archives, Series 3, Volume XXII, page 699. d0083/g0000004.html.

[4] Pennsylvania Archives, Series 3, Volume XXIII, pages 198-220.

[5] Continental Congress papers, No. 48, Folios 251-256, pages 89-96.

[6] http://listsearches.rootsweb.com/th/read/PAGREENE/1999-07/0931158294.

[7] http://www.ourfamilyhistories.com/hsdurbin/tax-lists/more-tax-census1.html.

[8] http://familytreemaker.genealogy.com/users/t/r/o/Craig-Trout/COL12-0112. html.

[9] *Associators & Militia, Muster Rolls, Washington Militia.1775-1781.* http://files.usgwarchives.org/pa/ Washington/military/must231-240.txt.

[10] Leckey, 144.

[11] Pennsylvania Archives. Series 6, Volume II, page 233.

[12] Pennsylvania Archives, Sixth Series, Volume II.

JOSIAH AND MOSES LAMBERT JR

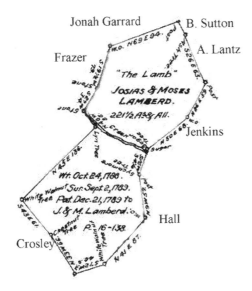

Moses Lambert Sr (abt 1710-1788) was born at Burlington County, New Jersey. In 1751 he was found in Frederick County, Virginia, where he surveyed for Dennis Springer who bought from John Frost a parcel of land lying on the Elk Lick branch of Back Creek in Frederick County, Virginia. The survey was signed by Dennis Springer, Thomas Chenowith, Francis Baldwin, and John Maury.

He was one of the early members of the Goshen Baptist Church that was formed in 1773. The Minute Book of the Goshen Baptist Church at Garard's Fort noted that in 1781 Moses Lambert Sr was received into the church by baptism when near death. He became a deacon in the Church in 1787, the year before he died.

Moses Sr was a private in Captain Daniel Piatt's Company of the First New Jersey Regiment commanded by Right Honorable Earl of Stirling located at the barracks at Elizabeth Town on January 7, 1776. He was on the Pay Roll of Captain Thomas DeWitt's Company in the Third New York Regiment commanded by Colonel Peter Ganswoort in May 1779 for which he was paid £2.[1]

When Moses Sr devised his Will in February 1782 he disposed of a legacy to John Martin's wife as directed by his father's Will, indicating that John Martin may have married Moses' sister. He referred to Ross Crosley as "my trusty friend and brother (in Christ)" and mentioned his wife, Osie, two sons, Moses Jr (the younger son) and Josiah (1742-

1820), and three unnamed daughters. Moses Jr was bequeathed a portion of the family farm on the west side of Stope Run adjoining Joseph Frazer, Jonah Garard, and Ebenezer Sutton. Josiah (the elder son) was bequeathed the main part of the family farm. The Will was witnessed by John Brown, Rachel Seal, and Ester Brown and recorded in the Washington County Will Book No. 1, page 9. It was probated in April 1782.[2]

Josiah was born in Hopewell, Hunterdon County, New Jersey, and died in Lawrence County, Ohio. He married Joannah Woodward (1745-1825) in 1766 at Shrewsbury, Monmouth County, New Jersey. Their children were Joseph, Anna, Hannah, Mary, Jonathan, Susannah, Richard, Priscilla, Job, and Abigail. During the American Revolutionary War Josiah served as an ensign on the privateer Retrieve which was captured by the British ship Milford and he was taken prisoner. Josiah also served as a guard in Philadelphia. After the war Josiah and family moved to western Pennsylvania in Washington County. Next they moved to Harrison County, Virginia, near what is now Clarksburg, West Virginia. The Lambert family ultimately settled on the Ohio River at what later became Ironton, Ohio, in 1800. Josiah and Joannah were buried in the Woodland Cemetery at Ironton, Lawrence County, Ohio.[3]

In 1787 the Goshen Baptist Church at Garard's Fort received Osie Griffith by letter from the Laurel Hill church. (Moses Lambert Sr's wife's first name).[4]

The deaths of Goshen Baptist Church members by the end of 1788 included Moses Lambert Sr. Ross Crosley and Osie Lambert appeared in court on November 4, 1788, to administer the estate of Moses Lambert Sr. His account settled, it was recorded in Washington County Book A, Volume 1, page 65. Moses Lambert Sr's tract of land near Garard's Fort, which was patented to his sons Moses Jr and Josiah, required that they pay £7.9s.2d for the 221 acres that they called The Lamb. The patent was recorded in the Washington County Patent Book 239, page 299.

In the Tax List for 1789 in Greene Township, Washington County, Pennsylvania, Moses Jr and Josiah were included on the list of the Persons Exonerated on the Frontiers of Washington County for having been distressed by the Incursions and Depredations of the Indians.[5]

By 1803 Moses Jr had moved to Kentucky where he married Nancy McGraw in Mercer County. They had nine children; Emily who married Samuel Sheets and ended up in Texas, Davis, Lewis, George, Andaville, Sally, Percival, Josephine, and Elizabeth. In 1806 Moses Lambert Jr and Nancy of Shelbyville, Kentucky, sold 125 acres of land to William Roberts of Greene Township, Greene County, on the waters of Whiteley

Creek situated next to John Burley. This land may have been Moses Jr's portion of the land left to him and his brother by their father, Moses Sr.[6]

[1] Rev War Rolls, NJ, First Regiment 1775-1776, folder 1, page 14 and folder 43, page 88.

[2] http://www.angelfire.com/my/crosleyconnect/ross.html

[3] http://www.findagrave.com.

[4] Corbly, Don. *Pastor John Corbly.* (Lulu Press, Raleigh, NC, 2008).

[5] http://listsearches.rootsweb.com/th/read/PAGREENE/1999-07/0931158294.

[6] http://www.angelfire.com/my/crosleyconnect/master4.html.

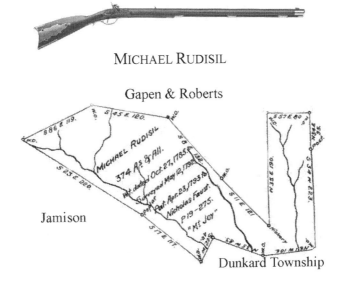

MICHAEL RUDISIL

George Philip Rudisil (1725-1758) was born in Weiler-Am-Stein, Germany, and was christened in Michelfeld, Baden, Germany. He died in Pennsylvania. He married Maria Barbara Miller (1722-1813) in 1745 in New Holland, Lancaster, Pennsylvania. She was born and died in Lebanon County, Pennsylvania, and was buried in Bindnagle, Lebanon County. Their son, Johann Michael Rudisil (1747-1791), was born in Lancaster, Pennsylvania. In 1765 he married Maria Angelica Engel Schaeferin (1737-1769) who was also born in Lancaster. Her parents were John Jacob Schaeferin and Maria Angelica Engel Kobel. The children of Johann Michael Rudisil and Maria Schaeferin were:[1]

    i. Maria Catharine (1766-1860),born in Lancaster, married John Jacob Fast and had seven children.

    ii. Eva Margaret (1769-1862), born in Albany Township, Berks Township, Berks County, Pennsylvania.

iii. Michael (1770-1859), born in Manheim Township, Lancaster County, Pennsylvania, died in Franklin County, Indiana. He married Susan Van Treese in 1797 in Hamilton, Ohio.

iv. Barbara (1772-1866), born in Middletown, Frederick County, Maryland. She married Conrad Cansler (1765-1813) who was born in Lincoln County, North Carolina, and died in Monroe, Tennessee.

v. Anna Maria (1773-1802), born in Middletown, Frederick County, Maryland, married John Van Blaricum (1796-1801).

vi. Christopher (1776-1848), born in Manheim Township, Lancaster County, Pennsylvania, died in Cincinnati, Ohio.

vii. Jacob (1782-1847), was born in Westmoreland, Pennsylvania.

viii. George (1788-1874), born in German Township, Fayette County, Pennsylvania, died in New Trenton, Indiana. He married Catherine Van Treese. They settled on government land in Whitewater Township, Indiana, in 1805. He was of German descent and was a Major General in the War of 1812.

On January 13, 1769, a land deed was delivered to Henry Smith, yeoman (landowner and farmer) of Heidelberg Township, Northampton County, Pennsylvania, from Michael Rudisil, yeoman of Penn Township of the same county.[2]

He served as a Private 6th Class in Captain Martin Weybright's Seventh Company in the Eighth Battalion of the Lancaster County Militia in June 1782, according to the Pennsylvania State Archives, Revolutionary War Military Abstract Card File.

Michael Rudisil signed the petition to form the new state of Westsylvania in 1782.[3] In Lancaster County about 1782 he owned 150 acres, three horses, and three cattle and was taxed £17.

Michael Rudisil bought 374 acres called Mount Joy on a warrant dated October 27, 1785. It was surveyed on May 12, 1792, patented on April 23, 1793, to Nicholas Fast, and recorded in the Washington County Patent Book P19, page 275.

JOHANN NICKLAUS FAST

Johann Nicklaus Fast (1727-1818) was born in Cocklingen, Kurpfalz, Germany, and died in Masontown, German Township, Fayette County, Pennsylvania. He was a Lutheran and a carpenter. He married Cadarina

Mararetha Doerner (1724-1796), daughter of Bernhard Dorner and Anna Pfuster. She was born in Ilbesheim, Germany, and died in Masontown, Fayette County, Pennsylvania. They emigrated from Germany in 1750 on the ship Royal Union to America. Cadarina's mother had a sister, Marie Cadarina Pfuster, whose Will stated that Cadarina had "married Nicklaus Fass (Fast) and gone to America." Nicklaus and Cadarina had eight sons and six daughters.[4]

About 1772 Nicklaus owned land on White Clay Creek near Smithtown, Washington County, Virginia (later Pennsylvania). They had a housekeeper named Ursala Clemens. Samuel Sackett was Nicklas' doctor. Thomas Shroyer built his coffin.

In 1781 Nicholas Fast was taxed $36 for 480 acres of vacant land in Greene Township, Washington County.[5] He bought tracts of land in Dunkard Township, Washington County, including 294 acres called Pleasure on a warrant dated February 7, 1785, which was surveyed on April 15, 1785, patented on February 3, 1787, and recorded in the Washington County Patent Book P8, page 243. He also purchased 183 acres called Pleasant on a warrant dated February 19, 1785. It was surveyed April 15, 1785, patented on November 1, 1785, and recorded in the Washington County Patent Book P4, page 76.

On October 27, 1785, Michael Rudisil bought 374 acres called Mount Joy on a warrant dated October 27, 1785, in Washington County. It was surveyed on May 12, 1792, and patented on April 23, 1793, to Nicholas Fast. The transaction was recorded in the Washington County Patent Book P19, page 275. A February 6, 1787, deed was owned by Nicklaus Fast for a tract of land called Hard to Find. It was recorded in the Washington County Patent Book 8, page 243.

He was included in the 1789 Greene Township List of Persons Exonerated on the Frontiers of Washington County for being Distressed by the Incursions and Depredations of the Indians.[6]

On April 17, 1794, an Indenture (a legal contract reflecting a debt or purchase obligation) from Nicholas Fast and his wife Catherine of German Township, Fayette County, Pennsylvania, was entered into with Ephraim Walter to purchase 106 acres next to Robert Ross and others on the east side of the Monongahela River south of Catt's Corner, now German Township, later Nicholson Township, near present day Masontown.[7]

Nicklaus Fast's Will was found in the Greene County Will Book 9, page 225, Waynesburg, Greene County, Pennsylvania.[8] Devised in January 17, 1816, in German Township, Fayette County, Pennsylvania, it read in part:

1st, Mary Weaver's share to be equally divided among her 3

children, dec'd wife of Frederick Wibel, 100 acres of land, Jefferson Co, OH being part of the one half section conveyed by my son Francis Fast to me, 6 Mar 1807, being #23, 11th Twp, Rg 4, from the west end of side half section, to be shared equally by the 3 children.

2nd, unto Henry Weaver, Frederick Wibel, and John Sears, each 50 cents. Remaining of my estate real and personal to be sold and equally divided in 7 shares and given as follows, viz. One each to:

(1) Jacob Fast (1762-1827).

(2) Francis Fast.

(3) Christian Fast (1762-1841), was born in Frederick County, Maryland. He married in 1783 Anne Barbara Mason (1787-). One of his sons, John Jacob (-1827), married Catherine, daughter of Michael Rudisil.

(4) Adam Fast.

(5) Barbara Aultman.

(6) Kathy Bowman.

(7) Catharina Weaver had eight children: Nicholas, John, Henry Jr, Jacob, Barbara, Mahdlana, Elizabeth, and Mary.

Supplementary Acct, Nicklaus Fast, June term 1820, by Francis Fast, Executor of Will, Nicklaus Fast late of German Twp, Fayette Co., PA. Valued $12,176.

Supplementary Acct, #11 Jun 18, 1827, Court. Value $370. Nicklaus Fast of Gocklingen, Germany, Robt Fast, 1894, page 143-148.

Nicklaus and Cadarina were buried in the Jacob's Evangelical Lutheran Cemetery, McClelland Town, German Township, near the Mason Town-Smithfield Road in Fayette County, Pennsylvania.[9]

The translation of their headstones from German to English read:

i. Cadarina Fast being born the 19 September 1729 has produced 8 sons and 6 daughters, 50 grand children, 8 great-grandchildren. (On reverse side) Died 8 May 1795, Age 65 Years 7 Months 18 Days.

ii. Nicklaus Fast Born 26 December 1727 Passed away 3 May 1818.

On October 31, 1939, the Records Department of the Pension Board stated that there were no records of claims for pension or bounty land for Jacob or Nicholas Fast.

[1] *Ancestors of Lowell Thomas Rudicel.* http://familytreemaker.genealogy.com/users/r/u/d/Lowell-T-Rudicel-IN/GENE1-0009.html.
[2] *The Joseph Downs Collection of Manuscripts and Printed Ephemera of Henry Francis du Pont,* Location 15C1-2, Folder 41: L V .301 (Winterthur Museum, Winterthur, DE).
[3] Leckey, Howard. *Tenmile Country and its Pioneer Families.* Rpt, (Closson Press, Apollo, PA. 2007) 144.
[4] Fast, Robert G. *Nicklaus Fast of Gocklingen, Germany.* (Thomson-Shore; 1st ed.) Dexter, MI, 1994).
[5] Effective Supply tax rates for Washington Co: Pennsylvania Archives, Series 3, Volume XXII, page 699.
[6] Washington County Tax Lists 1787-1789. http://listsearches.rootsweb.com/th/read/PAGREENE/1999-07/0931158294.
[7] Account of Estate of Nicklaus Fast, Orphans Court Index, (Uniontown, West Virginia, 1785-1885.) 76, 80.
[8] *Will of Nicklaus Fast,* http://bruce-bounds.com/full/aqwn11.htm
[9] Jacob's Evangelical Lutheran Cemetery. http://www.findagrave.com.

ABRAHAM COVALT JR

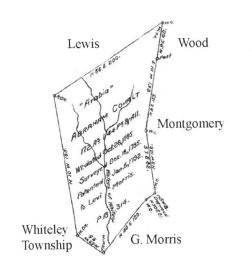

Lewis · Wood · Montgomery · Whiteley Township · G. Morris

Abraham Covalt Jr (1742-1791) was born in Great Egg Harbor, New Jersey. He was the son of Abraham Covalt Sr (1714-1780) and Elizabeth Gustin (1714-1805. At the age of 18 he joined the Royal Navy and took part in the storming of Martinico taking the Island of Martinique, part of the Lesser Antilles, from the French. After returning to Sussex County, New Jersey, he married Lois Pendleton in 1763. Their first child was born in Sussex County. In 1773 Abraham Covalt Jr and his family migrated to Bedford County in south central Pennsylvania where the rest of their 10 children were born and raised:[1]

    i. Cheniah (1768-1820).
    ii. Timothy Issac (1766-1844).
    iii. Abraham Jr (1769-1790).
    iv. Bethuel (1770-) .
    v. Mary (1772-1851).
    vi. Sophia (1775-).
    vii. Lucy (1778-).
    viii. Lois (1780-).
    ix. Ephriam (1782-1859).
    x. Jonathon (1786-1835).

Captain Abraham Covalt Jr commanded the 6th Company of Colonel George Ashman's 2nd Battalion of the Pennsylvania Line in December 1777. It was reported that he served as Captain of Indian Spies under Colonel John Piper from 1778 in Bedford County, Pennsylvania.

Abraham and Lois Covalt moved from Bedford County to Washington County, Virginia, and settled in the vicinity of present day Greene Township. On December 25, 1784, the Goshen Baptist Church received them by letter.

In 1785 Abraham Jr received four pay certificates totaling £73 for his service in the Bedford County Militia during 1785.[2]

On October 28, 1785, Abraham Jr and Lois Covalt bought and warranted Arabia, a tract of 172 acres of land in present day Greene Township. He had it surveyed on December 18, 1785, and then patented it on January 6, 1792, to Levi Morris, brother of George Morris. It was recorded in the Washington County Patent Book P18, page 314. The farm was situated on the Frosty Run branch of Big Whiteley Creek and was joined on the south boundary with the land of George Morris.[3]

In the 1789 Greene Township, Washington County Tax List Abraham Covalt Jr was included in the List of Persons Exonerated on the Frontiers of Washington County for being distressed by the Incursions and Depredations of the Indians.

In late 1789, five years after they had arrived at Garard's Fort, he and Lois received from the Goshen Baptist Church letters of dismission. Abraham's family and seven other families began building eight large flatboats on the bank of the Casselman River, a tributary of the Youghiogheny River in western Maryland and western Pennsylvania.

They were preparing to travel to what became Anderson Township, Ohio, where they founded the Garard-Martin Station.

The flatboats, with 45 souls aboard, some of their livestock, and what farm implements and furniture they could carry, set out from their farm homes in Bedford County for what was then called the Northwest Territory in Indian Country. They floated down the Casselman River into the Youghiogheny River and on to the Monongahela River. After they were well past Fort Pitt they entered the great Ohio River. On January 19, 1790, they poled their boats to the north bank of the Ohio River five miles east of what is now the center of the city of Cincinnati. From there they drove their livestock seven miles up the west bank and settled on 600 acres of land a half-mile south of present day Milford, Ohio, that Abraham Jr had purchased the year before. Living there in constant fear of the savage Shawnees who had been pushed to western Pennsylvania by earlier settlers, they set about building Covalt's Station, a fort to protect them. It was so well-built that the following year it housed a garrison of 20 soldiers from Fort Washington.[4]

By early 1791 the settlers had built 17 houses and four blockhouses at Covalt's Station. In addition, Abraham Covalt Jr brought in Joseph Hinkle, a miller from Pennsylvania, his wife, Lydia, and nine children between five and 25 years of age. After building a home for his family, Hinkle erected the first stone mill in the Little Miami Purchase.

One day, without the protection of the soldiers, Abraham Covalt Jr's party went hunting. They were attacked by the Indians and he and several others were killed and scalped near the station. One of the men, Mr. Wood, was sent to the station and a relief party started out at once, but without much effect. Daniel Doty, one of this party, left his recorded notes of the affair. He said he "saw for the first time a scalped man and was naturally much shocked." He recorded that "When a person is killed and scalped by the Indians, the eyebrows fall down over the eyeballs and give them a fearful look."

The killing of Abraham Covalt Jr was recorded in the journal of Thomas Fitzwater,[5] one of the hunting party:

> Towards noon on the first day in which Buckingham, Fletcher, and Covalt and others started on their hunt Covalt began to get very uneasy urged the others to return home saying there might be Indians about. The other two told him there was no danger, but this did not satisfy him. The nearer night approached the more importunate he became, and the more he urged them to return. This uneasiness in Covalt's mind was viewed as a bad omen. His entreaties finally prevailed on the others and they consented to return. They

left the 'licks' (salty deposits that the deer licked) in order to reach the station while it was yet daylight. Arriving opposite to Buckingham's mill, while Covalt and Fletcher were walking close together and Buckingham was about three rods behind, suddenly three guns were fired about twenty yards distant. Buckingham looked forward and saw Covalt and Fletcher start to run down the Miami and also saw three Indians jump over a log, yelling and screaming like demons. As Buckingham wheeled to run up the river he tried to throw off his blanket, but it hung over his shoulders like a powder horn as the strap passed over his head. When he did get it loose it took his hat with it. He ran up but a few poles, then took up the hill, the river and hill being close together. As he went up the hill he looked back several times, but saw no one in pursuit. When he arrived on the top he got his gun ready for emergency, then stopped, looked back, and listened. While thus standing he heard the Indians raise the yell down in the bottom thirty or forty rods distant, then he knew they had caught one or both of the others. When he found the Indians were that distance from him he knew that he could make tracks as fast as they could follow him. So he steered over the hills and came to the Miami at what is now Quail's railroad bridge. Getting to the station he found that Fletcher had got there before him. By this time it was night.

Lois Davis' declaration when applying for Abraham's pension No. R2742 read, in part:[6]

On October 21, 1837, at Fountain County, Indiana, appeared at the Fountain County Court, Loussa Davis, a resident of Shawnee TWP aged 92 years who doth on her oath make the following declaration to obtain the benefit of the provision made by Congress passes July 4, 1836, and the Act explaining it passed March 3, 1837. That she was married to Abraham Covalt, who was a Captain of Minute Men under the command of Colonel Pipes, that he entered that service in April or May in 1778 and left same only when the war was brought to a close. During 1778 he was on a tour for six months and allowed to return but once during that time for the purpose of attending to his harvest. He also served another tour of six months during which time he did not return at all.The reason why he was in the service so long was owing to the fact that he was then on the frontier and was ordered by Col. Pipes for the men placed under his command to act in the capacity of Minute Men or Indian Spies. During that time he was frequently called upon to go out, sometimes remaining four or five weeks, sometimes less, that being regulated by the nature and frequency of the Indian depredations.

That at the time in which he entered the service, he resided in the County of Bedford in State of Pennsylvania and that he was a volunteer. Further states that his services were rendered in and about Bedford County.

The applicant is not able to recollect the names of any officers other that the one mentioned above nor is she able to state whether he was ever in any battle nor whether there is any documentation in support of her claims. In relation to his commission all this affiant can say is that her husband was sent for by Col. Pipes, that he went, returned, and told her that he received his commission from Col. Pipes as Captain. That she frequently saw the commission but cannot tell who gave it or what become of it.

She further declares that she was married to the said Abraham Covalt on the 28th day of March in 1763 in New Jersey. That before said marriage was consummated it was published three Sabbaths successively in the church and to her knowledge there is no documentary evidence of the marriage. That her husband the aforesaid Abraham Covalt was killed by the Indians on the 31st of March 1791. That she was afterwards married to David Davis on the 12th day of May 1793 who died on the 14th of April 1808 and that she was a widow on the 4th Jay of July 1836 and still remains a widow as will more fully appear by a reference to the proof hereto annexed. Signed, Loassa Davis.

The Revolutionary War Record from the Pension Board for Abraham Covalt Jr, Pension Claim R2742, of Hamilton County, Ohio, follows:

The date and place of birth of Abraham Covalt and names of his parents are not given. He married March 28, 1763, in Sussex County, New Jersey, Loassa, Lois or Louisa. The date and place of her birth and names of her parents are not shown. Abraham Covalt and his wife, Loassa, resided in Bedford County, Pennsylvania, from 1773 until sometime in 1790 when they moved and settled on Little Miami in the then Northwest Territory that part called Covalt's

Station, Hamilton County, Ohio, where Abraham Covalt was killed by the Indians on March 31, 1791.His widow, Loassa, married May 12, 1793, David Davis, who died sometime in 1802 or 1803, all these dates are given. The widow, Loassa Davis, applied for pension.

Despite the declarations from Lois, his wife, and their sons Ephraim and Timothy, the Pension Board denied her claim on the basis that they had not produced adequate documentary evidence to substantiate that he had served the required minimum six months of duty.

HISTORY OF ABRAHAM COVALT BY HIS DAUGHTER, MARY

(First hand accounts of local historical events involving little known colonials is so rare that this had to be included here, regardless of its length.)

Mary Covalt (1772-1851), daughter of Abraham Covalt Jr and Lois Pendleton, was about 15 years old when she left Pennsylvania. She was born in Bedford County, Pennsylvania, and died at Fountain County, Indiana.

In 1791 Joseph Jones (-1815) emigrated from Pennsylvania to Hamilton County where he lived out his life. She married Joseph Jones in 1792 four years after she came to Ohio. Her parents had letters of dismission from the Muddy Creek Baptist Church of Pennsylvania. She lived 12 miles northwest of Covalt Station from the time of her marriage until her death.

This history of Covalt's Station and the Abraham Covalt family was written by Abraham Covalt Jr's daughter, Mary Covalt Jones, widow of Joseph Jones. Mary said that they made the trip from Pennsylvania to Ohio in 1788, but it was in 1790 that their flatboats began their trip down the Ohio River. Her journal is given here, as it was written.

MARY COVALT JONE'S JOURNAL.[7]

Spring of 1789. Latter part of April. Staid little better than a month. Then returned and came down again in the next spring, 1790. Mr. Covalt came down a little before I did, may be a few days. We went back together.

While here we came up to this place, and we looked at the lands. It was all surveyed by that time. David McKinney, Covalt, a surveyor and myself came up. There were 4 or 5 of us. Covalt had been up before and picked out where Ready's is and that same fall after he had come back, built a station.

Spring of 1790. McKinney, Clausen----3 asses for one dollar. Covalt had 4 blockhouses and four cabins and some picketed in. I helped to finish. Covalt, Hinkle, McKinney, Morris, Abel Cook, Riggs, Hickman, Claussen, Bailey, Bladlesey. Covalt had 2 or 3 young men grown, and most of them had pretty smart families. Some of them didn't stay long. The same year Tishman and Morris and Claussen, Badlely went down to Round Bottom and planted corn. I didn't know whether they planted ---- Joseph Bedle, Mr. Claussen, Levi Buckingham, Dick Fletcher.

Abraham Covalt. About last of May woods were right green. Had been up at mouth of Sycamore. Had gone up the night before and were there all night. There was a very large hollow Sycamore there and some of us lay on that. In the morning Bedle and Claussen started on down (Bedle killed a deer and had it on his back) to a lick on his way, and finding no deer, passed along the river and saw a deer standing in the river as they frequently found when not at the licks. While coming on down near a bend of the river which commands a 1/2 mile up the river, they saw three Indians crossing the Indian Ripples. They had just gotten by on the bank and saw the three perhaps drying on their moccasins below on the bank. Where we lay was not far from the stone meeting house there on the Sycamore. The Indians came up the bank and waylaid the band between the mouth of Sycamore and the Indian Ripples. When Bedle and Claussen started, I went up Sycamore to a fork and up the right fork to a lick where I shot a deer. I and ...came down Sycamore and along the bend of the river to where the Indians lay in ambush. Covalt and Fletcher in advance. I had----of the run throwing off my-----which had my cloak wrapped in it and was strapped over my shoulder. It fell into the river and getting it off my fur hat fell into the river too. (came off) I had my gun to carry and pushed on without seeing any Indians, though I looked back and stopped at the top of the hill, as I cut across to listen if I could hear them and rest. When they came for Covalt I came but my hat and load were gone. Fletcher took----and said as he turned to start, he blundered and fell and said he thought it wasn't worth the ----- Covalt, he then jumped, ran and got on before Bedle and Claussen. I got in just then and found the Garrison all in an uproar. Said Covalt were killed. He wouldn't go out with the rest for Covalt. I ran till I got to the top of the hill when I looked back and heard one gun. Then I knew someone was killed and got on out without seeing anyone. Covalt had run till exhausted and stopped by a fork of two logs which lay across the trace. The Indians on coming up, struck him in the forehead and knocked him over with the breech of the gun which was broken with the force of the blow. The Indians hid this under a log where it was afterwards found and took Covalt's rifle leaving him scalped on the ground. Covalt was the first sacrifice to Indian hostilities from the Miami settlement. The next day they were at the garrison. They next brought in furs and skins and traded for whiskey. There was a squaw that had on a white skirt who did all the business. She put down a grain of corn whenever they got a quart of whiskey.

Flinny lived between the railroad and Miami bridge on the flat about a mile from the garrison. Flinny had a station at Belpre. The tomahawk that Covalt had when he was killed slipped out of his belt as he ran but was found 30 or more years after. I could (verify) its identity for it had 2 edges and was made by a blacksmith Hinkle that was killed at Covalt Station. In the fall of 1790 we came to Covalt's brothers' family and myself and spent next summer there.

After St. Clair's defeat, the station broke up for the winter and moved back in again in the spring of 1791. Old Mr. Covalt and Mr. Hinkle were out on the hill opposite the station had felled a tree to make clapboards for a small hewed log house, (outside) he had put up outside the garrison. They were lying or sitting on the tree after felling it, (some men were working below, on the hill where they were at work) when a considerable company of Indians fell on them and tomahawked them with a fire. The men under the hill ran in and alarmed the garrison immediately. They (those men under the hill)-----tomahawked and scalped----they found the Indian trail seemed sill to be the largest. They supposed the Indians had had a design to attack the station. The men under the hill were firing a piece of the ground. I think for planting. Covalt had 4 sons, men grown. Hinkles family composed of small children.

In the fall of 1791, Timothy Covalt and Major Riggs went out and crossed the Miami down a little piece below the garrison, in sight, just across the creek, down below. Riggs, with a basket on his arm to put pawpaws and Covalt to hunt his horses-----used to be a great many over towards East-------and Riggs had gone towards the station for company and he said he thought his horses were over there, he believed he would go along, just as they were rising the opposite bank which was very steep, Riggs was-----and shot. We were eating dinner when we heard the shot. He fell over and lodged against a poplar on the steep side of the hills bank where the Indians scalped. The basket was still found hanging on his arm that he had taken to get pawpaws in. Covalt turned back and being behind reforded and got in. Neither had a gun. When I ran----- I had to carry a gun. Riggs left a wife, no children, I think. Hadn't been married long. Suppose it was after Riggs that Abel Cook was killed.

Demitt was taken after Cook was killed. Mr. Tichener was out with them at the time. Gabriel Hutching and Beddle were also there. Tichener hid Clemens under the leaves in the bushes. He had been shot in the knee. The artery of his leg was cut, he bled to death. And they got in the garrison with him. Demitt ran with an excellent rifle well loaded and harassed by some half dozen Indians. All in a string. He turned to shoot and might have killed some 3 or 4 but his gun would not go off. So he was taken. He was known to have killed an Indian and Tichener told him never to let himself be taken he would be burnt. And it is supposed he was. Mr. Rice preached the first sermon ever was preached at Round Bottom. Covalt's Station was settled before Round Bottom. Frances Bedle, it was that was taken. Jonas Coleman. I don't think there was any Jonathon Coleman there. Perhaps there was. Soon peace after Jennings was killed.

Mr. Covalt and Hinkle were out cutting a log for a mill. They had gotten down the tree and were sitting upon it when the Indians killed them. Mr. Tichener came to Columbia in 1790. Moved out of Round Bottom and from there to Lebanon, probably in ----.

Stites: 1742. John B. Stites family lived at Scotch plains near Elizabeth Town, New Jersey. From which he removed into [Bedford County, Pennsylvania.] ----(where I was born, now 70 years ago) into Buksley Co., near Middletown and lived there some 4 or 5 years. I was 3 years old when they left there (in 1775). Then he removed to the Redstone Country, on 10 miles, in Fayette County, on the water of the Monongahela. (About 18 miles above Brownsville. Brownsville named after Judge Ignatius Brown's father). That would be 1742 and 1775. We used to call it 20 miles to Washington, the county east of Fayette. Called Catfish for sometime, Old King Catfish had a great Indian camp there. Not laid out for sometime after we came, but then called Washington. Old uncle John Stites. Mayor of Elizabeth-Town, a man of wealth and influence, recommended him to Judge Symmes. In the Redstone country he was captain of a company of militia rangers and occupied Jackson's old fort. (right by where Waynesville now is) 3 months at a time. In 1786 he brought down a load of castings and iron & flour to Limestone. While there he went with a volunteer party in pursuit of some Indians that had been about Washington, stealing horses. He went so far, they rafted a creek in which the men had to join hands to get over. The water came up to their necks and they had to hold up their guns over their heads. While -----out he heard of the Miami country. Judge Symmes, then a judge in the Supreme Court of New Jersey. My father did not wish to (----) but for his information (---) as much as he would pay for, (---) any of the responsibility, (---) gave for this which was 5 shillings for asses, (----) which was equal to (----). My father went in from a good ways in, 4 men in a canoe to see if there would be any Indians there, waiting there for him, he kept out of the Kentucky side, till he should see them standing on the point. They got there perhaps one hour before we did, and found the bottom clear of Indians.

Arrived in 1788 18th of November, Sunday; we crossed, cleared away pawpaw bushes, stood sentry, seeing (----) wanted to prayer, and then went to work. My father and myself had ripped out clapboards at which he was first rate. (----) at Washington till he made a settlement and till after he had done the surveying. Built his house and next spring brought his family. He was son of John Gano, and Major General of first division. Ludlow was Symmes surveyor. Gano charges 105 lbs. Returned the plots of in and out lots, with charges on it. I saw it, dated 1788. Now in Samuel R. Miller's hands. (B.Z. Min, lawyer,----. Father took on spare boards (could get them for from $1 or $2 according to their size) to make floors for the blockhouses and also gates. We had four blockhouses, and space picketed in, the outsides jutting over. Had 7 or 8 boats. Quite a fleet. While we were getting out our boards Nehemiah Stites, my cousin, was employed by Morris; he & one Drake were making a settlement at Mayslick. As he was returning to Washington, where Morris lived, & had employed Stites, he saw another young man turned aside to kill a turkey, and were fired on by a party of Indians. Stites was shot right through the breast over one shoulder & out the back. His dog stayed to defend him, and the other young man fled and hid behind a bank to avoid pursuit; where he could hear the dog. The Indians however made their way to his (Stites) and scalped him, and struck their tomahawk into his head and struck it against a tree, where his brains were seen sticking. Capt. Baker raised a company and went out and brought him in on a horse. The dog followed me many a day after that. When we first came, ----March or Geo. March, and ----Indians one Blackfish came on Jacob Woolesy & one Spencer, on a bench of the hill above Mr. Covalt's where-----. These Indians had----gotten on to them before they saw them. This being down hill the two got the start. But down in the bottom the Indians could ride faster, and came on them, Blackfish and March in front, carrying their guns with the breech behind, nearly in view of the fort. Here Woolsey and Spencer tread (turned) seeing they would be taken, and were just at the point of firing when March hallooed not to shoot, they were for peace, they wanted to go in. They then gave up and March and one of them were first in, while the other was left. They had wanted to go in before, but had been afraid. My father then agreed with them, and appointed a day to give them a dinner but carefully clearing the blockhouses with the women and children. About 20 Indians and 10 squaws----us. The meal was cooked and ready for them. After this they went out and in trading all winter. My father had a ----. Shawnees and

Wyandots most of them. (March had been taken prisoner down by the falls when he was 10 years of age. Had light hair and had been fair skinned when he had on his clothes - could talk English as well as anybody, and was their interpreter. The Indians were peaceable, and we had seen none till the first snow fell on the ground, when the above Indians came.) On this first visit, they, this 7, were not admitted to the houses, and the men all stood armed at the----and what did come out, came out with their arms. After dark, and when they had stayed in late we----firing it at each to make them believe we had a big gun in each blockhouse. We fired frequently----a cabin by Louisville somewhere with his party and gotten shut inside alone when he was killed - and told me that I believed it.---- Jacob Woolery, towards Williamsburgh somewhere. Day of rejoicing when the fort was done. We fired our blunderbusses all day. Old judge Goforth had brought a keg of spirits, which probably made them more lively. Some hunting were down from Maysville----and heard the firing. They hastened back and Major Kinton and Col.---- came down day and night to our relief, as they imagined with----men. They were praised and entertained very kindly and then returned. There were 70 (said to be) in company with Judge Symmes, in March following. He came down in a large keel. I fired from the top of the house the large blunderbus (held a load of nearly a quarter of a pound of powder) which knocked me over. The ice was done running - river clear - pretty high - nearly up to our fort. Early in March.

Capt. Ephriarn Fidley. Commanded 80 spies under Wagons. Was a surveyor here the first winter.------ Bailey, 22------I paid his----where, it was torn when the Indians caught him when he jumped. Jas: Francis Bailey was out under Harmar. Went out to-----try to take prisoners and 4----. I was at Covalt Station when he came along, while Harmar was laying at Fort Washington before his campaign. (Bailey's Company) Lewis Whitaker, Capt. Jas: Vance, Matthew Fowles and Jack Fowles and Bailey, their leader) I had raised 4 men to go to protect Covalt Station, the Indians had killed so many there. Old Mr. Covalt and one Hinkle, right in sight of the fort. Lieut. McPherson was stationed there, but it was his business to guard the fort. He wouldn't go out to guard the men while they planted, so we came. Bailey's father and mother were at Covalt's Station, and he came after night to see and spend the night there, and hallooed first. Next morning went on and way laid their father but returned at night, after perhaps a week without seeing Indians. He died of the wounds he got in the campaign under Harmar as one of the ---- packhorse men was taken while under Captain Berkham who was packhorse man under---- I bought a------that I had to freeze, to get----. While I was on to---and----after the Indians came aong---and as far as

Muddy Creek---Clark and Hall the----side of the Miami. Kirby went on down till he fell on the Harmars trace----they heard a gun and knowing it was Indians, they took the Indians place and waylaid the trace. Presently the Indians, great big fellows, came along, loaded as heavy as they could carry. 9 took aim. All fired. And all hit, though one of the Indians ran some distance. When Kirby came up to him he said, brother But Kirby soon found a tomahawk into his head They had killed a possum for something to eat. (Who told me) Where John Smiths ad got back they put them up to sell. He was not one of the party. They however got some plunder, which they got something for, and he got his things for little or nothing, etc. The small----was prevailing, and they had had it at Smiths and had washed out all their bed clothes and hung them out. They were boiling sugar, and had left a kettle of sugar water over the fire. The Indians came along, and threw a couple of frogs into the water and them came round by one house, but finding nothing went on up by Smiths and took off the bed clothes. Capt. Kibby pursued. Reason Bailey was to drive packhorse and was going down to-----lots when he was intercepted at the forked alone by two Indians. Bailey could have managed the 2 but----they he didn't give up, they would stick their knives in him. They tied his arms behind at the elbow, and carried him on the top of the hills back from the river, but being afraid of waiting whites, they----and lowered his arms and ran a belt around his waist to hold him while he did so. Bailey suddenly thrust out his hand from his as if in the act of giving something to the Indians who deceived by this abrupt movement, let go of the end of the belt, and Bailey sprang and ran. It being dark, he had only to stop, and throw himself flat at the distance of about 100 yards, till the Indians passed and returned unable to find him. Towards midnight, when all appeared-----he returned, and came to our cabins. Came to where there was a dead cow. He and I down next morning to where he had the----at the Elm. I didn't go to Smiths, came right up to our house. Hallowed at the door, and after we talked a while we got and let him in. He was got down all alone early in the morning. Going to start out the day from town with the packhorses.

Father was poor and they had to stir about to make a living. Bailey----with trusting Indians an hour, up that hollow. Said the place was all worried round, as if horses had trodden there. I knew all the Baileys and Stites in the Redstone Country before I came here.

On Mrs. Spencer affair. Summer of 1792. Isaac Light was wounded in the shoulder. The three young men was killed----was brought up by the----and perhaps after..... She had jumped out into the opposite and, as where I then was. Hearing the fire of 2 guns I ran up to the house and got----Bailey was moving----. When he got to the----Indians started out, and took him, carried him back on the hills. He was then tied till night. The Indians then went to retire him for the night, untied him, where Bailey put his hands into his bosom and stretched it out quickly towards the Indians who supposed as it was intended he should, that he was going to hand or give him something. He let him go, and Bailey jumped away. It being dark, he could soon get out of the way. The other Indians caught him by the capps and tore a great slit. Between Harmars and St. Clairs Campaign, I think. Only 2 Indians. 3 hollows in the tree. Perhaps 1/2 dozen could hide in it. Off the sides half. They then thought of their guns, and he ran. As he passed along, he came to a log and threw himself into the fork of it. His capps being of the same color, he heard the Indians run along and back without seeing him. Made of grey cloth. I saw the capps, and where it was torn and sewed up. Know nothing of his being stopped. They made him to go over some-----. (Stopped this incident John C-----and others, were at work in John Smiths meadow, morning and they stopped to drink them. They were out far from-----. They were waiting, I think, to get something more. ----Fort St. Clair and Fort Hamilton.

After this----went on they heard the Indians say to stop their horses so they could shoot----. Stites threw himself down on his horses neck and the -----went right (my printer goofed up here for two lines so I can't read them!) forward so, he supposed the spurs ran into him so that he made-----start. Looking back he saw some Indians following and ----to Reeder, said, why don't you hurry on to the Indians with your gun. He said he couldn't, his young mare was not want to going without the whip, only threw up his head when the bridle was jerked. Stites knew their guns were empty or they would have shot him again and so he turned back, and on---to the horses flank, and so brought him off where they had jumped on, they looked back and saw the Indians standing on a-----ridge, looking after him. Silver spurs and high-topped boots. (Who had Bailey or----or Stites or the Indians. Indians near enough to throw their tomahawks. Reeder or the Indians? (That is, when they shot at Stites and Reeder). The Indians frequently wore----, & in their souts. The one that killed uncle-----had a caffs and cooked hat, he must have gotten it----.

This man had put in his family and didn't-----for a year or two for of He and-----had gone to Covalt's Mill----. His family was in the boat down in the fall, August 1789. He had----started and brought them all the way, and his-----bottom There he waited till his daughter & ----came up for him in nearly up to Round Bottom at that time. He said before he died, his fear of the Indians was done now. This happened while I took my wife on to Ct. (Cincinnati?)---- 18 years ago was living in Whitewater, below Connersville. Able Cook was----up to Round Bottom.

His family was there 3 or 4 miles from the other, above ----in the narrows, as he was returning from Columbia, he was shot by the Indians from the top of the point of a hill-----the only wound except the tomahawk. He had a good rifle but-----gone. Didn't know whether he had shot any Indians or not. He had rode down to Columbia & while he was at Red Bank the little bay mare died. I saw him skinning it out and I think he carried the hide down to Col. Spenner's tan yard at Columbia. It was while my father was east. I was up at Covalt's Station to guard while they farmed, and he came after I was there about a month. About sundown I heard of it, and I galloped through the narrows that night. After I got through, I heard a gun behind. They at the station thought it was me, and followed on till they came to the flats where they saw my track again and turned back. Whether Cook was killed after this or not, I cannot certainly recollect. I think after Covalt scoring trees to build a hewed-log cabin, and was shot in sight of the fort. After that I went into sawing and hewing. He was-----He had gone out where Shanes track was, and turned back and found Claussens Trace, which we continued till we came to a dr-----run-they-20 Indians from the Lakes crossed which was yet muddy. We agreed I should look forward and they to the right and I left, and if the Indians discovered us, we would turn back, and galloped out of reach of the trace. We followed on in that way till we came to where it turned down the hill; about 20 covered with tracks, right down to the river. We knew they were Indians. It was dreadful was their coming up, or we would before have tried to have gone round, but we knew we couldn't see to have gotten in. We now galloped into Fort Washington and I rode immediately up to the Sargents window, told him what I had seen and urged him to have a body ready by morning light, to scout the country, while we would go up to Columbia. Next morning the rain had washed all the traces away, and we scoured the hills in vain. The word of our night out have been believed but there were 3 of us, and I only waited every hour to have some stroke. They appeared to be still till the 3rd day, when we accordingly received an assurance from the Round Bottom Station, saying that Frances (-----) they followed to my track from Round Bottom. I am not certain what they did from the station or not. It was a mile above----and a soldier had been taken by the Indians. They had been into cutting timber for to repair their fort, and while in at dinner, the Indians attacked and took them prisoners. They----Round Bottom, (not Covalts) 17 of us pursued. We ascended the hill at the narrows, where they cut off the pursuit by going back on the point, to where they had left their----, and then crossed a tree over the hollow. When we got on it again, we followed to the mouth of Sycamore night------and we had to stop. Bedle said they were only about a mile ahead of us. In the thick back woods we had lost the trace, and it would have taken some time to find it. Since they were just 20 in number. That some were left to----and some had gone to watch a lick and then it was well we hadn't come on them. Some 2 or 3 weeks after, ----that summer, in the same flat. -----Round Bottom and Covalts a---Clarnens in his---into Round Bottom on his horse. They also took in Demitt cousin----little thought he would------after him. He was never heard of. The day Paul and Giffen were killed, we were out by Deerfield Ryrurson & myself with 2 Gregorys, Capt. Boyd, Jos. Bedle, & another, were out 25 miles, strait course, on Muddy Creek, =page 100=at (to follow after line 11 above), Frances Bedle was taken on the to Detroit & mourned so after his family he was sold to a British Lieutenant there, with whom he regularly served out his time. Found a piece of a Bible while there, which he said was a great consolation. About a year, I think a carpenter by trade. A good Presbyterian. But turned Shaker afterwards. I said then I would not have-----

We moored our boats at Columbia on the nineteenth of January. We did not have the gay steamer that now plies the wide waste of waters but the simple flat boat of our own construction. Captain Covalt had two boats, one 55 and the other 40 ft. long, the family occupied one, the other for his stock and farming implements for he came prepared for the wild woods. He had some 20 head of cattle, swine and sheep and 7 horses, the best ever came to the west. We met with very few incidents of interest on our voyage with exceptions of our boats becoming stranded on the ice and that filled our hearts with fear and terror. But with the united exertion of the men in the different boats we soon pursued our perilous journey. As I have said we landed on the 19th of January, we erected a tent on the banks of the little Miami in which place we remained for one week; while the men were erecting a temporary dwelling when it was completed, they came for their families. We then moved to our new home which was 7 miles from our tent and one mile below the town of Milford, now stands. The first night we stayed in our new home, there were 45 in number.

A fort was soon erected which consisted of seventeen dwelling houses and 4 blockhouses. It was called Covalt's fort. He was the proprietor and owned the land. His first purchase consisted of 600 acres of land.

My father built a mill, he brought the mill stones and a millwright whose name was Hinkle. This was the first mill in the Miami Purchase. During this time we had not been molested but once by the Indians. 5 days after we landed we had 5 of our horses stolen, each valued at $100. The sound of the axe was heard in the thick woods, to gell the sturdy oak and remove the wide spreading branches, from off the ground and prepare it for the summer crop.

We were unmolested during the summer. In the fall they came into the neighborhood but they did little damage. They killed one hog and roasted it and stole a horse from Mr. Batz. The Indians were pursued and one of them was overtaken--he had creased the horse so badly that he could not travel very fast. The Indian had a rope over his shoulder and was pulling it along. When the white men came near enough, three of them discharged their rifles and one of them felled him to the ground. They scalped him and took his gun, tomahawk, cap and knife and brought them to the fort.

Abraham Covalt and Abel Cook were chosen as their hunters to supply the inhabitants of the fort with game. Theirs was a perilous mission. During the winter and spring, the soldiers were often called to repulse the red foe, who would come so close to the fort that we could hear the noise and confusion at their camp for two or three days at a time.

Well, I do remember one night, whilst we were milking and the sentinels were guarding us, some Indians concealed behind a fence. They made their escape and when they arrived at their towns, they told the prisoners what had happened and how they acted. About this time the Indians became very troublesome. They attacked Dunlap's station (now cold rain) and told the soldiers they had taken Covalt's fort and had sent a company to take the fort at Cincinnati and that they might as well surrender for they were bound to take the fort. But they had a brave commander, one who was not frightened by their savage threats of cruelty. They fought with great bravery to defend their rites. Their commander was Lt. Hartshorn. During the siege he put his cap on a staff and elevated it above his place of concealment. The savages fired at it and it fell to the ground. The savages raised their well-known whoop and filled the air with their hideous cries.

By this time, Captain Covalt had sent to Cincinnati for reinforcements which were sent to their relief for the Indians attacked it again before relief had come, the besieged must have fallen prey to the tomahawk and scalping knife.

In June 1788 a company of five men went out on a hunting expedition they were A. Covalt, E. Fletcher, L. Buckingham, P. Beagle and Clemmons. After they had gone a short distance from the fort, Covalt said, "Boy, the Indians are not far off, we had better return to the fort and apprise them of the approach of the Indians, so they can repulse them before they come any nearer." Still they did not see the Indians but they started for the fort. The hunters had separated from each other Beagle and Clemmons were together when they came to Shawnee run, they saw two Indians sitting on the bank taking off their moccasins to wade over to the other side. Beagle wanted to shoot at them but Clemmons said "No, if you do I am dead man if they attack us. I am old and clumsy and I can't run and I must become a prey to their savage cruelty." Beagle did not shoot.

The Indians did not go more than twenty yards up the ravine when they came on contact with the other three Indian men. The Indians fired before the white men saw them. Covalt was wounded, Fletcher and him ran together about a hundred yards when Covalt said, "For God's sake Fletcher make your escape for I am a dead man." He was shot through the breast--he did not expire immediately after he fell. He had fought the Indians as long as he had strength he had received several wounds in the face. The tomahawk did its work of death. They took his rifle and powder horn. He threw away his tomahawk. It was found some 20 years later by his companion, Levi Buckingham. Thus ended the life of one of the brave sons of Pennsylvania as ever inhaled the morning air. He was as undaunted as a lion and as active as a deer that bounds through the forest. In his deportment he was genteel and affable. He was beloved by all that knew him. He left many friends to bemoan his loss.

The other four hunters got to the fort safe, they soon called their little band together to go search for Covalt. They brought him to the fort to pay last tribute of respect to so brave a man. They did not pursue the foe, for their number being too small to be divided.

In about a month from the time spoken of, the Indians were again seen prowling about the banks of the Miami. Abel Cook had been on a visit to his friends at Columbia, on his return home to Covalt station the Indians attacked and killed him. He was alone, his companions at the fort soon found him and interred his body by the side of his hunting Compton with whom in life he roamed the dreary forests.

We were not molested again until March of 1789. When they again invaded the Little Miami valley. Captain Covalt wishing to live a more retired life had got the timber ready for his house but the framing was not complete. He with his two sons and Joseph Hinkle were making Shingles when they were attacked by the Indians. Hinkle was not shot but his head was cut half off by the tomahawk and then scalped. Captain Covalt was wounded in two places--one ball passed through his breast--the other through his arm. He told his sons to make their way to the fort, that he was wounded. He ran with axe in hand, about a hundred yards and fell across a log with arm under his head. The scalping knife soon robbed it of the auburn locks that clustered round his noble brow. But his spirit ascended to the God who gave it. I will now invite you back to the year 1743, to Captain Covalts native place where he was born in New Jersey, near Egg Harbor. And was a resident of the place until he was 18 years old--he then embarked on board a ship to fight for his country's cause. He was at the storming of Martinico. In a short time afterwards, he returned to his native place.

There he became acquainted with a lady by the name of Louisa Pendleton on whom he bestowed his fondest affection which were duly reciprocated by her and they were joined in wedlock bands by the reverend M. Fuller in Boundbrook,, New Jersey. After he was married left the place of his nativity for Bedford County, Penn. There he was elected Captain which office he filled during the Revolutionary War. After the war was closed, he came to this western country to seek a good location and return for his family. He made the purchase previously spoken of then returned to Penn. to make preparations to move. He was blessed with six sons and four daughters. All of his children came with him to endure the trials of the western wilds. But alas, he was cut down in the midst of life. He was a man that feared God with all his heart and his prayers and alms were held remembrance. Well might the widows hear bleed at the loss of so good a husband and the children mourn the loss of so kind a parent. When they beheld him weltering in his gore, they brought him to the fort. There to pay last tribute of respect to one so brave and noble and brave they buried his remains on his farm where his grave can be seen to this day. This is but a small sketch of his life and character. The inmates of the fort were like sheep without a shepherd. They knew not what to do their leader was gone.

His widow survived him until the year 1838, when she died at the advanced age of 100 years. She was a true child of God. She was blest with her mental powers to the last. After the death of Captain Covalt, the Indians did not invade our borders again until 1790. In November 1791-- Gen. St. Clair called out soldiers to battle all that could be spared from every station. I do not know the number that went from Covalt's station-- they were commanded by Lt. Spears. Our number was decreased so much that we all retired to Garard-Martin Station and did not return until February 1792.

(Garard-Martin Station, 1790. Site of the first fortified settlement in Anderson Township and one of the first in the Virginia Military District. John Garard and Joseph Martin were the founders of this Station, who, with Elias Garard, Joseph Frazer, and others, came by two flatboats with families and livestock from Garards Fort, Pennsylvania, via the Ohio and Little Miami rivers. The contingent from Garard Fort landed there on December 23, 1790, and proceeded to erect the fortification. Other early inhabitants include the families of Captain James Flinn, Stephen Betts, Joseph Williamson, Stephen Davis, Richard Hall, Jacob Bachofen, and

John Corbly Jr. Three years later, in 1793, Anderson Township was officially established with the first Township officers coming from the Garard/Martin Station. A private militia was formed to protect early settlers from Indian attacks until well after the Greenville Treaty of 1795. The Station was later disbanded as new settlements in the area emerged.)

Then we got reinforcement again and returned to our fort. Through that summer the Indians were very troublesome. The Indians took three of the most efficient prisoners. There names were Beagle, Coleman, and Murphy. They were taken to Detroit and Beagle and Murphy were sold to the British, but they would not part with Coleman. When he parted with his companions, he wept like a child because he knew his doom--it was to be burned at the stake. Beagle returned home in three (months?). Murphy never returned and Coleman was never heard of after he parted with his companions. Beagle said when they were taken prisoners, that they were not more than a quarter mile from the fort. Murphy was the sentinel. Beagle would not have been taken but as he was running he caught his foot under a grape vine and fell. The savages were like panther in pursuit of prey the moment he fell they sprang upon him and bound him.

Not being content with their prisoners they killed a soldier by the name of Gockey but his loss was not regretted. It was supposed he was a traitor. The soldiers being always in readiness at the report of guns started in the direction of the sound in pursuit of the Indians. The savages saw them coming, they ran round the hill and attacked the fort knowing that the soldiers would have to return to the fort to protect it. They shot several shots in the gate of the fort. I (Mary) was the one that shut the gate, the men being all absent. But there was none injured. The Indians still continued to prowl around the banks of the Miami and in the immediate vicinity of the fort. Not long after the invasion of the fort, Major Riggs and T. (Timothy) Covalt crossed the Little Miami, Covalt in search of his horses and Riggs to hunt pawpaws. On their way home Covalt stopped to look for horse tracks--Riggs stepped in the path before him in a moment the report of rifles were heard and Riggs fell. Covalt wheeled and ran to the river. Where he was met by the soldiers.

In the winter of the same year, men had been grinding at the mill. One night they returned to the fort and that night the Indians came to the mill, emptied the grain out of the sacks on the floor, then they took down some tobacco from the rack that had been hung to dry and crushed some of it into the flour and took the rest and sat down to stem it and wait for the approach of the miller. But the miller was detained until late and thus saved him life. S. Gustin was the miller. They did no other damage at this time with the exception of killing one cow.

About this time Gen Harmer called the soldiers of the different stations together to go to the river St. Marys to assist in the burying those that were left died on the field of battle after St. Clairs defeat. I heard those say that were in the battle that the day before the battle there were 1600 men and of those 900 returned to their homes. One of those that was there said on the morning of the battle before daybreak the Indians raised the war cry which filled the soldiers heart with animation and courage. Their courage was soon tested. They fought like brave men and fell in a glorious cause. When the word retreat was passed around it caused their hearts to quake with fear--they ran in every direction amidst the shower of rifle balls. As one of the soldiers and his companion were ascending a hill his companion was shot dead and fell at his feet--he said, if he had ran fast before he ran faster afterwards. That was the last he saw of the Indians. Of all that left Covalts station but one returned, they left in great hopes of conquering the foe but never returned. The one that returned was Cheneniah Covalt. In the spring of 1792, a company of men were hired by the government to treat with the Indians. They were Wm. Smalley and Truman and his servant, J. (John Garard) Gerred and one Captain James Flinn. Wm. Smalley had been a prisoner with the Indians for 11 years. Before Smalley and his company got to the Indian towns, they were overtaken by two Indians who said they would pilot them to their towns. When night came on the Indians said they were three white men and but two Indians that they must tie up one of them--the other two had got separated from three--unthoughtedly they consented. They tied the hands of the servant.

Truman being overcome by fatigue, wrapped himself in a blanket and went to sleep. The Indians now had the advantage of the white men. They killed Truman and his servant. Smalley ran to make his escape. The Indians called him to come back-..he said, they would kill him. They told him no, to come back. He came back and asked them what they killed the other men for. They said wanted the money and if they went to the towns, they would get but little and now they had it all. Smalley went with them to the towns. He expected to fall victim to their savage cruelty but to his great joy there he met with his old Indian brother who sent him back to the station. Gerred and Flinn were never heard of after they left their comrades.

In October, the Indians invaded our neighborhood again and took one young man whose name was Pelser (?) prisoner. The men were plowing in the field about two hundred yards from him when he was taken but they were not attacked. We lived quite peaceably through the winter and until the spring of 1794. The inhabitants had begun to build their houses and improve their farms and live like free men again but this peace was but of short duration. The first notice that we had of their approach--two of the men had been to Columbia and were on their return to the fort when the Indians attacked them. One of them--Jennings was wounded but he arrived at the fort--the other whose name was Crist went to the Round Bottom fort to apprise them of the approach of the Indians. Being apprised so soon of their approach of the Indians, they did but little damage. This was their last invasion. Old Gen Wayne soon compelled them to bury the hatchet and retire to peace.

Now, the inhabitants began to disperse and the woodsman's axe was heard in every direction. The wilderness of Ohio became the home of some of Pennsylvania's bravest. Much has been said concerning the settling of Ohio. Some has stated that half a century ago, Cincinnati was a wilderness but they have been wrong informed. In 1791, there were five small cabins and the garrison. And the Covalts fort had been erected three years.

(If this Journal falls in the hands of friends of old pioneers they will think of the many hairbreadth escapes and trials of their ancestors and consider it an honor to be known as their descendents.)

[1] Rockey, J. L. *History of Clermont County, Ohio, with illustrations and biographical sketches of its prominent men and pioneers*. (British Library, London. Rpt 2010).

[2] Pennsylvania State Archives, Revolutionary War Military Abstract Card File.

[3] Leckey, Howard. *Tenmile Country and its Pioneer Families*. Rpt, (Closson Press, Apollo, PA, 2007) 596.

[4] Ford, Henry A., and Ford, *Kate B. History of Hamilton County Ohio, with Illustrations and Biographical Sketches, 1881*. (Rpt., Higginson Book Co., Salem, MA. 1993).

[5] Rockey.

[6] Pennsylvania Archives, Revolutionary War Pensions, Pennsylvania, Abraham Covalt.

[7] http://archiver.rootsweb.ancestry.com/cgi-bin/search. [OHHAMILT] Covalt Station and Round Bottom.

JONAH GARARD

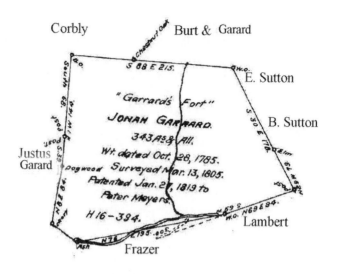

Corbly   Burt & Garard   E. Sutton   B. Sutton   Justus Garard   Lambert   Frazer

George Morris explored Whitely Creek Valley in 1764 and was so favorably impressed with the country that he built a hunter's lodge on land he wished to claim there. He returned to Virginia and after legal settlements were made concerning the former Indian lands, he influenced John Corbly, the Garard brothers, and others to come to that part of Washington County, Virginia.

In 1766 John Garard Sr (1720-1787) and his sons Jonah (1750-1782), Justus (1755-1828), and Isaac (1757-1794) undoubtedly followed the road that Christopher Gist had blazed in 1753 for the Ohio Company. It followed an old Indian route from the mouth of Will's Creek, a tributary of the North Branch of the Potomac River in Pennsylvania, to the mouth of Red Stone Creek on the Monongahela River. When they arrived at White Clay Creek, (later called Whiteley Creek) John Garard found Conrad Sykes' abandoned cave where he lived while trapping furs with Augustine Dillinger from 1760 to 1763.

He and his followers chose land to their liking and tomahawked their claims along White Clay Creek. John Garard claimed the land containing the cave and lived in it while nearby on Jonah's claim they built a one-hundred-foot square stockaded fort with a strong palisade near the creek, a mile north of the ancient Warrior Trail. Once their protection from the Indians was secured, they lived in the fort while they built a log church which was also to be used as a school. A cemetery was laid out a few rods to the east of the fort. They cleared and made claims to land, built cabins, tilledthe land, and then commenced to build a Meeting House.

According to Evans[1] it was built thusly:

Long, straight logs were split in halves. They were stood upright in a trench on the outer boundary. The logs of the outer row were placed with the flat side out, close together. They stood fifteen feet above ground and four or five feet below. An inner row of such half-logs stood within; close up to the outer row. These had the split side inward and one in each space between the logs of the outer row. There was only one entrance. This was closed by a large heavy gate that swung on heavy, strong, wooden hinges. There were no windows outward. There were several small lookout holes and also small portholes through which to fire on an approaching enemy. The woods near by were cleared to an extreme gunshot distance from the fort, not even a stump or log was left that would shelter an enemy from a gun that was shot from the fort. The actual site of that old fortification was about one-eighth of a mile from Garard's residence in rather a northeasterly direction therefrom. There, on a delightful plateau, in the center of a beautiful and picturesque valley which widens out into respectable proportion, an acre or two of land was enclosed with a system of cabins stockaded and palisaded after the most approved plan of the day.

The fort was later enlarged to 200-feet-square (the size of a city block) to house up to a hundred families as the community's population increased. The cabins within the fort were arranged along the palisades, their doorways pointing to the center of the fort. Rocks lined the entrance of the secret escape tunnel. The Indians murdered many settlers within the adjoining settlements, but the fort was never successfully attacked due to its superior construction. It was reported to be the oldest fort in what became Greene County.[2]

Jonah's claim was southeast of Conrad Sykes' claim with the old cabin that John Corbly later bought and made ready for his children who he had left with his neighbor, John Rice, on the Great Cacapon River where he and Abigail Kirk had begun to raise their family.[3]

He signed the Petition for a New State of Westsylvania to be formed on the lands that became Fayette, Washington, and Greene Counties in Pennsylvania, and Ohio and Monongalia Counties in Virginia.

He was recruited as an Ensign in Captain John Huston's Company of the First Battalion of the Washington County Militia in February 1782 and was in Lieutenant Mill's Company of Militia on a scouting party when he was killed. George Morris, Jonathan Morris, and Levi Harrod were also Privates in that scouting party.

Jonah left a Will which was filed in Washington County on July 2, 1782, naming his wife, Chloe (Frazer) Garard, a minor son, Jacob, and a daughter not named as heirs. Chloe was reputedly a sharp-tongued lady who was several times cited by the Goshen Baptist Church. Witnesses were Thomas Douglass, Elias Garard, and John Jones. The Will was filed in the Washington County Will Book 1, page 11. Jonah Garard's land was later patented to Peter Myers.

Jonah's claim was southeast of Conrad Sykes' claim with the old cabin that John Corbly later bought and made ready for his children left with John Rice on the Great Cacapon River where he and Abigail Kirk had begun to raise their family.

He signed the Petition for a New State of Westsylvania to be formed on the lands that became Fayette, Washington, and Greene Counties in Pennsylvania and Ohio and Monongalia Counties in Virginia.[4]

He was recruited at Garard's Fort as an Ensign in Captain John Huston's Company of the First Battalion of the Washington County Militia in February 1782 and was in Lieutenant Mill's Company of Militia on a scouting party when he was killed. George Morris, Jonathan Morris, and Levi Harrod were also Privates in that scouting party.

Jonah's Will was filed in Washington County on July 2, 1782, and named his wife, Chloe (Frazer) Garard, a minor son, Jacob, and a daughter not named as heirs. His brother-in-law, Jacob Frazer, was named executor.[5] Witnesses were Thomas Douglass, Elias Garard, and John Jones. The Will was filed in the Washington County Will Book 1, page 11. Jonah Garard's land was later patented to Peter Myers.

[1] Evans, L. K. *Pioneer History of Greene County.* Rpt. (Greene County Historical Society, Waynesburg, PA, 1941) 2000.
[2] Corbly, Don. *Pastor John Corbly.* (Lulu Press, Raleigh, NC, 2008) 62.
[3] Corbly, 81.
[4] Continental Congress papers, No. 48, Folios 251-256, pages 89-96.
[5] Pennsylvania Archives, Series 6, Volume II, pages 217, 247.

GEORGE MORRIS

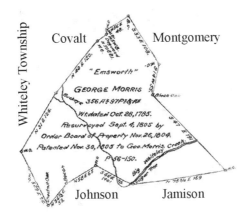

Richard Morris and Mary Porter had a son, Joseph (1727-1788), who was born in England. He came to America at the age of 16, settled in Springfield, Burlington County, New Jersey, and married Hannah (Lee) Asson (1723-1783) in 1744 in Burlington County, New Jersey. Joseph and Hannah Asson's children were:[1]

i. George (1745-1842) was born in New Jersey and died in Greene County, Pennsylvania. He married Margaret Corbly (1758-1833). They lived at Garard's Fort and were buried in the cemetery there. Their daughters, Priscilla and Margaret (1797-1810), were also buried in the Garard's Fort Cemetery.

ii. Levi (1749-1783) was born in Sussex, New Jersey. He was the head of a family consisting of two males under 16 years of age and two females in the Greene Township Census of 1790. On January 6, 1792, he patented a tract of land which had been warranted to Abraham Covalt Jr on October 28, 1785, and called it Arabia. It was situated on the Frosty Run branch of Big Whiteley Creek and joined with his brother George's land, also at the mouth of Frosty Run.

iii. Joseph Jr (1750-1823) was born in Burlington County, Virginia, and died in Rush County, Indiana. He was married to Elisabeth…in 1783 in Washington County, Pennsylvania. He was taxed with his father in the Greene Township Assessment Rolls for 1784. They had a son, Joseph (1793-1804). In the Census record of 1790 he was listed as the head of a family consisting of one adult male, three males under 16 years of age, and three females. His cabin was on the Woods Run branch of Whiteley Creek.

iv. Amos (1751-) was born in Greene County, Pennsylvania.

v. Jonathan (1753-1841) was born in Virginia and married (1)

Sarah Davis (-1798) before 1778 in Winchester, Frederick County, Virginia. He next married (2) Hannah Bradford before 1802. He married (3) Mary Robbins after 1816. He was buried in Dunkard Township, Greene County, Pennsylvania. His father had borrowed some money from John Neville in 1771 which he had partially paid back with goods and two roan mares. Jonathan paid back the rest of the loan in 1789. On December 1788 David Bradford was paid 15s. for advising Jonathan and Joseph Morris Jr in the appraisal of their father's estate.

In 1765 Joseph Morris Sr, his wife Hannah, and their children were living in Monongalia County, Virginia. Jonathan was 10 or 12 years of age.[2] George explored the White Clay Creek and was so impressed with the country around the abandoned Eckerlin settlement that he claimed land on Dunkard Creek about eight miles from the mouth of White Clay Creek for himself, built a hunter's cabin on it, and then left to return the following year. Written testimony bears out this claim, for in his pension application of March 17, 1834, Jonathan, brother of George, stated that he was born in Virginia on June 15, 1753, and was brought to what became Greene County by his father, Joseph Morris, when he was about 10 or 12 years of age, at which time his brother, George, was already settled there.[3]

In 1768 Joseph Sr settled the family on the Big Whiteley Creek in Washington County. They lived out their lives there and were buried in the Garard's Fort Cemetery.

Dunkard Creek had a long history before George Morris discovered it. In 1747 the French Governor of Quebec sent Creaux Bozarth to establish a settlement on Eckerlin Creek, known also as Dunkard Creek, where the abandoned French Fort Louis I was located.

Christopher Gist, who had guided George Washington at Great Meadows, led Bozarth, his family, and 20 Indian runners along the ancient Warrior Trail which passed westward over the Alleghenies to the Monongahela River and Eckerlin Creek.

Creaux Bozarth dug a cave for his family on the bank of Eckerlin Creek and supported them by trapping for furs. For two years he tried to improve the French fort but, the project being too large for him alone to accomplish, he abandoned the place in 1754. He had also been charged with inciting the Indians against the settlers. Before returning to Quebec, he and his family lived with the Indians while he advised them how best to wage war against the frontier settlers.

According to Bittinger[4] the families living on Dunkard Creek at that time included Clark, Cox, Evans, Hall, Henderson, Hostatler, Keckly, Andrew Lantz, Martin, Peter Myers, and Thomas Province. Some of these families had migrated from the Cacapon River Valley and South Branch Valley of Berkeley County. Several other families later migrated to the White Clay Creek area. The Indian threat was very real this far beyond the Monongahela River and the only protection for these settlers was Fort Dillinger on the Monongahela River about two miles east of the mouth of Dunkard Creek.[5]

The Goshen Baptist Church was built in 1771 and organized by 30 members. The number of inhabitants in the settlement at Garard's Fort increased rapidly during 1773. Everything appeared prosperous and the settlement enjoyed peace and plenty; but in the early spring of 1774 war hung like a pall upon the country as Indians marauded and slaughtered families almost within the confines of the fort itself, including the Spencer family who were inhumanely butchered.

George Morris become the militia captain in command of Garard's Fort and he had his problems. His officers served only for short periods of time after which other officers were elected by the men in the ranks. This made training difficult and disrupted his chain of command. When the Indian attacks were at their peak food was very scarce; they lived for weeks without bread. Their farms could be tended only while the workers were protected by armed men. Additional guards were required inside the fort for its protection. Selected groups of frontiersmen were formed for scouting duties and pursuit of attacking Indians.

The crowded living conditions within the fort were so severe that some families had to live on their farms and depend on the scouts to warn them when to flee to the fort. Life along Whiteley Creek was so tenuous that many families preferred to live in Garards Fort. It was not safe for anyone to work the fields or venture out from the fort without a large armed escort. Lyman Draper, the historian, preserved this letter which described the situation:[6]

> Dear Sir: I am Now at Garards Fort with 12 Men only, and am intirely without Ammunition, and also without my full Quo of men. I hope you will send by Van Sweringen Some Ammunition and flint and as the Times is So Hazardous I hope the men may be ordered to Come here Immediately, as the People are much put to it to get their Harvest up the creek, and it is not in my power to go on a scout with so few men and leave men to guard the People. I am Sn Yr 'bl Servt. Wm Jacobs. 1774.

Before 1774 George Morris had established himself, his parents and brothers Jonathan and Amos on Big Whiteley Creek.

George served in Governor Dunmore's army in 1774 and had accepted a Captain's commission from him which he destroyed when he learned that the Governor was planning to use the militia on the side of the British. He continued to serve as a scout in the Revolutionary War and became one of the best scouts of the frontier, usually in the company of his brother, Jonathan. Jonathan was later granted a pension, but because his application was almost identical with Jonathan's, George's application was initially refused. Amos also got a pension on his claim of having served under his brother George. Many other applicants for pensions mentioned having served under George Morris in the greater Garard's Fort area.

He was a great hunter, a brave Indian scout, a Revolutionary War soldier, a successful farmer, and an upright Christian citizen. Once while on scout duty near the Ohio River, he evaded a large body of savages and succeeded in warning the settlements of their danger. At another time he was ambushed in his cabin, but escaped to Garard's Fort by felling one Indian with his rifle and outrunning the rest of them. In 1775 he was baptized by Pastor John Corbly and for 67 years was a member of the Goshen Baptist Church.

Meantime, Joseph Morris Sr sold his grant in Monongahela County on August 5, 1777, to Robert Rutherford of Berkeley County for £30 and recorded the transaction in the Berkeley County Patent Deed Book 11, page 435.

George served in March 1777 during the Revolutionary War in the Third Pennsylvania Regiment and in Stockley's Rangers in the Washington County Militia on the frontiers during 1778 to 1783.[7] He was the Captain of the company which followed the band of Indians that murdered the family of his father-in-law, Pastor John Corbly, in 1782. The Indians' escape was made so rapidly that they reached the western side of the Ohio River before being seen by their pursuers. The following information of the George Morris and Margaret Corbly Morris family was found in the Morris family Bible.[8]

> Rev. John Corbly was born Feb. 25th, 1733, died June 9th, 1803, aged 70 years, 3 months, 12 days, buried at Whiteley, Pa. Abigail, first wife of Rev. John Corbly, died about 1768, was the mother of two daughters, Margaret and Rachel. Margaret married George Morris Dec. 19, 1774, was the mother of Levi Morris and the grandmother of Major J. B. Morris, of Mt. Morris, Pa. Rachel married Justice Garard, was the mother of Elizabeth Garard and grandmother of

Corbly Fordyce, of Tine Bank, Pa. Elizabeth Corbly, the second wife of Rev. John Corbly, and her four children, Nancy, Isaac, Mary Ann, and Katherine were killed. Elizabeth and Delilah were scalped by the Indians on the 10th day of May 1782, at Garards Fort, and are buried in the church cemetery.

Margaret Corbly (1758-1842) was born near Winchester, Virginia, and died at Garard's Fort, Pennsylvania. She married at Garard's Fort in 1774 to George Morris. They and her sister, Priscilla, and her husband, William Knight, lived in their homes inside the palisaded walls of Garard's Fort. Another sister, Rachel, and her husband, Justus Garard, lived on their farm adjacent to John Corbly's farm about a mile north of the fort. Margaret and George were buried in the Garard's Fort Cemetery. The children of George and Margaret Corbly were:[9]

    i. Amelia (1775-1856) married in 1790 Samuel Gustin (1767- 1852).

    ii. John (1777-1852) married in 1800 Margaret Mundle (1783-1846).

    iii. Hannah (1779-1851) married in 1795 Elkanah Gustin, (1769- 1852).

    iv. Jonathan (1781-) married Sarah Clymer.

    v. Levi (1783-1842) married in 1809 Lucretia Stephens (1790-1885).

    vi. Isaiah (1785-1858) married in 1812 (1) Rachel Carpenter (-1819), in 1822 (2) Catherine Trimble (-1828), and in 1840 (3) Rhoda Corwin.

    vii. George Jr (1788-) married Elizabeth....

    viii. Rachel (1790-1814) married in 1810 to Justus Wright (1789-1873).

    viii. Huston (1792-1879) married in 1822 (1) Ann Devers (-1828), and in 1829 (2) Melchia Smith (1805-1879).

    ix. Priscilla (1794-1810).

    x. Margaret (1797-1810).

Shortly after John Corbly's ordination in 1775 the Goshen Baptist Church received George Morris, James Crookes, Moses Tyler, James Moore, James Moredock, and William Crawford (nephew of Colonel Crawford, personal friend of George Washington), all leading pioneer citizens in the Garard's Fort area. In July 1776 the Minute Book of the Goshen Baptist Church recorded that "it was agreed that church meetings be altered holding them in the future the Saturday before the preparation for communion. Mary Ives excommunicated. George Morris and William Crawford baptized and received into Goshen Church."

In the 1781 Greene Township, Washington County Effective Supply Tax Rolls George Morris was assessed for 500 acres of land, one horse, and two cows for a value of $89. He was listed on the 1784 Assessment Roll for Greene Township, Washington County.[10]

He bought 356 acres of land in Washington County which he called Emsworth. The warrant was dated October 28, 1785. The tract was resurveyed September 4, 1805, patented November 30, 1805, and recorded in the Greene County Patent Book P56, page 150.

In April 1788 the Goshen Baptist Church Minute Book recorded that the Church "Met at Muddy Creek according to appt and proceeded to business viz...Bro Robert Jones, Jo's Frazer, Elias Garard, Dan'l Clark, Jeremiah Gustin, and David Price to meet at Brother Frazer on Wednesday next to settle a matter betwixt Brother George Morris and Elijah Moore."

On July 26, 1788 the Church "met at Whitely according to appointment and proceeded to business viz....A report brought to the Church by the Brothers appointed to hear the affair between Brother Elijah Moore and George Morris. Namely Robert Jones, Joseph Fraizey, Elias Garard, Daniel Clark, Jeremiah Gustin, David Price. The Church concluded that Brother Morris keep his place in the Church and Sarah Hill appeared before the Church but gave no satisfaction. The Church referred the matter to the next meeting for business."

On April 18, 1789, the Church "met at Whitely according to appointment....Likewise the Church from the report of Brother Robert Jones, Jo's Frazer, Ross Crosley, Jeremiah Gustin concerning to Brother George Morris and Elijah Moore be laid under the censure of the Church." On November 28, 1789, the Church "met at Whitely according to appointment and proceeded to business viz... Likewise George Morris to cite Baley Johnson to come to the next monthly meeting." On March 28, 1790, the Church "met according to appointment and proceeded to business viz....Bro George Morris and Jacob Frazer to cite Baly Johnson to attend the next meeting. Bro Henry Johnson laid under censure for drinking to excess."

The 1789 List of Persons Exonerated on the Frontiers of Greene Township, Washington County for being distressed by the Incursions and Depredation of the Indians included the four Morris brothers; Joseph, Levi, George, and Jonathan.

George Morris was listed on the 1790 Greene Township census as the head of a household of five males under 16 years of age and four females.

On April 6, 1794, he received 200 acres of Donation Land for his service as a Private in the Third Pennsylvania Regiment during the Revolutionary War. [11]

In the 1797 Greene County Tax Book made by Joseph Willford, Assessor, assisted by Elias Stone and Stephen Gapen, George Morris was assessed for 750 acres of land at $750, 20 acres of cleared land at $20, one house at $5, one barn at $2, two horses at $30, and one cow at $6. The following year he was assessed for 248 acres of land at $200, 30 acres of cleared land at $24, one house at $10, one barn at $10, two horses at $20, and five cows at $30. In 1799 he was assessed for 250 acres of land at $200, 40 acres of cleared land at $40, one house at $6, two cabins at $2, and five cows at $30.

The list of voters residing in Greene Township, Greene County, who voted in the Annual Election held at the house of John Burley on October 13, 1801, included George, Levi, and Joseph Morris. On October 14, 1806, Joseph and George Morris voted at the house of John Campbell. [12]

The Goshen Baptist Church Minute Book recorded on May 26, 1804, that it "met and after the usual introduction proceeded to choose Brother Herrod moderator, Thomas Wright not being there. Brother Morris made the proposition that the Church should appoint three members to go to Levi Morris and inquire of him the bargain between the two brethren and himself and after hearing of him if not satisfied to proceed to view the land and the division of said land. And if such brethren then think that Brother Morris has any advantage of Brother Wright then the said brethren shall make report according to the best of their judgment how much and he will make it up. The Church agreed to Brother Morris's proposals and appointed Brothers Minor, Rudolph, and Curl to examine the same and make a report to our next meeting….Also Brother Morris to call on Brother Nicholas Johnston to attend our next meeting to give some satisfaction concerning some conduct respecting of himself and others." [13]

In 1803 during the administration of the estate of his deceased father-in-law, Pastor John Corbly, an unvalued share of John Corbly's books were left to George. [14]

At the age of 96 years he made a center shot demonstrating his skill with a rifle. During the War of 1812 a recruiting officer came to his home. George declared, "I have six sons old enough to enlist and unless three of them volunteer, I'll go myself." Jonathan, Levi, and George Jr enlisted and served in Captain Seely's Cavalry.

Five of his children, two sons and three daughters, were among the early pioneer settlers in Ohio and Indiana.

In 1834 Henry Yoho, George Morris' neighbor, signed an affidavit that he knew George Morris was a Lieutenant in Dunmore's War under Captain Huston's Company of Volunteers and that his company met at Wheeling Creek. Their General did not meet them there and after several days of waiting they moved to the mouth of Grave Creek and stayed there a day or two and then returned home. Yoho further declared that George Morris was at Jenkin's Fort in Greene County for four or five years and was always ready to march against the Indians when called upon. Another neighbor, Matthew Herman, declared that he and George Morris were in Captain John Minor's Company for six months, George as orderly Sergeant, and after they were discharged they both forted at Garard's Fort for a few years until the end of the Indian war. Corbly Garard, a Justice of the Peace, certified that Matthew Herman was as long as he could remember an unimpeachable character, honest, and upright.

Jonathan Morris, in 1834, declared that he and George served in Captain Wilson's Company stationed at VanMeter's Fort on Muddy Creek when some settlers were murdered by the Indians. He and George, then a Sergeant, pursued the Indians and then returned to VanMeter's Fort. They later marched against some Indian towns. He declared that George Morris was in service over eight months. A year afterwards he and George assisted in building Garard's Fort and forted there for six years. During that time he and George spied against the Indians.

On March 3, 1841, the Treasury Department, under the Act of April 1838 placed George Morris on the Pensioner Roll of the Philadelphia agency at the rate of $8 per month.[15]

[1] Leckey, Howard. *Tenmile Country and its Pioneer Families.* Rpt, (Closson Press, Apollo, PA. 2007) 596.
[2] National Archives S.7247.
[3] Leckey, 57.
[4] Bittinger, Emmet F. *Heritage and Promise: Perspectives on the Church of the Brethren.* (Published by Church of the Brethern General Board, Elgin Ill, 1970).
[5] Leckey ,578.
[6] Fordyce, Nannie L. *The Life and Times of Reverend John Corbly, 1953.* (2nd ed., Leola Wright Murphy, Mayhill Publications, Knightstown, IN: 1970).
[7] Pennsylvania Archives, Series 3, Volume XXIII, pages 198-220.
[8] Evans, L. K. *Pioneer History of Greene County.* 1941. Rpt. (Greene County Historical Society, Waynesburg, PA, 2000) pages 152-155, 164-165.
[9] Fordyce.
[10] Leckey, 135.
[11] Pennsylvania Archives, Series 3, Volume VII, Chapter; Donation Lands granted Soldiers of the Pennsylvania Line.

[12] http://www.cornerstonegenealogy.com/greene_county_voter_lists_1801.htm.
[13] http://www.uh.edu/~jbutler/gean/goshenbaptist.html.
[14] Corbly, 267.
[15] Pennsylvania Archives, Revolutionary War Pensions, Pennsylvania, George Morris, page 23.

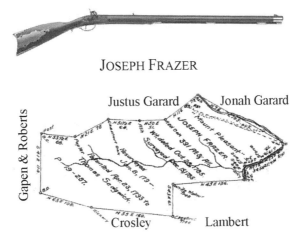

JOSEPH FRAZER

Joseph Frazer (1750-1793) was born in Burlington County, New Jersey, and died in Ray's Hill, Bedford County, Pennsylvania. He was the son of Stephen Frazer and Sarah Allen. He married Mary Pearsall (1761-1858), the daughter of John Pearsall and Mary Andrews, about 1778 in New Jersey. She was born in New Jersey and also died in Bedford County, Pennsylvania.

He witnessed the Will of Richard Garrety, a shopkeeper in Philadelphia on September 10, 1771, which was proved September 18, 1771.[1]

In a Montgomery, Wythe County, Virginia Court David Finley appeared and:

> ...claimed a right of settlement and pre-emption to a tract of Land lying on the northeast side of Dick's River about 3 Miles below the mouth of Falling Creek including two small springs by building a Hut and raising a crop of Corn on the premises in the year 1776. William Frazer contested the claim by Joseph Frazer and alleged the said Frazer has a prior improvement to the said land. Sundry Witnesses were sworn and examined in consideration of which the Court are of the Opinion that the said Finley has a right only to a pre-emption of 1,000 Acres of Land including said improvement

and that a Certificate be issued for same and that the said Finley recover of the said Frazer his Costs.[2]

Joseph Frazer was taxed $55 for 100 acres of land, two horses, two cows, and three sheep in 1781 according to the Effective Supply Tax Rate Book for Washington County.[3] In 1783 Joseph Frazer of Cecil County, Maryland, was assessed for 50 acres of land.

He moved that year or early next, for in 1784 he was listed on the Assessment Roll for Greene Township, Washington County, Pennsylvania.[4]

He bought 391 acres of land in Washington County and called it Mount Pleasant. His warrant was dated October 28, 1785. He had it surveyed on December 15, 1785, and patented it on April 23, 1793, to Thomas Sedgwick. The patent was recorded in Washington County Patent Book P19, page 287.

In May 1788 the Goshen Baptist Church "met at Muddy Creek according to appt and proceeded to business viz ...Bro Robert Jones, Joseph Frazer, Elias Garard, Dan'l Clark, Jeremiah Gustin, David Price to meet at Brother Frazer on Wednesday next to settle a matter betwixt Brother George Morris and Elijah Moore." In July the Goshen Baptist Church "met at Whitely according to appt and proceeded to business viz: A report brought to the Church by the Brothers appointed to hear the affair between Brother Elijah Moore and George Morris. Namely Robert Jones, Joseph Frazer, Elias Garard, Daniel Clark, Jeremiah Gustin, and David Price." The following month the Goshen Baptist Church "met at Muddy Creek/Whitely according to appt and proceeded to business viz. Negro Jane/ Brother (Elijah) Moore's affair to stand as it is, only Brother Moore to decline communion. Brother Jo'h Dunn's to be continued as he has Association letter to be prepared. Brother Jones, Brother Frazer, Brother Jon'n Morris, Brother Corbly, and Moredock Messengers. Brother Price to prepare the letter."

Nearly a year later on April 18, 1789, the Goshen Baptist Church "met at Whitely according to appt...Likewise the Church from the report of Brothers Robert Jones, Joseph Frazer, Ross Crosley, and Jeremiah Gustin concerning Brothers George Morris and Elijah Moore be laid under the censure of the Church." In February 1790 the Goshen Baptist Church "met at Muddy Creek according to appt and proceeded to business viz. The Church appointed Brothers Ross Crosley, Joseph Frazer, Justice Garard, and Jonathan Morris to examine into a complaint made against Eli Mundle for bad conduct and singing vulgar songs and to cite him to come to the next monthly meeting where they are to make a report." [5]

In the Washington County Tax Lists of 1787-1789 Joseph Frazer was included in the List of Persons Exonerated on the Frontiers of Washington County for being distressed by the Incursions and Depredations of the Indians.

In the 1790 Greene Township Census Joseph Frazer was listed as head of a household with two males under 16 years of age and four females.[6] In that year Joseph Frazer, John Corbly Jr, Joseph Martin, John and Jonan Garard, and Elias Garard departed Goshen Baptist Church on two flatboats with their families and livestock from Garard's Fort via the Ohio River and the Little Miami River to settle near Cincinnati, Ohio. They founded Garard-Martin Station in Anderson Township, Virginia Military District. Other early inhabitants of Anderson Township at that time included Captain James Flinn, Stephen Betts, Joseph Williamson, Stephen Davis, Richard Hall, and Jacob Bachofen.[7]

In 1799 Joseph Frazer, John Frazer, Richard Davis, and John Riley were appointed to view a road from the upper end of Jonathan Woods's field along a stony ridge until it intersected the Mockerson Road. They reported that it was a much better road than the former and ordered it to be cut.[8]

An Orphans Court was held in Bedford County, Pennsylvania, in November 1808 before Jonathan Walker, Esquire, President, and James Martin, John Dickey, John Scott, and John Moore, Esquires, Judges of the Court. Thomas Runyan, Administrator of the estate of Joseph Frazer, deceased, produced his account of Administration as settled by the Register of Bedford County showing a balance of £113.11s.7 ½d. which he was directed to distribute according to law.

On March 12, 1821, a settlement between Thomas Runyan, Administrator of Joseph Frazer, late of Bedford township deceased, and the heirs of Joseph Frazer, filed by which it appeared that John Frazer, Samuel Frazer, Jacob Tanner and Charity his wife, Daniel McLain and Mary his wife, Elishas Barton and Anna his wife, and Joseph Frazer, heirs and legal representatives of said Joseph Frazer, deceased, respectively received their share of said estate. Mary Bishop and Frances Moore were witnesses to the signing of Joseph Frazer's Will.[9]

THOMAS SEDGWICK

Mr Joseph Gwyne, Collector of Taxes of Cumberland Township, Washington County for 1781 received this notice, "You are hereby authorized and required to notify every person in your respective township what their taxes is either personally or in writing as expressed in your duplicate at least five days before the appeal which will be held at home of Henry VanMetre, Esquire, Friday 16th of May." Thomas Sedgewick was one of the people notified.

His estate was placed on the Assessment Rolls for Cumberland Township, Washington County, in 1784 and 1788. He bought 206 acres in Cumberland Township on a warrant dated December 23, 1785, and called it Mount Rock. It was surveyed on April 24, 1786, and patented on June 6, 1787. The transaction was recorded in the Washington County Patent Book P10, page 177.

Thomas Sedgwick was listed in the 1790 census for Cumberland Township, Washington County, as the head of household with two males under 16 years of age, four males over 16 years of age, and two females.[10]

On April 23, 1793, Thomas Sedgwick bought Joseph Frazer's 391 acres farm called Mount Pleasant. Frazer had purchased it on a warrant dated October 28, 1785, and had it surveyed on December 15, 1785. The transaction was recorded in the Washington County Patent Book P19 on page 287.

In the roundup of the southwestern Pennsylvania Whiskey Rebels in 1794 Thomas Sedgwick, a Justice of the Peace in Washington County near Garard's Fort, was one of the prisoners arrested and confined in Fort Pitt; only 18 of the prisoners, including him, were sent to Philadelphia for trial. While the court in Philadelphia took the matter under consideration a motion was made for a writ of habeas corpus on behalf of John Hamilton and Thomas Sedgwick.

The first step was to get Hamilton, the Sheriff of Washington County, and Sedgwick, a Justice of the Peace from the same county, discharged from prison or released on bail. The writ was issued by order of the Court and no objection was raised by the government. Three days later the federal marshal brought the two prisoners into court for the second phase of the proceeding, an examination into whether sufficient cause existed to detain them. Thomas' attorney, William Lewis, under a writ of habeas corpus, got him released from prison because he was a Justice of the Peace.[11]

On March 9, 1796, Justices of the Peace were commissioned for Greene Township. Thomas Sedgwick, along with John Guthery and Samuel Hyde, received commissions signed by Governor Thomas Mifflin and they were sworn in on July 13, 1796.[12]

In the 1798 Greene Township Assessors Book made by Joseph Willford, Elias Stone and Stephen Gapen assessed Thomas Sedgwick for 180 acres of land at $150, 40 acres cleared at $35, 2 houses at $10, one barn at $5, one horse at $10, two cows at $12, one grist mill at $40, and one sawmill at $30. The following year his assessment was for 80 fewer acres of land of which 50 acres were cleared. He had acquired an additional house, a horse, and two more cows.

[1] http://www.usgwarchives.org/pa/pafiles.htm.
[2] Finley, Carmen J. *John and Mary Finley of Montgomery, Wythe County, Virginia*, in J. F. Dorman, *The Virginia Genealogist.* (Washington 1957-2006.Volume 34) 243-255; (1991: Volume 35) 18-33, 122-35, 173-85, 251-262.
[3] Pennsylvania Archives, Series 3, Volume XXII, page 699.
[4] Maryland State Archives, Indexes of Assessment of Cecil County, 1784.
[5] Corbly, Don. *Pastor John Corbly.* (Lulu Press, Raleigh, NC, 2008) 281-283.
[6] Leckey, Howard. *Tenmile Country and its Pioneer Families.* Rpt, (Closson Press, Apollo, PA, 2007) 159.
[7] Corbly, 161.
[8] Russel County, Virginia, Law Order Book 3, Part 1, page 51. 1700-1808.
[9] http://genforum.genealogy.com/hawthorne/messages/1410.html.
[10] Leckey, 157.
[11] Fleming, George Thornton. *History of Pittsburgh and Environs, from Prehistoric days to the Beginning of the American Revolution, 1855-1928.* (The American historical society, New York, Chicago, 1922). Volume 2.
[12] Walkinshaw, Lewis Clark. *Annals of southwestern Pennsylvania,* (Lewis Historical PubliShinng Co, New York, 1939) Volume 2.

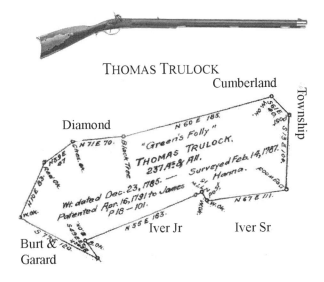

THOMAS TRULOCK

Thomas Trulock was married to Elizabeth Ivers, daughter of Richard Ivers Sr and Mary Hudson. He was listed as a Private on the Muster Roll of Captain Thomas Cook's Company in Colonel Daniel Broadhead's 8th Regiment of Foot of the Pennsylvania Line during June through August 1778 at Fort Pitt.[1]

He served as a Private 4th Class in the Third Company of the First Battalion of the Washington County Militia in October 1781, according to the Pennsylvania State Archives, Revolutionary War Military Abstract Card File. He was a Private 4th Class in Captain Crawford's Company in Lieutenant Colonel Thomas Crooke's Fifth Battalion of Militia in the district lying upon the Monongalia River between Whiteley and Muddy Creeks on October 16, 1781. The men were enlisted from the vicinity of Carmichael Town in Washington County.[2]

He signed the 1782 Petition for the New State of Westsylvania to be erected out of Fayette, Washington and Greene Counties, Pennsylvania, and Ohio and Monongalia Counties, Virginia. He was listed on the 1784 Assessment Roll for Greene Township, Washington County.[3]

Thomas Trulock bought 237 acres called Green's Folly on a warrant dated December 23, 1785. It was surveyed February 14, 1787, patented April 16, 1791, to James Hanna and recorded in the Washington County Patent Book P18, page 101. He bought tracts of 150 acres, 100 acres, and another 209 acres called William Paul in Washington County, all on a warrant dated December 23, 1785. The William Paul tract was surveyed on July 11, 1786, but there was no record when, or if, the latter three tracts were patented.[4]

He was listed on the 1789 Greene Township List of Persons Exonerated on the Frontiers of Washington County for being distressed by the Incursions and Depredations of the Indians and was listed on the 1790 census for Greene Township as head of household with two males under 16 years of age and three females.

Captain Thomas Trulock was listed on the Return of Officers of Company Eight, Second Battalion, Washington County Militia on November 1, 1792.[5]

He apparently moved from Washington County, Pennsylvania, by 1796. The Freeman's Journal was published in Hamilton County, Ohio, from 1796-1799. On October 31, 1796, Thomas Trulock posted the following notice in it, "Found two brindle steers Cluff Creek."[6]

JAMES HANNAH

James Hannah (1760-1821), son of Francis S. Hannah and Sarah..., was born in Chester County, Pennsylvania, and died in Vincennes, Knox County, Indiana. He married Mary... (1773-) in Washington County, Pennsylvania. They lived there from 1777 to 1808 when they moved to Vincennes, Knox County, Indiana. His Will was probated on March 23, 1822, and the inventory and appraisal of his estate were filed in the Knox County records. He and Mary were buried in the lower Indiana

Presbyterian Churchyard in Knox County. The children of James Hannah and Mary were:[7]

i. Jane (1792-1846) born in Knox County, Indiana; in 1810 she married John Barrickman (1785-1857) who was born in Westmoreland County, Pennsylvania, and died in Knox County, Indiana.

ii. Nancy (1793-1858) born in Greene County, Pennsylvania, died in Knox County, Indiana. She married (1) Abraham Rodarmel (1784-1833) and (2) Abraham Westfall. Nancy and Abraham Rodarmel were buried at the Lower Indiana Church, Vincennes, Knox County, Indiana.

iii. Sarah (1796-) born in Greene County, Pennsylvania, married Samuel Marshall in 1820 in Knox County, Indiana.

iv. Margaret (1798-1835) born in Greene County, Pennsylvania, died in Vincennes, Knox County, Indiana. She married William Burtch in 1819 in the Lower Indiana Church, Knox County, Indiana.

v. Peter (1799-) born in Greene County, Pennsylvania, married Elizabeth Light in 1820 in Knox County, Indiana.

vi. Elizabeth (1800-) born in Greene County, Pennsylvania, married...Hamilton.

vii. Minerva (1802-1873) born in Greene County, Pennsylvania, married Joseph Roseman (1793-) in 1822 in Knox County, Indiana.

viii. Mary (1805-1879) was born in Greene County, Pennsylvania, married (1) Thomas Docker and then (2) William Burtch (1793-1880) who was born and died in Vermont. Her sister, Margaret, was previously married to Burtch.

ix. Indiana (1807-1887) born in Greene County, Pennsylvania, married Esau McFall in 1831 in Knox County, Indiana.

x. William (1808-1838) born in Knox County, Indiana, married Diana Flowers in 1834 in Knox County, Indiana.

xi. Isabel (1810-1888) married John A. Kurtz in 1830 in Knox County, Indiana.

xii. John B. (1812-1884) married Mahala Profit in 1848 in Vanderburgh County, Indiana. They were buried in the Walnut Hill Cemetery at Petersburg, Pike County, Indiana.

xiii. Francis (1814-).

xiv. Maria L. (1819-) was born in Greene County, Pennsylvania and married John Barrickman.

Private 2nd Class James Hannah served in Captain George Sharp's Company of Colonel David Williams' Third Battalion of Washington County Militia in September 1781. Private 1st class James Hannah served in Captain William Scott's Company in Lieutenant Colonel John Marshall's Fourth Battalion of Washington County Militia which was ordered to rendezvous on March 1, 1782. Private 7th Class James Hannah served in Captain William Fife's Company in the Second Battalion of the Washington County Militia which was ordered to rendezvous on June 14, 1782. Private 2nd Class James Hannah served in Captain Samuel Shannon's Company of the Washington County Militia which was ordered to rendezvous at Leet's Mill and Tanyard (near present day Chickamauga Creek, Georgia) on July 13, 1782.[8]

In 1788 he was listed as a single man in the Cumberland Township Tax List, Washington County, Pennsylvania. Between 1797 and 1808 he was taxed in Cumberland Township, Greene County, Pennsylvania.

In 1791 he patented 237 acres called Green's Folly on Whiteley Creek on the line of Greene and Cumberland Townships, Washington County, Pennsylvania. It was previously owned by Thomas Trulock. In 1806 he and his wife, Mary, sold 115 acres of Green's Folly to James Hank Jr and recorded it in the Greene County Patent Book 2, page 104.

He was a farmer but the 1793 tax list for Washington County confirmed that he was also a whiskey distiller, as were about 20 percent of the settlers in Washington County. James Hannah and Thomas Sedgewick were distillers who sold whiskey at the same place on the same day. It was reported, "This was a busy day for the distillers for James Hannah brought in 15 1/2 gallons that was under proof and Thomas Sedgewick traded out 33 gallons of the good stuff in the same day."[9]

On April 1, 1823, an act was passed to exonerate the estate of the late James Hannah Esquire, deceased, from the payment of certain monies.

> Whereas, the late James Hannah Esq., dec. in his lifetime, viz: In the year 1817, as brigade inspector of the 2nd brigade composed of the counties of Somerset and Cambria, in the 12th division of the militia of this state, put into the hands of Jacob Mason, then the constable of Somerset twp., Somerset county, a warrant for the collection of fines against delinquent militia men, amounting to $717.00, of which James Hannah received

$5.00 only by reason of the constable having, shortly after his house and papers burnt and in consequence of his losses, becoming insolvent, and his bail having paid the amount of their bond to other creditors of the constable, therefore the executors of James Hannah, are hereby exempted from the payment to this commonwealth of the uncollected part of the warrant.[10]

There was no record that James Hannah applied for, or received, a pension for his service during the Revolutionary War.

[1] New York Historical Society. *Collections of the New York Historical Society for 1915.* (Printed for the Society by John Watts DePeyster Publication Fund, New York, 1916).

[2] Pennsylvania Archives, Series 6, Volume II, page 165, 166.

[3] Leckey, Howard. *Tenmile Country and its Pioneer Families.* Rpt, (Closson Press, Apollo, PA. 2007) 136, 142.

[4] Egle, William Henry. *Warrantees of Land in the Several Counties of the State of Pennsylvania, 1730-1898, Volume III.* (William S. Ray, State Printer of Pennsylvania, 1899).

[5] Pennsylvania Archives, Series6, Volume IV.

[6] http://www.rootsweb.ancestry.com/~ohhamilt/news/1796.html.

[7] Roster of Soldiers and Patriots of theAmerican Revolution Buried in Indiana. 1980, page 25. http://www.genealogy.com/.users/m/c/k/MichaelMckleroy/FILE/0010text. txt.

[8] Associators & Militia, Muster Rolls, 1775-1781. http://www.usgwarchives.net/pa/ Washington/military.htm.

[9] Leckey, 500.

[10] The Statues at Large of Pennsylvania, Harrisburg PA, 1911. Laws passed Session 1822/1823. http://files.usgwarchives.org/pa/1pa/xmisc/1823laws.t xt

RICHARD IVERS SR AND JR

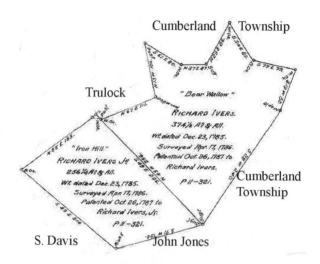

Richard Ivers Sr (1730-1806) was born in Ireland and died in Greene Township, Greene County, Pennsylvania. Before 1750 he married Mary Hudson (-1806) in Ireland. She was a daughter of Joshua Hudson who emigrated from Wales. Richard Ivers Sr appeared on the tax list in Lancaster County, Pennsylvania. He left a Will that was probated May 19, 1806, and recorded in the Greene County Will Book 1, page 53. The children of Richard Ivers Sr and Mary were:[1]

> i. Charlotte Jane (1756-1806), who married John Bozarth (1774-1840) in 1770. They lived at Old Redstone Fort south of Ten Mile Creek. She was born in Ireland and died in Zenia Township, Greene County, Ohio. Upon her death he married Ann Volath and then died in Fulton County, Indiana.
>
> ii. John (1752-) was in Captain William Crawford's Company of Militia and signed the petition to form the new state of Westsylvania.
>
> iii. Robert (1750-1800) also served in Captain William Crawford's Company of Militia and signed the petition for a new state of Westsylvania.
>
> iv. Richard Jr (1754-1837), born on Whiteley Creek, Greene County, Pennsylvania, married Deborah Leslie (-1836). Their children were Charlotte, Maria, Mahala, Eliza, Thomas, Virginia, William, and Samuel. He also signed the petition to form the new state of Westsylvania.
>
> v. Mary (1758-1810) married Jeremiah Long (-1820) who died on Dunkard Creek.They were buried in the Garard's Fort Cemetery.

vi. Elizabeth (1760-) married Thomas Trulock who was a member of Captain Crawford's Company.

vii. Sarah (1762-) married...Woods.

viii. Ann (1764-1823) married...Steele.

ix. William (1766-1832) was born and died in Tyler County, Virginia. He married (1) Priscilla Israel (01796), (2) Druscilla Brady (-1822), and (3) Sarah McCoy (-1858). He was a whiskey distiller in Greene County, Pennsylvania, and signed the petition to form the new state of Westsylvania. His Will was probated in 1832.

Richard Ivers Sr was probably too old for service in the Revolutionary War; however, two of his sons were in Captain William Crawford's Militia Company. The Muddy Creek Ledger shows that his son, William, was in the distilling business as early as 1793.

About 1782 Richard Ivers Sr signed the petition for a new state of Westsylvania to be formed out of present day Fayette, Washington, and Greene Counties, Pennsylvania, and Ohio and Monongalia Counties, Virginia. Richard Ivers Sr was on the 1784 Assessment Roll for Greene Township, Washington County, Pennsylvania.[2]

Richard Ivers Sr and his son, Richard Jr, bought adjoining tracts of land in Washington County on warrants dated December 23, 1785. Richard Sr's land was called Bear Wallow and Richard Jr's land was called Iron Hill. Both tracts were surveyed on April 17, 1786, patented on October 26, 1787, and recorded in the Washington County Patent Book 11, page 321.

Richard Sr was included on the 1789 Greene Township List of Persons Exonerated on the Frontiers of Washington County for being distressed by the Incursions and Depredations of the Indians. Richard Jr was listed on the 1790 Greene Township Census as the head of a household with one male under 16 years of age and one female.

Richard Ivers Sr was listed in the 1797 Greene County Tax Book made by Joseph Willford, Assessor, assisted by Elias Stone and Stephen Gapen. He was assessed for 200 acres land at $200, 30 acres of cleared land at $30, two cabins at $2, and one horse at $15. The next year he was assessed for 330 acres of land at $230, 20 acres of cleared land at $30, one cabin at $1, and house at $10, and two cows at $12.

In 1801 Thomas Wilkinson and James Seaton witnessed a deed of sale of land between Richard Ivers Jr and his wife Deborah...(-1836) of Greene Township, Greene County, Pennsylvania, to Josias Lowry of Cumberland Township, Greene County, Pennsylvania. The sum of $420 was paid for 105 acres of land in Greene Township. The deed was recorded on February 1, 1802.

The Will of Richard Ivers Sr,[3] found in the Washington County Will Book I, page 53, was probated May 19, 1806, and read as follows:

In the name of God, Amen, I, Richard Ivers of Washington County and state of Pennsylvania being weak in body, but of sound and perfect mind and memory, blessed be Almighty God for the same, do make and publish this my last will and testament, in manner and form following;

First, I give and bequeath unto my beloved wife Mary Ivers one third of all my real and personal property during her life.

Secondly, I do also give and bequeath to my eldest son John Ivers the sum of fifteen shillings; I do also give and bequeath to my son Richard Ivers the sum of five shillings, I do also bequeath unto my five daughters Jane Bosher, Mary Long, Elizabeth Trulock, Sarah Woods, and Ann Steel, the sum of five shillings each, which said several legacies or sums of money I will and order shall be paid to the said respective legatees within one year after my decease; I do also give and bequeath unto my son William Ivers all the rest, residue and remainder of my personal estate where I now live containing seventy four acres of land be there more or less; and lastly I give and bequeath to my son William Ivers all the rest of all my real and personal estate of what kind and nature soever.

I give and bequeath to my son William Ivers, who I hereby appoint sole Executor of this my last will and testament, hereby revoking all former wills by me made, in witness whereof I have hereunto set my hand and seal this twentysixth day of January in the year of our Lord one thousand seven hundred and ninety three.

Signed, sealed, published and declared by the above named Richard Ivers to be his last will and testament in the presence of us who have hereunto subscribed our names as witness in the presence of the testator, Stephen Gapen, Benjamin Titus, Rachel Gapen Titus.

[1] Leckey, Howard. *Tenmile Country and its Pioneer Families.* Rpt, (Closson Press, Apollo, PA. 2007) 627.
[2] Leckey, 135.
[3] http://files.usgwarchives.org/pa/greene/wills/iver0001.txt.

JOHN AND TABITHA DAVIS

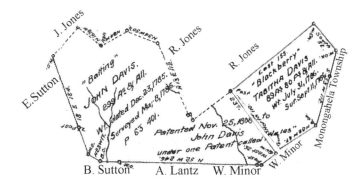

"By the 1758 Laws of Virginia in the County of Augusta, Virginia, in the reign of George II, John Davis (1754-1825) received £2.15s. for provisions furnished to the inhabitants of the said county."[1]

He settled in Washington County, Virginia, by 1772.[2] In October 1776 the several companies of militia and freeholders of Augusta County forwarded to their representatives in the Legislature their sentiments on the subject of religious liberty. They demanded, "All religious denominations within the Dominion be forthwith put in full possession of equal liberty without preference or pre-eminence." The paper was signed by John Davis and others.[3]

John Davis served in Stockley's Rangers of Militia in Washington and Northampton Counties from 1778 to1783.[4] In 1781 he was recruited in the vicinity of Carmichael Town, Washington County, to enlist in the First Battalion of the Pennsylvania Militia.

In the 1781 Effective Supply tax rates for Greene Township, Washington County, John Davis was taxed $158 for 300 acres of land, two horses, three cows and three sheep.[5] In 1781 Mr Joseph Gwyne, Collector of the Taxes of Cumberland Township, Washington County, received the following notice, "You are hereby authorized and required to notify every person in your respective township what their taxes is either personally or in writing as expressed in your duplicate at least five days before the appeal which will be held at home of Henry VanMetre Esq, Friday 16th of May." John Davis was one of the people notified.

Private 5th Class John Davis served in Captain Crawford's Company of Washington County Militia in the District lying upon the Monongalia River between Whiteley and Muddy Creeks in October 1781.

William Davis (-1789) of Chester County, Pennsylvania, married Elizabeth Wolison and died in Cumberland Township, Washington County, Pennsylvania. In his Will, which was probated December 1, 1789, he named his daughter Tabitha (1753-1803) who married John Davis. The Will was filed in the Greene County Will Book 1, page 104.

About 1782 John Davis signed the petition for a new state which was circulated through Fayette, Washington, and Greene Counties, Pennsylvania, and in Ohio and Monongalia Counties, Virginia. [6] He was listed on the 1784 Assessment Roll for Greene and Amwell Townships, Washington County, Pennsylvania.[7]

Ensign John Davis served in the Seventh Company of Colonel Benjamin McVeagh's First Battalion of the Philadelphia County Militia in March 1784.[8]

On July 7, 1785, he bought 300 acres of land in Cumberland County. In August 1789 he received Warrant No. 561 good for 300 acres of Donation Land for service as a Captain of the Pennsylvania Line during the Revolutionary War.

He was listed in the 1790 census for Greene Township as the head of a household which included one male less than 16 years of age, one male between 16 to 25 years of age, and five females.[9]

The Tax Book for 1797 in Greene County was made by Joseph Willford, Assessor, assisted by Elias Stone and Stephen Gapen. John was assessed for 300 acres of land at $360, 80 acres of cleared land at $80, two houses at $15, a cabin at $1, one barn at $10, two horses at $40, and four cows at $24. In 1800 he was assessed for 300 acres of land at $330, one house at $8, a barn at $10, two horses at $50, and seven cows at $42.

Land records show that he acquired 3,237 acres of land in Washington County between 1776 and 1838.[10]

He resided in Westmoreland County in 1825 when he was pensioned under the Act of Congress of March 18, 1818. He began receiving a pension on May 12, 1820. John and Tabitha Davis were buried in the Garard's Fort Cemetery. His Will was recorded in Greene County Will Testators Record, Volume 1, page 275. His son-in-Law, James Morrison, married to their daughter Elizabeth, was the executor of his Will in which he left these bequests:

i. Mary Davis Long, $500, married Elial Long (1756-1835).

ii. Hannah Davis Lesley (1779- 1853), $ 500.

iii. Elizabeth Davis Morrison, $1,000.

iv. Sarah Davis Morrison, $1,200.

[1] http://vagenweb.org/hening/vol07-09.htm.
[2] Pilcher, Margaret C. *Historical Sketches of the Campbell, Pilcher and Kindred Families,* (Marshall & Bruce Co., Nashville, 1911) 96.
[3] American Archives, Fifth Series, Volume II, page 815.
[4] Pennsylvania Archives, Third Series, Volume XXIII, pages 198-220.
[5] Pennsylvania Archives, Series 3, Volume XXII.
[6] Continental Congress papers, No. 48, Folios 251-256, pages 89-96.
[7] Leckey, Howard. *Tenmile Country and its Pioneer Families.* Rpt, (Closson Press, Apollo, PA, 2007) 135.
[8] Pennsylvania Archives, Series 1, Volume X, page 219.
[9] Leckey, 156.
[10] Pennsylvania Archives, Series 3, Volume XXVI.

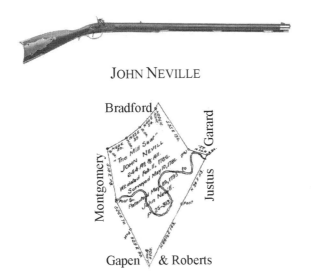

JOHN NEVILLE

General John Neville (1731-1803), son of George Neville and Ann Burroughs, was born in Prince William County, Virginia. In 1754 he married Winifrede Oldham (1736-1797), daughter of John Oldham and Anne (Conway) Oldham. She was born in Virginia and died at Pittsburgh, Pennsylvania. General and Winifred (Oldham) Neville had two children:[1]

i. Presley Neville (1755-) was a distinguished military officer during the Revolutionary War, became a colonel, and as aide-de-camp to the Marquis de Lafayette participated in most of the principal battles. He died on land granted him for his military services at Neville,

Clermont County, Ohio. He married October 15, 1782, to Nancy, daughter of General Daniel Morgan, and they had 14 children.

ii. Amelia (1763-1849) was born in Winchester, Virginia, the only daughter of General John Neville. She married in 1785 to Major Isaac Craig. They were the parents of 13 children, three of whom died in infancy. She survived him nearly a quarter of a century, dying on Long Island in the Ohio River which had been renamed Montour's Island. Their son, Neville B. Craig, was born March 29, 1787, in the old redoubt erected by Colonel Bouquet in 1764 at Pittsburgh and used during Major Craig's occupancy of the post as officer's quarters. His wife was Jane Ann Fulton.

In 1754 John Neville served under Major George Washington in the ill-fated campaign against the French at Jumonville in present day Fayette County, Pennsylvania, which was then claimed by Virginia. The defeat of Washington's forces by the French marked the beginning of the French and Indian War. In 1755 he served under General Edward Braddock in the unsuccessful attack on Fort Duquesne in present day Pittsburgh, later renamed Fort Pitt.

He was a delegate from Augusta County, Virginia, to the Provincial Convention of Virginia which appointed George Washington, Peyton Randolph, and others to the Continental Congress at Philadelphia, but sickness prevented his attendance.

On August 7, 1775, Colonel Neville was ordered by the Provincial Convention to march with his Fourth Virginia Regiment to take possession of Fort Pitt.

On May 16, 1775, John Neville was chosen a member of the Committee of Observation at Pittsburgh for the Washington County Militia for that part of Augusta County on the west side of Laurel Hill.

On December 23, 1776, he was commissioned under Virginia authority a Justice of "Yohoganie" County Court, but the boundary dispute between Virginia and Pennsylvania and his position under Continental authority as commandant at Fort Pitt made him decline the appointment.

He fought in the battles of Trenton, Princeton, Germantown, and Monmouth and was captured in the Battle of Charleston in 1780.

In the 1781 Effective Supply Tax Book of Greene Township, Washington County, he was assessed for 400 acres of land at $48.

In 1783 he was brevetted a Brigadier General by the Continental Congress and elected to the Supreme Executive Council of

Pennsylvania from Washington County. Two years later he became a member of the State Board of Property.

John Neville bought 244 acres called The Mill Seat on a warrant dated February 11, 1786. It was surveyed May 10, 1786, patented May 29, 1795, and recorded in the Washington County Patent Book P25, page 313. He bought 406 acres in February and 290 acres in August 1786 in Washington County. On October 6, 1786, he bought 400 acres on Shirtie (Chartier) Creek. On April 3, 1788, he bought 400 acres between Peter's Creek and Chartier's Creek in Washington County.[2]

In 1789 and 1790 he was a member of the convention that ratified the Federal Constitution and adopted the Pennsylvania Constitution.

In 1791 he was appointed inspector of United States Revenue for the Fourth District of Pennsylvania at Pittsburgh and held that position during the Whiskey Insurrection of 1794 when his house and other buildings were besieged and burned to the ground by the rebel mob.

General John Neville, who lived in Washington County a mile south of the Allegheny County line, was listed in the 1790 Census as head of a household with one male under 16 years of age and two females.

In 1791 the Federal Government, seeking ways to repay the debt incurred by the American Revolution, passed an excise tax on whiskey which was fiercely opposed by the people along the Monongahela River.[3] John Neville was called by President George Washington to be the Inspector of Revenue for that district and demonstrate that the excise tax on distilled spirits initiated in 1791 by Alexander Hamilton would be collected west of the Allegheny Mountains.

The settlers in the region had very little money and lived on the barter system. Their primary means of getting hard cash was by distilling their excess grain into whiskey. They transported their whiskey by packhorse over the Alleghenies to the affluent eastern Pennsylvanians and bartered to obtain staples such as salt and gunpowder which they could not produce. By the 1780s a small still was a fixture on many farms on the western frontier and life was still hard, but somewhat peaceful. That is, until Treasury Secretary Hamilton passed the Whiskey Tax Act. Under that Act, what little money they were able to gain by selling their whiskey was lost in taxes which were used by the new federal government to offset expenses of the recent Revolutionary War. The stage was set for discontent and violence in Pittsylvania Country.

In 1794 General Neville bought a large tract of land in Washington County, built his home on it, and called it Bower Hill. He set about collecting taxes on whiskey from the settlers. To accommodate violators of the tax law, Congress established a United States District Court for

Western Pennsylvania at Pittsburgh instead of transporting violators to York or Philadelphia. Major David Lenox, a United States Marshal, was sent to Pittsburgh to take command. Major Lenox successfully served all of the warrants handed to him by General John Neville, the Tax Inspector, except one. On July 10, 1794, Major Lenox went to Pittsburgh with General Neville to serve it on a distiller named Oliver Miller who lived near Peter's Creek. Miller fired at them as they left his house, but missed both of them. Miller later said that he was incensed that the Marshal had brought the despised General Neville to his door and that he would have to spend $250 to make the trip to the court in Philadelphia. It was later said that if the Marshal had gone there alone to serve the warrant there would have been no trouble.

Angry farmers demanded Neville resign his commission and destroy all tax records. Led by Oliver Miller Jr and James McFarlane, a militia of approximately 500 men surrounded Bower Hill. The militia was met by armed slaves and soldiers sent by the federal government. Shots rang out and Bower Hill was set on fire. By morning, Bower Hill was smoldering and McFarlane and Miller were dead.

General John Neville and Major David Lenox promptly reported the rebel attacks to President Washington and Secretary of the Treasury Hamilton who was the operational authority behind the excise tax law. General Neville alleged that over $4,600 in excise receipts had been taken from his home. The attack upon the Neville homestead and its destruction, the deaths of Major McFarlane and Miller, and other overt acts in the vicinity sharply drew the line between the federal government and the rebels and set the stage for a confrontation. Notice of the attack on General Neville's property was sent to the Judges, Justices of the Peace, Sheriffs, and Brigade Inspectors of Westmoreland, Washington, Fayette, and Allegheny Counties. Neville and other plantation owners in the Chartiers Valley moved away. Neville went to Montour's Island in the Ohio River.

The disgruntled Friends of Liberty raised their own militia, terrorized Pittsburgh, and tarred and feathered tax collectors. Violence escalated and in 1794 President Washington, reacting to this challenge to Federal authority, called out several states' militia and raised an army of more than 13,000 troops which moved west under his personal command to quell the uprising.

Neville was appointed agent for the sale of lands at Pittsburgh under the Act of Congress passed March 18, 1796. He died on Montour's Island, present day Neville Township, Allegheny County, Pennsylvania, on July 29, 1803. He and Winifred (1797) were buried in the burial ground at the Trinity Episcopal Church in Pittsburgh.

JOHN HOLTON

In 1795 John Neville and Winifred "Winnie" Oldham Neville, his wife, sold The Mill Seat to John Holton for 5s. In 1798 General Neville also sold his 1,000-acre Kentucky land grant to John Holton for $1 and other considerations. John Holton of Greene County, Pennsylvania, was apparently an associate of General John Neville.

John Holton was a single freeman listed in Springhill Township, Bedford County, Pennsylvania, in 1772. He married Lydia Evans, daughter of David Evans and Mary Lewis, first known to be in southwest Pennsylvania about 1775. Holton apparently moved to Kentucky and used the name of John H. Neville, which was on the land patents to General Neville, perhaps to help establish his claim to the land which was in conflict with an earlier Virginia land grant.

[1] Jordan, John W. *Colonial and Revolutionary Families of Pennsylvania.* (Clearfield Co., Pub, Baltimore, MD, 1978).
[2] Egle, William Henry. *Warrantees of Land in the Several Counties of the State of Pennsylvania, 1730-1898, Volume III.* (William S. Ray, State Printer of Pennsylvania, 1899).
[3] Corbly, Don. *Pastor John Corbly.* (Lulu Press, Raleigh, NC, 2008) Chapter Seven.
[4] http://www.oldsaintlukes.org/neville_history.htm.

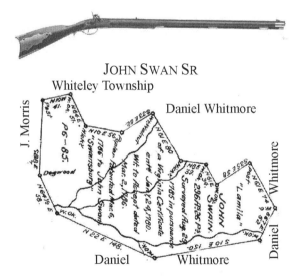

JOHN SWAN SR

John Swan Sr (1721-1799) was born in Pennsylvania, the son of John Swan (1690-) and Elizabeth (Greene) Foster (1683-). In 1744 he married

Elizabeth Lucas (1724-1805) who was born in Prince George's County, Maryland. They were buried in the Swan Cemetery near Rice's Landing in Carmichael Town, Greene County.[1] Their children were:

    i. John Jr (1744-1780), in 1769 married Elizabeth VanMeter (1752-1848), daughter of Jacob and Letitia. She was born in Frederick County, Virginia.

    ii. Thomas (1747-), was born in Maryland, married …VanMeter.

    iii. Charles (1749-1832) married Sarah VanMeter (1758-1825), daughter of Henry and Martha VanMeter. He was buried in the Swan Cemetery in Greene County.

    iv. Elizabeth (1751–1825), born in Maryland married Thomas Hughes (1749-1823). They died at Jefferson, near Carmichael, Pennsylvania, and were buried in the old Presbyterian Cemetery there.

    v. Richard (1753-1822) married Martha VanMeter (1754-1836), daughter of Henry and Martha VanMeter.

    vi. Sarah (1755-1838), born in Maryland, died in Howard County, Missouri, married in 1775 to Joseph Hughes 1753-1837), brother of William Hughes.

    vii. Martha (1760-1783) married William Hughes, (1760-1828), brother of Joseph. They died in Howard County, Missouri.

    viii. William (1762-1835) married Sarah Harrod (1766-1822), daughter of Colonel William Harrod Sr and Amelia Stephens.

In early 1768 John Swan Sr, his wife Elizabeth, and sons John Jr and Charles Swan; Felix and Thomas Hughes; Jacob VanMeter and his wife Letitia (Strode); William Harrod, Coleman Brown, John Rice Jr, James Kincaid, Richard Chenowith, Elias Garard, and David Heaton moved from Winchester, Virginia, to the Ten Mile Country near present day Brownsville, Pennsylvania. Jacob VanMeter, John Swan Sr, Thomas Hughes, and Henry VanMeter, brother of Jacob, were granted headrights for transporting migrating families.

They traveled toward George and Margaret Hupp's cabin on Ten Mile Creek, the stopping point for most settlers who came to that region. Jacob VanMeter and some other VanMeters settled on Pumpkin Run while others became the first settlers on Muddy Creek. Felix Hughes and Thomas Hughes built their cabins nearCarmichael Town. Charles Swan selected a place one mile west of Carmichael Town and JacobVanMeter, the patriarch, settled on the lower Muddy Creek in then Augusta County,

Virginia.

Their top priority was the construction of forts. Jacob VanMeter built Fort VanMeter on Muddy Creek. John Swan Sr built Fort Swan on Swan's Run, and Henry VanMeter also built his Fort VanMeter on Swan's Run not far from John Swan's fort. This land in 1772 was included in Spring Hill Township, Washington County.

Jacob and Letitia VanMeter lived by Muddy Creek for several years and then moved south near Garard's Fort. He participated in the organization of the Goshen Baptist Church at Garard's Fort. Among the church's original founders were 10 members of the Van Meter family and John Swan Jr and his wife, Elizabeth.[2]

John Swan Sr served in the First Company of the Third Battalion of the Washington County Militia in September 1781, according to the Pennsylvania State Archives, Revolutionary War Military Abstract Card File. He was a Private 4th Class in Captain Samuel Shanon's Company of the Third Battalion of the Washington County Militia in September 1782 and also signed the petition to form the new state of Westsylvania.[3]

The principal fort in the Garard's Fort's general area was Jackson's Fort on the south fork of Ten Mile Creek. Ross and John Ankrom's Fort was also on the south fork. Jacob VanMeter's Fort was on Muddy Creek; Clegg's Fort was on Dunkard Creek; William Minor's Fort was on Big Whiteley Creek; Guthrie's Fort was on Big Whiteley Creek; John Swan's Fort and Henry VanMeter's Fort were on Swan's Run; Henry Enoch's Fort was at the forks of the Ten Mile Creek; and Bell's Fort was on Rough Creek.[4]

John Swan Sr bought 399 acres in Cumberland Township called Roach. It was surveyed June 3, 1785, on a Virginia certificate which was entered January 24, 1780, patented March 6, 1786, on a warrant to accept dated March 2, 1786, and recorded in the Washington County Patent Book PA6, page 84.

In 1788 in Cumberland Township, Washington County, Mr Joseph Gwyne, Collector of the Taxes, received this letter: "You are hereby authorized and required to notify every person in your respective township what their taxes is either personally or in writing as expressed in your duplicate at least five days before the appeal which will be held at home of Henry VanMetre Esq., Friday 16th of May." John Swan Sr was one of those so notified.[5]

John Swan Sr was assessed in 1781 in Cumberland Township, Washington County, for 270 acres, two horses, four cows, and 12 sheep at $303. He refused to give property, but paid taxes of $30 for 300 acres of vacant land in Greene Township, Washington County.[6]

In the Cumberland Township 1790 Census John Swan was listed as head of household with one male under 16 years of age, one male over 16 years of age, one female, and six slaves. He was living in Cumberland Township when he filed his Will in the Greene County Will Book, Volume 1, page 23.

John Swan Sr (1721-1799) and Elizabeth were buried in the Swan Cemetery near Rice's Landing at Carmichael, Greene County, Pennsylvania.[7] Their headstone inscriptions read:

Here lies the body of Elizabeth Swon, died 17th day of October 1822 aged 83 yrs - no footstone.
Here lies the body of John Swon, died 29th day of December 1799 aged 78 yrs - no footstone.

[1] Leckey, Howard. *Tenmile Country and its Pioneer Families.* Rpt, (Closson Press, Apollo, PA. 2007), 169-185
[2] Corbly, Don. *Pastor John Corbly.* (Lulu Press, Raleigh, NC, 2008) 72.
[3] Continental Congress papers, No. 48, Folios 251-256, pages 89, 96.
[4] http://freepages.genealogy.rootsweb.ancestry.com/~mooreorless/harrod.htm.
[5] http://www.ourfamilyhistories.com/hsdurbin/tax-lists/more-tax-census1.html.
[6] Effective Supply tax rates for Washington Co: Pennsylvania Archives, Series 3, Volume XXII, page 699.
[7] http://www.easternusresearch.com/easternusresearch/cemet/cem3.html.

ROBERT MORRISON

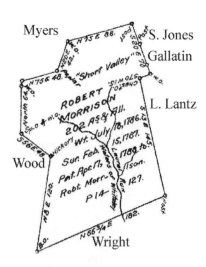

John MacPherson Morrison's son, William Morrison (-1760), born in Ayr, Scotland, married Elizabeth Hamilton of Ayr, Scotland, in 1743. Their son, Robert Morrison (1750-1832), was also born in Ayr, Scotland.

Robert Morrison married Elizabeth Culbertson (1753-1816) in 1771 and then immigrated to Greene County, Pennsylvania, near Carmichael Town. Elizabeth, the daughter of Elder Robert Culbertson and Sarah Seeley, died in Pennsylvania. The children of Robert Morrison and Elizabeth Culbertson were:[1]

i. Sarah married John Huston.

ii. William (1780-1862), born in New Castle, Delaware, died in Armstrong County, Pennsylvania, married (1) Margaret Barnes and (2) Martha Johnson.

iii. Elizabeth (1782-1862) married James Montgomery (1777-1844) in 1812.

iv. Thomas (1772 – 1790) married Mary Jennings.

v. Andrew married Margaret Crozier.

vi. Agnes married…Hughes.

vii. John married Nancy Barnes.

viii. Alexander married Hannah Dunlap.

ix. Robert married Sarah Galbreath.

x. Ruth married John Cree.

xi. Margaret married David Rich.

On November 1, 1777, Robert Morrison was a Private in Captain Henry Darrah's Company of the Bucks County Militia commanded by Lieutenant Colonel John Lacey; and later commanded by Colonel William Roberts in 1778.[2]

After the Revolutionary War he moved to Washington County, Pennsylvania, near Garard's Fort.

Jennings[3] wrote that after the Revolutionary War Robert Morrison, one of the "blue hen's chickens," as soldiers from Delaware were called, took his wife, Elizabeth Culbertson, an English woman, and two children and went west. General Washington asked him to take his tract of 600 acres in the northwestern part of Fayette County, Pennsylvania, lying on the Youghiogheny River. He looked at the land, but thought it too exposed to incursions from the Indians and continued his journey about 50 miles farther southwest into Greene county where he bought out the McClungs who went with their slaves to Kentucky, as Pennsylvania had passed an ordinance of gradual emancipation in 1780. There they lived, reared a family of 10 children, and he died at the age of 82 years.

In the 1781 Effective Supply Tax Rate Roll for Washington County, Pennsylvania, he was taxed $8 for two horses and one cow.[4]

Robert bought 202 acres in Washington County called Short Valley on a warrant dated July 18, 1786. It was surveyed on February 15, 1787, patented on April 17, 1788, and recorded in the Washington County Patent Book P14, page 127. He also bought 388 acres called Toft on November 1, 1787, in Washington County.[5] In 1793 he sold 250 acres of it to William Jones.[6]

He was listed in the 1790 Greene Township Census as head of a household of four males under 16 years of age and four females.

During the Whiskey Insurrection, General John Neville established his headquarters for Washington County in the house of William Faulkner at Washington and attended to his tax collection business there two days a week. Faulkner was advised by several local settlers that he was making a mistake in allowing a revenue office in his house and was urged to discontinue it. Faulkner was alarmed by this warning and set about learning the public's opinion of the matter. At Benjamin Parkinson's place Robert Morrison confronted him with a copy of the Pittsburgh Gazette in which Neville had advertised the location of the excise office in Washington and Faulkner admitted its accuracy. Robert roundly damned him as a rascal and public enemy and threatened that the Association, comprised of 500 members, would make an example of him. Later that day at David Hamilton's house Robert met a group of settlers who strongly opposed the Whiskey Tax. Faulkner said in his later deposition, "David Hamilton then came forward and after giving a whoop or two caught hold of some of the hair of this deponent on the top of his head and asked him if he understood the meaning of being scalped." Faulkner understood perfectly and promised to withdraw his permission for the use of his house.[7]

In 1796 Robert Morrison ran a tavern on Louther Street, Carlisle, Cumberland County, Pennsylvania.[8] In the 1797 Greene County Tax Book made by Joseph Willford, Assessor, assisted by Elias Stone and Stephen Gapen, Robert Morrison was assessed for 200 acres of land at $100, 30 acres of cleared land at $30, one cabin at $1, one barn at $2, three horses at $30, and four cows at $24. The following year he was assessed for 200 acres of land at $100, 30 acres of cleared land at $25, two cabins at $2, three horses at $30, and three cows at $18.

A deed from William Jack to the burgesses and inhabitants of the borough of Greensburg, Greene County, Pennsylvania, dated April 18, 1803, described a lot, "upon which a log schoolhouse was erected by and at the expense of certain inhabitants of said borough and its vicinity." After the custom of that day it was "built near a spring, and was a rude log cabin about 18 by 24 feet, one story high, with a Shinngle roof. The furniture consisted of wooden benches of oak plank and as long as the house would admit. The writing desks were made of broad inch boards, and were fastened to the walls around the inside of the building. They extended entirely around the room except at the door. In this house were three or four small eight by ten light windows. Among the early teachers were Robert Williams and Robert Morrison. Williams taught a long time, perhaps down to 1816 or '17. The third teacher was probably Robert Montgomery."[9]

Robert Morrison was a member of the Board of Trustees of the New Providence Church, Greene County, which was incorporated in 1804 nearCarmichael Town.[10] He was one of the voters in Greene Township who voted at the house of John Campbell on October 14, 1806.[11]

Robert Morrison was buried in the Glade Cemetery in Cumberland Township, Washington County.[12]

The Bureau of Pensions, War Department, on May 10, 1928, replied to a questioner that no record of a pension for Robert Morrison was in their files.[13]

[1] http://familytreemaker.genealogy.com/users/d/a/v/Richard-JDavis/FILE/0001 text.txt.

[2] Pennsylvania Archives, Series 5, Volume V, Muster Roll of Bucks Count, pages 405-409.

[3] Jennings, William H. *A Genealogical History of the Jennings Families in England and America,* (Hard Press PubliShinng Co., Lenox, MA, 2010).

[4] Pennsylvania Archives, Series 3, Volume XXII, page 699.

[5] Egle, William Henry. *Warrantees of Land in the Several Counties of the State of Pennsylvania, 1730-1898, Volume III.* (William S. Ray, State Printer of Pennsylvania, 1899).

[6] Crumine, Boyd. *History of Washington County, Pennsylvania: with biographical sketches of many of its pioneers and prominent men,* (L. H. Everts and Co., Philadelphia, PA, 1882).

[7] Baldin, Leland D. *Whiskey Rebels : the Story of a Frontier Uprising,* (University of Pittsburgh Press, Pittsburgh, PA, 1939).

[8] http://files.usgwarchives.org/pa/cumberland/history/local/carlisletaverns01.txt.

[9] Boucher, John Newton, and Jordan, John W. *History of Westmoreland County, Pennsylvania, Volume One,* (The Lewis PubliShinng Company, New York, Chicago, 1906).

[10] http://listsearches.rootsweb.com/th/read/CRAGO/2001-04/0987922226.

[11] http://www.cornerstonegenealogy.com/greene_countyvoter_lists_1801.htm .

[12] http://www.easternusresearch.com/easternusresearch/cemet/revwarcem2.html.

[13] Pennsylvania Archives, Revolutionary War Pensions, Pennsylvania, Robert Morrison.

JOHN SCHRYER

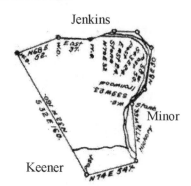

John Schryer bought 197 acres in York County, Pennsylvania, on a warrant dated May 31, 1762. It was recorded in the York County Deed Book AA-No. 6, page 401.

Very little is known about John Schryer's marital status. The only credible record stated that he married Christianna Fetter in Allegany County, Maryland, in 1795. She may have been born in Hagerstown, Maryland, and was probably underage because a letter was required to support her right to marry. There were no credible records to support her birth, parents, or siblings nor any formal account of John and Christianna's children.[1]

In 1778 Jacob Stoner, York County, Pennsylvania, agreed to buy 144 acres from John Schryer, but Schryer died before he conveyed the deed. Jacob Stoner lived in York County. Stoner and Schryer were farmers.[2]

John Schryer took the Oath of Allegiance to the State of Pennsylvania in Lebanon Township, Lancaster County, Pennsylvania, on June 2, 1778.[3] In 1779 he was a Private 7th Class in the 7th Company of the 9th Battalion of the Lancaster County Militia, but in May the Muster Roll's remarks column recorded him as "gone," according to the Pennsylvania State Archives, Revolutionary War Military Abstract Card File.

In 1780 in York County, John Schryer was taxed £10.16s. for a horse and a cow and £6.13s. for a house.[4]

In 1782 Private John Schryer served in Captain John Guthrey's Company in the First Battalion of Washington County's Militia.[5]

On July 31, 1786, John Schryer bought 94 acres in Washington County called Germany. It was surveyed on March 25, 1789, patented on

June 9, 1794, and recorded in the Washington County Patent Book P21, page 309. He owned 200 acres of land on July 31, 1798, in Greene County, Pennsylvania.[6] He was listed in the 1809 Dunkard Township, Greene County Tax Book made by Joseph Willford and assistants Elias Stone and Stephen Gapen. He was assessed for 110 acres of land at $440, two horses at $24, and two cows at $12.

In August 27, 1812, in the Monongalia County Court, William Jones was summoned to answer John Schryer in a plea of debt for $40 and $10 damages. A promissory note was signed for $40 and witnessed by William McColloh. William Jones was also summoned to answer John Schryer in a plea of debt for $98.68 and $10 damages. A ninety-day note was signed by Jones to Schryer dated December 27, 1810, for $96.68 and was secured by Davis Shockley and Jacob Foulk on September 21, 1812. In the May 1813 court term, judgment was for plaintiff for $96.68 with interest from September 27, 1811, and judgment for plaintiff for $40 with interest from January 27, 1811.[7]

On September 8, 1832, he was named Administrator of the estate of Joseph Schryer, Greene County, Pennsylvania. He also was the Administrator of the estate of Mary Sedgwick, Greene County, Pennsylvania.[8]

[1] Scharf, Thomas. *History of western Maryland: Being a history of Frederick...1882. Volume II.* (Heritage Books Inc., CD. Westminster, MD, 2002).

[2] http://freepages.genealogy.rootsweb.ancestry.com/~midmdroots/county/frederick/equity/js10.htm.

[3] Muster rolls and papers relating to the Associators and Militias of the county of Lancaster, Series 2, Volume XIII, page 409.

[4] *Returns of Taxables of the County of York for the years 1779, 1780, 1781,* (Pub. BiblioBazaar, Charleston, SC, 2009).

[5] Pennsylvania Archives, Series VI, Vol. 2, pages 18, 19, 271.

[6] Pennsylvania Archive, Series 3, Volume XXVI, *Provincial Papers, Warrantees of land in the Several Counties of the State of Pennsylvania, 1730-1898,* page 608.

[7] Zinn, Melba Pender. *Monongalia County, (West) Virginia, Records of the District, Superior and County Courts, Volume 7: 1808-1814.* (Heritage Books Inc., Westminster, MD, 2009) 227.

[8] http://www.indgensoc.org/publications/IGSquarterly.pdf.

RICHARD HALL

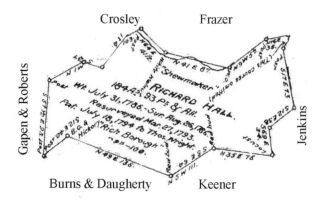

Crosley   Frazer

Gapen & Roberts   Jenkins

Burns & Daugherty   Keener

In 1750 Richard Hall bought 400 acres of land from John Harrison Jr on Meadow Creek, a branch that flowed from Blacksburg, Virginia, into the Woods River (New River) near Montgomery County, Virginia. That land had been patented to John Harrison in 1746. He also bought land near Drapers Meadow in 1750 in Augusta County, Virginia, now present day Blacksburg, Montgomery County, Virginia.

Richard Hall (1729-1821) came to Stouble's Creek at the junction of the South Branch and North Fork Creeks in Botetourt County, Virginia, about 1752. He had married Phebe...in Hamilton County, Ohio.

In 1752 Richard Hall appraised Israel Lorton's land and in 1768 he did another appraisal for the James Conley estate.[1]

Christopher Gist was an explorer for the Ohio Company and a guide for Major George Washington in 1753-1754 when he was sent by Governor Dinwiddie of Virginia to negotiate with French military forces with the purpose of keeping them out of the Ohio Valley which Virginia claimed. Richard Hall was mentioned in Christopher Gist's Journal:[2]

> Monday 13. Set out southeast two miles, east one mile, southeast three miles, south 12 miles to Richard Halls in Augusta County. He was one of the farthest settlers to the westward on the New River.
> Tuesday 14. Stayed at Richard Halls and wrote to the President of Virginia & the Ohio Company to let them know I should be with them by the 15th of June.
> Wednesday 15. Set out from Richard Hall's south 16 miles.
> Friday 17. Set out southwest three miles, then south nine miles to the dividing line between Carolina and Virginia where I stayed all night, the land from Rich Hall's to this

place is broken.

On March 8, 1753, Richard Hall bought 58 acres of land in Philadelphia County. It was patented on September 24, 1754, and recorded in the Philadelphia County Patent Book A, page 291. In that year he petitioned the Chester County Court for a license to trade in Conestoga, Donegal, and Paxtang Counties of Pennsylvania.[3]

When British General Braddock was defeated on the Ohio River in July 1755 the whole frontier of western Virginia was thrown open to the ravages of the Indians. Richard Hall lived in 1756 about 30 miles from Fort Prince George which was then an uncompleted fort at present day Pittsburgh in Allegheny County, Pennsylvania. The site was originally a trading post established by William Trent in the 1740s. It was the first of five forts that were built to control the strategic Forks of the Ohio River. The French built Fort Duquesne there and the British captured it and renamed it Fort Pitt.

In December 1757 "An Indenture was made between John Walker of Albemarle County, Virginia, and Richard Hall of same County...doth sell Richard Hall land lying on south side of Fluvanna River containing by estimation 50 acres in Albemarle County being heretofore granted unto William Cabell by patent...Witness: John Hunder, Edward Hunder, Richard Taylor."

In 1763 Richard Hall, a house carpenter of Halifax County, Virginia, patented 400 acres of land on Drapers Meadow to Abraham Chrisman of Frederick County, Virginia.[4]

Richard Hall's family was living in the Dunkard Creek area in 1768 when George Morris claimed land there for himself and built a hunter's cabin on it. According to Bittinger[5] other families living on Dunkard Creek at that time were Clark, Cox, Evans, Henderson, Hostatler, Keckly, Andrew Lantz, Martin, Peter Myers, and Thomas Province. Some of them had migrated from the Cacapon River Valley and South Branch Valley of Berkeley County, Virginia. Many other families later migrated to the White Clay Creek area. The Indian threat was very real that far west of the Monongahela River and the only protection for those settlers was Fort Dillinger, an emergency fort built on the Monongahela River about two miles east of the mouth of Dunkard Creek.

The Great Bethel Regular Baptist Church, the first Baptist church organized west of the Alleghenies, was one of the first religious faiths established within the boundaries of present day Fayette County, Pennsylvania. Elders John Sutton and Henry Crosbye founded that church on November 8, 1770, at present day Uniontown, 22 miles east of Garard's Fort. There were six charter members; Jacob VanMeter and his wife Leticia (Strode) VanMeter, Richard Hall and his wife Phebe, Jeremiah Blackford, and Rachel Sutton. The Great Bethel Regular Baptist Church was a member of the Ketocton Association until 1776. Its Record Book contained this early entry, "That this Church was Constituted by me, Nov. 7th, 1770, and that the Bearer was licensed to Preach before me, or in my Presence, as witness my hand this 8th day of Nov., 1770. Henry Crosbye."[6]

Captain George Morris, who lived at Garard's Fort, learned in 1774 that the Governor of Virginia, Lord Dunmore, was aiding and abetting the British interest by enlisting Indians to attack the settlers in Pittsylvania Country. He tore up the commission from Lord Dunmore which had made him a Captain in the British service. He remained, however, a soldier and patriot. At the close of Dunmore's war, during which he fought as a patriot Militiaman, he returned to Garard's Fort to farm and function as a scout when necessary. On one occasion he, Richard Hall, and John Keener were on a scouting expedition and were fired upon by Indians concealed in thickets near John Lantz's meadow. Keener was killed, but Morris and Hall escaped to the fort, Morris having received a slight wound. They had returned the fire and killed and scalped an Indian who Henry Sykes found the next day.[7]

The messengers from the various Baptist Churches in southwest Pennsylvania went to the annual Redstone Baptist Association meeting at the North Ten Mile Baptist Church in Great Bethel, Monongalia County, Virginia, in present day Fayette County, on October 13, 1777. The following messengers attended from their respective Baptist Churches: Turkey Foot—Richard Hall and Henry Abrams; Pike Run—William Wood, James Rogers, and Morris Brundy; Forks of Cheat—Samuel Luallen; Simpson Creek—William Davis and Dana Edwards; Georges Creek—Joseph Barnet and Peter Jones; and Cross Creek—William Taylor.[8]

Richard Hall was among the Westmoreland County Rangers on the Frontier from 1778 to 1783. His son, David (1754-), was an infantry Corporal in Colonel Bufford's Division from 1779-1781 during the Revolutionary War.[9]

Just before the massacre of the Corbly family in 1782 the following event took place in the Garard's Fort area. Colonel John Minor, commander of military operations, sent out a party of scouts each successive morning to observe the surrounding country and report upon the situation. Upon one occasion Amos Morris, Richard "Dick" Hall, and a man by the name of Mahanna were sent up the creek. The three scouts had proceeded on their way to John Lantz's farm when they were fired on by concealed Indians. Mahanna was killed on the spot; Morris was wounded in the arm, but shot one Indian and escaped.

When Morris and Hall returned to the fort Colonel Minor organized about 500 men to pursue the Indians. This army arrived at the place where the scouts had been fired on and found Mahanna stripped of his clothing and so mutilated and cut to pieces that his remains had to be rolled into a sheet for burial. They placed the body under a fallen tree, covered it with earth, and called it a burial.

The army then formed into a line of skirmishers to search out the Indians. Henry Sykes, in an advanced guard preceding the main army, was on the south bank of a creek when he found an Indian trail. He followed it to some shelving rocks under which he observed some loose stones covering a dead Indian, the one Hall had shot the previous day. Seizing him by his top-knot, he dragged him into the light, scalped him, and gave a war whoop. It was said that in less than five minutes he was surrounded by the whole of Minor's army.[10] Sykes lost his personal rifle in the melee and was reimbursed £7 according to the Pennsylvania State Archives, Military Abstract Card File, Ledger B, page 686.

In 1782 Richard Hall signed the petition for the new state of Westsylvania to be formed from present day Fayette, Washington, and Greene Counties in Pennsylvania and Ohio and Monongalia Counties in Virginia.[11]

Richard Hall bought 184 acres called Shewmaker on a warrant dated July 31, 1786. It was surveyed March 27, 1793, and patented on July 18, 1794, to Thomas Wright as Rich Borough. The transaction was recorded in the Washington County Patent Book P22, page 108.

He was included on the 1789 Greene Township List of Persons Exonerated on the Frontiers of Washington County for being distressed by the Incursions and Depredations of the Indians.

In 1790 John Corbly Jr, Joseph Martin, John and Jonah Garard, Elias Garard, and Joseph Frazer departed the Goshen Baptist Church on two flatboats with their families and livestock from Garard's Fort via the Ohio and the Little Miami Rivers to settle near Cincinnati, Ohio. They founded the Garard-Martin Station in Anderson Township in the Virginia Military District. Other early inhabitants of Anderson Township at that time included Captain James Flinn, Stephen Betts, Joseph Williamson, Stephen Davis, Richard Hall, and Jacob Bachofen.[12]

Richard Hall received 50 acres of Donation Land for his service in the Pennsylvania Militia during the Revolutionary War.

In his application for a pension for military service, he made a Declaration which was recorded thusly:

I lived in Washington County, Pennsylvania, when enlisted in the Penn Troops as a Private, was an Indian Spy at various forts and on several expeditions for three months during 1777-1778, six months during 1778-1779, three months in 1780, and six months in 1782. During 1781 went to Kentucky and served under General George Rogers Clark and as a Captain in an Indian Expedition under General Wilkinson. married in Hamilton County, Ohio, to Phebe...

Richard died in December 1821 in Clermont County, Ohio. His widow, Phebe, applied for his pension on June 1840 in that county but her claim was denied because the date of their marriage was not satisfactorily established. The person who performed the marriage forwarded an affidavit to the Pension Board that was satisfactory and she received a yearly pension of $40 until her death.

[1] Extracted from the Court Records of Augusta County, 1745-1800. (Genealogical PubliShinng Company, Baltimore, MD, 1999)Volume 2.

[2] Darlington, William M. *Christopher Gist's Journals with Historical, Geographical, and Ethnological Notes and Biographies of his Contemporaries,* (J. R. Weldin & CO., Pittsburgh, PA, 1893) First Journal 1750 to 1751.

[3] Hanna, Charles A. *The Wilderness Trail, or, The Ventures and Adventures of the Pennsylvania Traders on the Allegheny Path...*(G. P. Putnam's sons, New York, London. 1911) Volume 1, page 179.

[4] Chalkley, Lyman. *Chronicles of the Scotch-Irish Settlement in Virginia:* Extracted from the Original Court Records of Augusta County,1745-1800. (Genealogical PubliShinng Company, Baltimore, MD, 1999) Volume 2.

[5] Bittinger, Emmet F. *Heritage and Promise: Perspectives on the Church of the Brethren,* (Church of the Brethern General Board, NP) 1970.

[6] Ellis, Franklin. *History of Fayette County, Pennsylvania...*(J.R. Lippincott & Co., Phil, PA) Volume 1, 74

[7] Evans, L. K. *Pioneer History of Greene County, Pennsylvania.* (Waynesburg, Republican Press, Waynesburg, PA, 1941) 128-129.

[8] Crumrine, Boyd. *History of Washington County, Pennsylvania with Biographical Sketches of Many of Its Pioneers and Prominent Men,* (L. H. Leverts & Co., Phil, PA, 1882) 652-672.

[9] Lucas, Roderick Lewis. *A valley and its people in Montgomery County, Virginia,* (Southern Print. Co., Blacksburg, VA, 1973)

[10] Evans, 104-105.

[11] Continental Congress papers, No. 48, Folios 251-256, pages 89-96.

[12] Asplund, John. *The annual register of the Baptist denomination, in North America; to the first of November, 1790...*(Church History Research and Archives (1979) 161.

Robert Montgomery

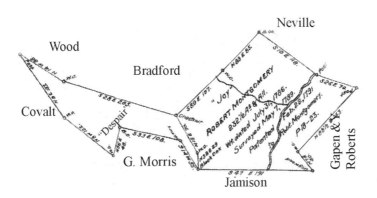

John Montgomery (1719-1795), born in Londonderry, Northern Ireland, died in Augusta County, Virginia. He was a son of James Alexander Montgomery (1690-1750) and Ann...(1689-). He married in 1738 in Earl Township, Lancaster County, Pennsylvania, to Esther Houston (1724-1790) who was also born in Londonderry, Ireland, and died at Augusta, Virginia.[1] Their children were Isabella, James, John, Margaret, Esther, Ann, Dorcas, Jane, Robert (1763-1815), Alexander, and Thomas.

Robert (1763-1815) was born in Augusta County and died in Washington County, Virginia, where his Will was dated and proved. He married in 1784 to Sarah J. Colville (1761-1839). In the Revolutionary War he fought at Kings Mountain.[2] Their children were:

i. Mary "Polly" (1784-1805).

ii. Jane Hays (1784-1805).

iii. Esther (1784-) in 1800 married David Hays.

iv. Sarah "Sally" (1806-1882).

v. James W.(1784-1805) married Mary....

vi. Andrew C. (1793-1874) born in Washington County, Virginia, died in Blount County, Tennessee. He married (1) Ann Houston, (2) Evaline C. Green, and (3) Rebecca Thompson Porter.

vii. Juliet (1795-) before 1813 married John W. Craig.

viii. John C. (1786-1804).

He was buried in the Garard's Fort Cemetery. A gravestone there bears the name Robert Montgomery and date of death August 9, 1815. Sarah was reportedly buried in the Fall Creek Cemetery, Highland County, Ohio.[3]

Under the 1781 Effective Supply Tax Rates he was taxed $168 for 200 acres of land, two horses, and two cows in Cecil Township, Washington County, Pennsylvania.[4]

On February 8, 1785, a warrant was issued to Robert McCloskey for 217 acres of land called Fressan on a branch of Chartier's Creek. It was surveyed on the following 8th of March. McCloskey lived on this farm and in about 1799 sold Robert Montgomery 3.5 acres of it on the creek on which Montgomery built a fulling-mill. The land was part of the military patent of Crawford and Neville.

Robert Montgomery bought 232 acres in Washington County called Joy. The warrant was dated July 31, 1786. It was surveyed on May 7, 1789, patented on February 28, 1791, and recorded in the Washington County Patent Book P18, page 23.

He was included in 1789 in the Greene Township List of Persons Exonerated on the Frontiers of Washington County for being distressed by the Incursions and Depredations of the Indians. He was listed in the 1790 Greene Township Census as head of a household with two males over 16 years of age and two females.

Robert Montgomery bought an adjacent 97 acres of land next to his previous purchase of Joy. He called the new land Despair. It was purchased on a warrant dated February 19, 1793, surveyed on June 18, 1793, patented on November 23, 1804, and recorded in the Greene County Patent Book P55, page 158.

In the Greene County Tax Book made by Joseph Willford, Assessor, in 1797, assisted by Elias Stone and Stephen Gapen, Robert Montgomery was assessed for 300 acres of land at $300, 50 acres of cleared land at $50, one house at $5, one barn at $10, two horses at $40, and three cows at $18. The following year he was assessed for 625 acres of land at $300, 40 acres of cleared land at $30, one house at $10, one barn at $10, three horses at $30, and four cows at $24.

Robert Montgomery was listed in the Greene County Will Testators Book PA30, page152. He was included on the List of Voters Names residing in the Township of Greene, Greene County, who voted in the Annual Election held at the house of John Burley on October 13, 1801. On October 14, 1806, he voted at the house of John Campbell.[5] He filed his Will in the Greene County Will Book, Volume 1, page 152.

[1] Anderson, Beulah H. *John and Esther Houston Montgomery, 1719-1973.* (Brazos Printing Co., Maryville, TN, 1974) p. 30.

[2] Wulfeck, Dorothy. Marriages of Some Virginia Residents 1607-1800, Volume II. "A History of Rockbridge County Virginia" by C. F. Morton(1920) 512.

[3] Summers, Lewis P. History of Southwest Virginia and Washington County; Annals of Southwest Virginia. (DMK Heritage pub., Austin, TX, 2004).

[4] Pennsylvania Archives, Series 3, Volume XXII, page 699.

[5] http://www.cornerstonegenealogy.com/greene_county_voter_lists_1801.htm.

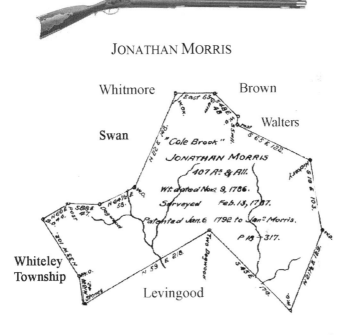

JONATHAN MORRIS

Richard Morris and Mary Porter Morris had a son, Joseph Morris (1727-1788), who was born in England. He came to America at the age of 16, settled in Springfield, Burlington County, New Jersey, and married Hannah (Lee) Asson (1723-1783) in 1744.

Two of Joseph and Hannah's sons were Jonathan Morris (1753-1841) and George Morris. Jonathan stated that he was born in Virginia and was about 12 years of age when he was brought by their father, Joseph Morris Sr, to Washington County where his older brother George had already settled.

Joseph Morris Sr had borrowed some money from John Neville of Washington County in 1771 which he had partially paid back with goods and two roan mares. Upon his father's death, Jonathan paid back the rest of the loan in 1789.

Jonathan Morris married (1) Sarah Davis (-1798) before 1778 in Winchester, Frederick County, Virginia. He married (2) Hannah Bradford before 1802. He married (3) Mary Robbins after 1816. Sarah and Jonathan Davis' children were:[1]

i. Samuel (1778-1871) was born in Washington County, Pennsylvania. He married in 1802 to Sarah Garard (1782-1865), daughter of Justus and Rachel (Corbly) Garard. They had 12 children.

ii. Joseph (1780-) received land in Luzerne Township, Fayette County, Pennsylvania, in settlement of his father's estate.

iii. Owen (1783-1860) married Abigail Wilson (1795-1875). They settled near Casstown. Miami County, Ohio, and had five children.

iv. Lucretia Louisa (1787-1867), born in Waynesburg, Washington County, Pennsylvania, married in 1807 to James Roberts (1785-1864). They lived and died in Le Harpe, Illinois.

v. Mary (1790-) was born in Washington County, Pennsylvania.

vi. Sarah (1793-1853) was born and died in Washington County, Pennsylvania.

vii. Abner (1796-) born in Greene County, Pennsylvania (Washington County became Greene County in 1796).

viii. Jonathan Jr (1796-) was born in Cambridge, Ohio and married Mary Bice.

ix. Elizabeth (1798-) was born in Greene County, Pennsylvania, and married Cephas McClelland. Both were buried in the Fairmont Cemetery near Newark, Ohio. Sarah Davis, Jonathan Morris' first wife, died during this childbirth.

x. Levi (1802-) was born in Greene County, Pennsylvania. (This was Jonathan's first child by his second marriage to Sarah Clymer (1793-1824.)

xi. Isaiah (1806-1906) was born in Greene County, Pennsylvania, and died in Hancock County, Illinois. He married Eleanor McCormick.

Jonathan Morris served as a Private and Corporal in 1778 and as a Sergeant in 1779. He was promoted to Captain and commanded a

Company of Foot in the Seventh Regiment of the Maryland Line during the Revolutionary War. He was discharged on August 16, 1780.[2] He was a member of Stockley's Rangers in the Washington County Militia from 1778 to 1783.

In 1781 he was listed in the Supply Tax Book of Greene Township, Washington County with 300 acres of land taxed at $36.

Recruited in 1782 he was a Private from Washington County in Captain Benjamin Stites' Company of Foot in the First Battalion of Washington County's Militia.[3]

In 1784 he was listed on the Assessment Roll in Washington County although he was living outside of Greene Township.

On November 9, 1786, he bought 407 acres he called Cole Brook on Frosty Run in Washington County. He lived at the mouth of Dutch Run on land adjoining that of his brothers, George and Levi Morris. It was originally patented to Jacob Frazer. It was surveyed on February 13, 1787, patented on January 6, 1792, and recorded in the Washington County Patent Book P18, page 317.

On December 1788 David Bradford was paid 15s. for advising Jonathan and Joseph Morris Jr in the appraisal of their father's estate.

Jonathan was included on the 1789 Tax List of Persons Exonerated on the Frontiers of Washington County for being distressed by the Incursions and Depredations of the Indians.

He was an active member of the Goshen Baptist Church at Garard's Fort as shown by entries in the church's Minute Book:[4]

i. 24 December 1785: Bro Robert Jones and Brother Jonathan Morris were chosen Deacons to assist Bro Moredock in the business of the church.

ii. August 22, 1788. Met at Muddy Creek/Whitely according to appointment and proceeded to business viz. Association letter to be prepared. Brother Jones, Brother Frazer, Brother Jon'n Morris, Brother Corbly and Moredock Messengers.

iii. August 1, 1789: Met at Whitely according to appt and proceeded to business viz Appointed Brother John Corbly, Levi Harrod, James Moredock, Jonathan Morris, Azariah Davis, Charles Anderson, and brother Robert Jones Messengers to the Association at Great Bethel and Brother David Price to prepare the letter.

iv. February 1790: Met at Muddy Creek according to app't and proceeded to business. The Church appointed Bro Ross Crosley, Bro Joseph Frazer, Justus Garard, and Bro Jonathan Morris to examine into a complaint made against Ely Mundle for bad conduct and singing vulgar songs and to cite him to come to the next monthly meeting where they are to make a report.

v. September 4, 1792: Met at Whitely. Bros Corbly, Crossley, Harrod, Morris, Jones, Brown and Fordyce appt'd messengers to ass'n at George Creek. Bro Corbly to write letter.

vi. 1793: Met at Muddy Creek. Trouble between Brother Myers and Jonathan Morris...Bros Henry Crosley, Herrod, Jones, Davis and Charles Anderson heard matter between Myers and Morris.

vii. August 30, 1794: Met at Whitely Creek. Bros Corbly, Crosley, Harrod, Jones, Fordice, Jonathan Morris, Davis and Abner Mundle apptd messengers. Bro Corbly to write letter.

viii. February 24, 1798: Met at Thomas Wright and after singing and prayer proceeded to business when Jonathan Morris reported that he had talked with Brother John Guthery and received no satisfaction therefore the Church agreed to lay him under censure. After Brother Morris reported he had talked with David Long he confessed his conduct had been unbecoming and would attend next meeting but he neglected.

ix. January 4, 1802. Met according to appointment and after singing and prayer proceeded to business. Bro Wright when laying in his charges against Bro Jonathan Morris respecting some dealings between them, the Church upon the whole on both sides unanimously was of the opinion there was nothing in Bro Morris's conduct that ought to break Bro Wright's fellowship with him, agreed that Bro Morris take his place.

x. February 4, 1802. Church met sung and prayed when Bro Morris layd on a charge against Wright for speaking reproachfully of him to more members seen at last meeting postponed til next meeting.

xi. March 27, 1802. Met according to appt and after singing and prayer proceeded to business. The former charge against Bro Wright by Bro Morris brought and Bro Wright could not make good his charge, together for his conduct towards the Church at different times, with that of certificate from Mr Hesten. The Church did unanimously lay him under suspension.

xii. August 27, 1802. Met and after singing and prayer proceeded to business as follows. Church app'd Bros Jonathan Morris, Abner Mundle and Abia Minor to go and inquire of Ely Mundle his reason for leaving this Church and gaining the Methodist Society and make report to our next meeting of business. (P290)

xiii. March 24, 1804. The Church met and business between Jonathan Morris and Thomas Wright left unsettled.

xiv. October 24, 1807. Met at Whiteley. Resolved that Bro Jonathan Morris has affirmed that he heard Bro John Rudolph say that he and Morris had bad luck with their flour that some part of the greater part which they had made for Superfine Flour was condemned to common flour and he said he did not think it was fair for a man that used spectacles to inspect flower for it made the specks appear larger. Bro John Rudolph being duly qualified before Jacob Black Esq upon solemn oath Delevereth that no such conversation ever passed between Jonathan Morris and himself. It is therefore required of him the said Morris to obtain the deposition of Joseph Morris, Robert Ross Esq, and of such other, if any there be, that can prove or confirm in any way the truth of his assertion and present the same to our next meeting of business. Likewise we appoint Brother Hersey to write immediately to Brother John Rudolph and inform him the process of the business and cite him to our meeting of business in January next.

xv. September 27, 1823. The Church met and Heard the experience of Jonathan Morris and recd him into full fellowship and union in the Church and baptism next day.

Jonathan Morris was listed in the 1790 Greene Township Census as head of a household with two males over 16 years of age, six males under 16 years of age, and nine females.

The Washington Mechanical Society was organized May 12, 1792, with Jonathan Morris as president and David Reddick as secretary. The object was to create a fund and loan money for a term not exceeding three months for charitable, political, and generous purposes at six per cent. In 1795 the secretary was directed to open a correspondence with the Philadelphia Mechanical Society for the purpose of encouraging foreign mechanics to immigrate to this country.

In 1798 a committee consisting of Robert Hamilton, Samuel Clark, and D. Cook was appointed to report the best mode of procuring tin for a tin manufactory. The mode and manner were approved and a quantity was brought to Washington.[5]

In the 1797 Greene County Tax Book made by Joseph Willford, Assessor, assisted by Elias Stone and Stephen Gapen, Jonathan Morris was assessed for 227 acres of land at $180, 20 acres of cleared land at $20, one house at $5, one barn at $2, one horse at $15 and two cows at $12. Two years later he was assessed for 120 acres of land at $75, 14 acres of cleared land at $15, one house at $8, one cabin at $1, two horses at $25, and five cows at $30.

Jonathan Morris was included in the List of Voters Names residing in the Township of Greene, Greene County, who voted at the Annual Election held at the house of John Burley on October 13, 1801.[6]

On January 22, 1802, Pastor John Corbly and Jonathan Morris appraised the estate of John's good friend, Pastor William Wood, deceased, at a value of $376.35.[7]

In the war of 1812 there was a unanimous feeling of hostility against England. A company of cavalry was formed and entered the service of the United States under the command of Captain Seeley. Jonathan, Levi, and George Morris, John P. Minor, Joseph Masters, and Thomas Clark were members of this Company.[8]

In his application for a pension for his services during the Revolutionary War in 1834 he made a declaration:

> ...moved to Greene County with his father at age 12 and settled on Whiteley Creek. There was no other family west of them. They forted a year at VanMeter's Fort on Muddy Creek. It became more convenient to fort at Garard's Fort. To his memory there was no other man than his brother, George, who was in Greene County when they first arrived there. Jonathan forted at Garard's Fort during the Revolutionary War except two years when he lived in Fayette County. Jonathan went out as an Indian Spy to the Ohio River and also served in Captain Wilson's Company in pursuit of Indians for six months during Dunmore's War. They had no regular officers at the time because the whole fort turned out to fight Indians. Jonathan spied on Indians for two years. He served one month at Fort Laurens on the Tuscarawas River in Ohio and guarded prisoners. He stated that his entire service amounted to more than two years.He declared that he had never received a discharge and said that Stephan Gapen, Abner Mundle, and George Morris would verify his proof of services and that Corbly Gerrard would vouch for his veracity.

His brother, George Morris, submitted an affidavit stating that Jonathan Morris had served with him including several years service in the Revolutionary War at Garard's Fort which they helped build. Stephen

Gapen and Abner Mundle testified to similar service (National Archives, Pension Claim No. S.7247).

Jonathan Morris was active in the Goshen Baptist Church and died in Greene County where he left a Will which was devised on August 2, 1838, and probated on April 1, 1841. He died on March 20, 1841 (Greene County Will Book 2, page 137).

The War Pension Office, in the award of his pension, made the following statements.

> That his pension claim number was S.7247. He was born 1753 in Va, and moved to Greene CO, PA at age 10-12 and settled on Whiteley Creek at Muddy Creek settlement. Later they lived at Garrard Fort which Jonathan assisted in building. He lived in the Fort during the Rev War except two years while living in Lancaster Co, PA. Jonathan served 10 weeks against the Indians during Dunmore's War on the Ohio. He served as Indian Spy and scout, serving under Capt Wilson and Crawford of the Penns Troops. His served more than two years total.

By a Resolution of the Pennsylvania Senate on March 3, 1835, Jonathan Morris received a pension for his services as an Indian spy during the Revolutionary War. He received the pension while living in Dunkard Township, Greene County, Pennsylvania. Certificate No. 26318 was issued at the rate of $80 per year.[9]

Jonathan Morris left a Will which was signed on August 2, 1838, and probated April 1, 1841. He died March 20, 1841, and the Will was filed in the Greene County Will Book 2, page 137. He was buried in the Old Dunkard Cemetery, New Town site, Dunkard Township, Greene County, Pennsylvania.[10]

---

[1] Leckey, Howard. *Tenmile Country and its Pioneer Families.* Rpt, (Closson Press, Apollo, PA. 2007) 598.

[2] http://files.usgwarchives.net/pa/1pa/military/revwar/sorrolln-z.txt.

[3] Leckey, 35.

[4] Corbly, Don. *Pastor John Corbly.* (Lulu Press, Raleigh, NC, 2008) 275.

[5] Creigh, Alfred. *History of Washington County from its first settlement to the present time...* Rpt. (Washington, PA, 1870.Nabu Press, Charleston, SC, 2010) 232.

[6] http://www.cornerstonegenealogy.com/greene_county_voter_lists_1801.htm.

[7] Corbly, 194.

[8] Evans, L. K. *Pioneer History of Greene County, Pennsylvania.* (Waynesburg, Republican Press, Waynesburg, PA, 1941) 164-165.

154

[9] Pennsylvania Archives, Revolutionary War Pensions, Pennsylvania, Jonathan Morris.
[10] http://www.easternusresearch.com/easternusresearch/cemet/dargraves.html

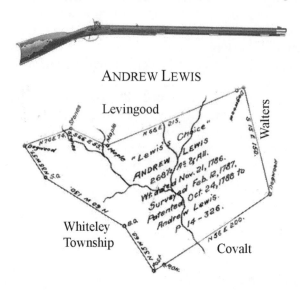

ANDREW LEWIS

John Lewis Sr (1678-1763) was born in County Donegal, Ireland. In 1720 he killed his landlord and a steward by crushing their heads with a shillelagh (he was later cleared of the charge) and fled to America, finally settling in Augusta County, Virginia, where he founded the village of Staunton. His Quaker family was among the founders of the Tinkling Spring Meeting House there which gathered in a log cabin measuring 24 feet by 50 feet that also served as a fort and a recruitment center for soldiers.

John Lewis Sr soon became a Colonel of Militia in Augusta County and had at least three sons; Andrew, Thomas, and Charles. In 1743 an Order of Council placed 30,000 acres of public land in the control of James and Henry Robinson, Esquires, Colonel James Wood, and Thomas and Andrew Lewis, the sons of Colonel John Lewis Sr. It was very important to secure the aid of influential men in places of authority. The Robinsons were aristocratic planters of Tidewater Virginia. Colonel Wood was the surveyor of Frederick County and a prominent landowner. Thomas and Andrew Lewis, then 25 and 23 years old respectively, were sons of Colonel John Lewis Sr, the leader of the Staunton settlement in Augusta.

Andrew Lewis Sr (1720-1781) married about 1746 to (1) Martha Teas and (2) in 1749 to Elizabeth Anne Givens of County Antrim, Ireland. He and Elizabeth established a home near present day Salem, but later moved to the Shenandoah Valley and built a home called Bellefonte on a creek that bore the Lewis name. He was tall, agile, very strong, and had a commanding presence.[1] The children by Andrew Lewis Sr and Elizabeth Givens (1724-) were:

    i. Samuel (1748-1763).

    ii. John (1750–1788).

    iii. Thomas (1752–1800) married Nancy Evans.

    iv. Andrew Jr (1759–1844) was born in Staunton, Augusta County, Virginia. He gained a basic education and learned the skills of a surveyor. On June 10, 1792, he married Margaret Briant of Botetourt County, Virginia.[2]

    v. Anne (1760-)

    vi. William (1764–1812).

    vii. Charles (c.1768-1781).

An Order of Council authorized the Lewis brothers and their partners to survey the 30,000 acres in an indefinite number of tracts, all lying in the basin of the James River above the mouth of the Cowpasture River below Fort Lewis in western Virginia. Of the 91 tracts surveyed by the Lewises in 1745-1746, only 15 were in Alleghany County.

By 1745 Andrew Lewis had became well known as a frontiersman and surveyor. He spent 15 years developing his farm in southwestern Virginia, surveying land throughout the valley, and helping open new lands in what are now Botetourt and Roanoke Counties. He surveyed much of the Greenbrier District of Augusta County, later Greenbrier County, West Virginia. He became a Lieutenant and later Captain of the Augusta County Militia during several years of protecting the settlement against Indian raids. He became a General and gained fame in defeating the Indian Chief Cornstalk, in the Battle of Point Pleasant, the only major battle during Dunmore's War.[3]

On June 4, 1766, Thomas Tosh and Mary...,for £100, patented to Andrew Lewis 269 acres situated on the south side of the Roanoke River known as Goose Creek. Two days later he witnessed the transaction of John Dailey to David Stewart and Samuel Cowdon, a mortgage. The consideration was grantees going bail for grantor in a suit in general court brought by Keppen and Company for £250 to convey the land Dailey lived on called Hart's Bottom, 270 acres, part of 400 acres patented to Silas Hart, and by Hart sold to William Anderson, and by Anderson to Dailey Ray.

On November 21, 1766, he signed as witness to the case of "Thomas Bullett of Fauquier County of the 1st part and Thomas and Andrew Lewis of the 2nd part. The parties had taken up 300 acres including the

Little Warm Springs and entered into agreement in regard to a division thereof and management, forming a deed of partition delivered from John Kinkead to Gabriel Jones £100; the mortgage containing 530 acres, part of 1,061 acres, one moiety of which John sold to John Kinkead of Albemarle, the moiety hereby conveyed being whereon John now lives on the Calfpasture."[4]

In 1772 Edward McMullin bought from Andrew Lewis 325 acres in Allegheny County for £30.[5]

He was listed on the 1784 Assessment Roll for Cumberland Township, Washington County, Pennsylvania.[6]

On a warrant dated November 21, 1786, Andrew Lewis bought 268 acres of land in Washington County near Garard's Fort called Lewis' Choice. It was surveyed February 12, 1787, patented on October 24, 1788, and recorded in the Washington County Patent Book P14, page 326.

Andrew Lewis was listed in the 1790 Cumberland Township census as head of household with three males over 16 years of age and two females. In the 1797 Greene County Tax Book made by Joseph Willford, Assessor, and assisted by Elias Stone and Stephen Gapen, Andrew Lewis Jr was assessed for 275 acres of land at $200, 30 acres of cleared land at $30, and one cabin at $1. The following year he was assessed for 273 acres of land at $200, and 30 acres of cleared land at $24.

The files of the Pension Board of the War Department contained the following document regarding the Revolutionary war pensioner, Andrew Lewis, who enlisted in Botetourt County, Virginia.[7]

His application for pension was designated case W. 3431.On February I, 1777 while a resident of Botetourt County, Virginia Andrew Lewis Jr enlisted as a private in Captain Joseph Crockett's Virginia Company and was discharged May 28, 1777. He enlisted May 25, 1779 in Captain James Barnet's Company in Colonel Hugh Crockett's Virginia Regiment and was discharged July 28, 1779. He enlisted August 20, 1779 in Captain William McClanahan's Company in Colonel William Preston's Virginia Regiment and was discharged October 3, 1779. He enlisted January 31, 1781 in Captains Gillian and McClanahan's Company in Colonel Hugh Crockett's Virginia Regiment, fought at Whitsell's Mills on Ready Fork in Halifax County, Virginia and was discharged on June 4, 1781. He was allowed a pension on his application executed April 29, 1833 while a resident of Montgomery County, Virginia. The place of his birth and the name of his mother was not given. He married

June 10, 1788, Margaret Briant of Botetourt County, Virginia. He died September 25, 1844. As the widow of Andrew Lewis Jr, said Margaret Lewis was allowed pension on her application executed January 23, 1845, while a resident of Montgomery County, Virginia, aged 79 years.

G. H. SWEET, Executive Assistant to the Administrator.

Pennsylvania Archives, Revolutionary War Pensions.

[1] Morton, Oren F. *A Centennial History of Alleghany County, Virginia,* (J. K. Reubush Company, Dayton, VA, 1923).

[2] http://files.usgwarchives.org/va/botetourt/vitals/marriages/mar1770grooms.txt Botetourt Co. VA, Marriages 1770-1803.

[3] Johnson, Patricia G. *General Andrew Lewis of Roanoke and Greenbrier.* (Walpa Publications, Blacksburg, VA.) 1980.

[4] Chalkley, Lyman. *Records of Augusta County, Virginia, Original Petition and Papers in Court 1745-1748, Volume III,* Rpt. (Genealogical PubliShinng Co, Baltimore, MD, 1965) 69,440-449.519.

[5] http://genealogytrails.com/vir/alleghany/history.html.

[6] Leckey, Howard. *Tenmile Country and its Pioneer Families.* Rpt, (Closson Press, Apollo, PA. 2007) 132.

[7] Revolutionary War Pensions, Pennsylvania, Andrew Lewis.

WILLIAM BURT AND ISAAC GARARD

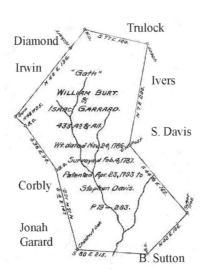

William Burt was born in Berkley County, Virginia, which bordered Maryland in the upper panhandle of what is now West Virginia. He married Isabel Alison on March 9, 1755[1]. In 1744 his father, Richard Burt, made his final Will which follows, in part:

Item. I give to my son William Burt three negroes Daniel, Will, and Pheney all the remainder of my estate I give to be equally divided between my two sons Josias Burt and William Burt and I do appoint my two sons Josias and William Burt my Executors of this my last Will and Testament as Witness my hand and Seal this twenty first of February one thousand seven hundred and forty four. (his) Richard R Burt (mark). Witnesseth in the Presence of us, Richard Pate & John Coman.

William Burt was listed in the Assessment Roll of Bedford County before Westmoreland County was erected out of it in 1773. He was one of the early Virginia settlers who migrated west into Pittsylvania Country and pledged allegiance to Virginia, rather than to Pennsylvania. Others who settled at that time in what became Greene Township, Greene County, Pennsylvania, were Leonard and Frederick Garrison, Aaron Jenkins, John Jones, John Long, George Morris, Isaac Sutton Sr, Isaac Sutton Jr, John Swan Sr, John Swan Jr, Thomas Miller, and John Williams.[2]

In 1775 the records of the Goshen Baptist Church at Garard's Fort show that William Burt, Jemima Burt (relationship not proven), Isaac Garard, and Rachel Garard became members of the church by baptism. William and Jemima Burt were later excommunicated. Jemima Burt was found in the 1820 Census living in Ross Township, Green County, Ohio, with two young males and one young female in her household. She was not found on a census after 1820.

William Burt enlisted for three years in the Continental Army during the Revolutionary War. He received pay dated from Camp Pennsylvania in February 1777; from Peekskill, New York in February 1777; from Cross Roads, Bucks County, Pennsylvania, in August 1777; and from Camp Whitemarsh Church, 13 miles northwest of Philadelphia, in November 1777. In May 1777 he was listed as a Matrofse gunner (Private) in Colonel Drake's Regiment of Artillery. During May and June 1778 he was at Valley Forge. He was paid £8.30s.90d. on the October 1778 Payroll.

He was a Private in Captain Winthrop Sargent's Company in Colonel John Crane's Third Regiment of Artillery from June to October 1778 when he received $8.30/90ths pay. In July and August 1779 he was at Pound Ridge in Westchester County, New York, in August and September at Lower Salem, Massachusetts, and at Camp Bedford, Pennsylvania. After his three-year enlistment he moved to Virginia where he was a Private of Infantry in the Virginia Line and received pay of £18.5s.8d. in September 1783 to settle his military pay account.[3]

During those years of military service the 1781 Effective Supply Tax Book of Greene Township, Washington County, showed that William Burt was taxed for 250 acres of land, three horses, two cows, and four sheep.[4]

William Burt's Will was filed in Washington County on July 2, 1782, without naming Chloe, his wife:[5]

In the Name of God Amen. I William Burt Sr of Greensville County and State of Virginia being of sound mind and Memory praise be to God for the same do make this my last Will and Testament in manner and form following, to wit.

i. First I will that my Debts and funeral charges be paid.

ii. Item. I give and damise to my Son William Burt Jr all my Plantation whereon I now live on Fountains Creek with all and Singular the appurtenances thereunto belonging to hold to him the said William Burt his heirs and assigns forever containing four hundred Acres more or less also I give and bequeath to my Son William Burt one negroe man named Lewis and one negroe woman called Polly to him and his heirs forever

iii. Item. I give and bequeath to my daughter Mary Tooke one negroe Woman called Kate and her child called Sylvia and their increase to her and her heirs forever.

iv. Item. I give and bequeath to my daughter Lucy Haley twenty Six Shillings.

v. Item. I give and bequeath to my Daughter Mary Tooke one bed and furniture.

vi. Item. I lend to my daughter Elizabeth Kelbie during her natural life One fourth part of the following Negroes hereafter named to be Sold and after her death I give and bequeath to my Grand Son William Gibbs the one fourth part which I lend my daughter Elizabeth Kilbie after her death to the said William Gibbs his heirs and assigns forever.

vii. Item. I give and bequeath to my three children after deducting one fourth part of whatever the following negroes may Sell for which part I have lent my daughter Elizabeth Kelbie during her natural life and after her death to return to the said William Gibbs his heirs and assigns forever.

viii. Item. I give and bequeath to my three children, to wit, Harwood, William, and Mary after deducting one fourth part which I have lent my daughter Elizabeth Kelbie during her natural life and then to my Grand Son William Gibbs as before mentioned Viz Finnie, Robin, James, Bob, Rachel, Pegg, Ailee, Daniel, little Rachel, Kate and their increase to be sold and equally divided amongst my said children Harwood William and Mary after deducting one fourth part of whatever the aforesaid Negroes may Sell for which one fourth part I have demised as before mentioned.

ix. Item. All the rest and residue of my estate in possession remainder and reversion of what nature or kind so ever or wheresoever situate I give and bequeath to my Son William Burt to him and his heirs forever Lastly I nominate and appoint my two sons Harwood and William Burt Executors of this my last Will and Testament In Witness whereof I have hereunto set my hand and seal this 15th day of October one thousand Seven Hundred and Eighty two. Signed and sealed) William Burt Senr in presence of William Finnie, Jeconias Parks, and Walter C. Ballard.

Isaac Garard, son of Reverend John Garard, was given a 433-acre farm called Gath on Big Whiteley Creek in his father's Will. The warrant, dated November 24, 1786, in the Washington County Land Records Office was taken out by William Burt and Isaac Garard. Gath, surveyed on February 4, 1787, was situated east of John Corbly's farm and north of Jonah Garard's tract which he called Garard's Fort. William Burt, by deed dated April 13, 1791, conveyed his prior right to Gath to Isaac Garard who then patented the land on April 23, 1793, to Stephen Davis and recorded it in the Washington County Patent Book P19, page 283.[6]

William Burt served in Colonel Drake's Regiment of Foot and received pay of £4. at Puck Hill, New York, on January 10, 1786.[7]

On February 17, 1786, the Goshen Baptist Church "laid William Burt under Censor for further consideration due to fornication."

On July 8, 1786, "Elizabeth Burt was received as a member by baptism. William Burt was cut from the fellowship of the church on November 10, 1787." Elizabeth Burt was one of several persons who applied for Letters of Dismission on September 25, 1790. A list of members of Goshen Church prior to 1799 included Jemima Burt, dismissed; Elizabeth Burt (his wife, having remarried) dismissed; and William Burt, excommunicated.

The 1789 Tax List of Greene Township, Washington County, included William Burt in the List of Persons Exonerated on the Frontiers of Washington County for being distressed by the Incursions and Depredations of the Indians. He was listed in the 1790 Census in Greene Township as head of household with two males under 16 years of age and three females.[8]

He died before 1792 and was survived by his widow, Elizabeth, who married on December 8, 1792, Colonel Covington of Artillery in the Continental Army who died on October 10, 1810. She did not marry again.

ISAAC GARARD

Isaac Garard (1757-1794) was born in Berkeley County, Virginia, and migrated to present day Greene County by 1772 to occupy the 433-acre farm, Gath, on Big Whiteley Creek which he had inherited in his father's Will (Reverend John Garard). It is unclear why William Burt joined in the warrant unless he had a part ownership in the land.

Isaac Garard was received into the Goshen Baptist Church by baptism on September 8, 1785, along with William Burt, Azariah Davis, Margaret Morris, Rachel Garard, and Jemima Burt.[9]

Isaac married Rachel Hays (1775-1825) by about 1790 and they both died in Greene County, Ohio. He was listed in the 1790 Greene Township Census as the head of a household with two males under 16 years of age and three females.[10]

[1] Chalkley, Lyman. *Chronicles of the Scotch-Irish Settlement in Virginia, Extracted from the Original Court Records of Augusta County, 1745-1800.* (Genealogical PubliShinng Company, Baltimore, MD, 1999) Volume 2, 270-279.
[2] Walkinshaw, Lewis Clark. *Annals of southwestern Pennsylvania.* (Lewis Historical Pub. Co,, New Castle, DE, 1939) Volume 1.
[3] Pennsylvania Archives, Revolutionary War Rolls, Continental Troops, 1777-1779.
[4] Pennsylvania Archives, Series 3, Volume XXII, page 699.
[5] Washington County Will Book, entry July 2, 1782.
[6] Leckey, Howard. *Tenmile Country and its Pioneer Families.* Rpt, (Closson Press, Apollo, PA. 2007), 601.
[7] Pennsylvania Archives, Series 3, Volume 13, page 177.
[8] Leckey, 158.
[9] Corbly, Don. *Pastor John Corbly.* (Lulu Press, Raleigh, NC, 2008) 279.
[10] Leckey, 159.

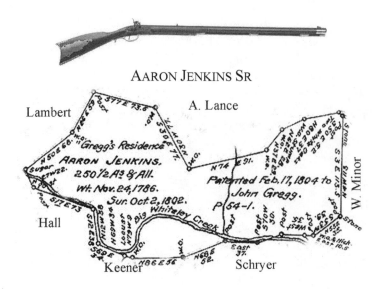

In 1731 Charity Harlan married (2) Francis Baldwin Jr and moved to Berkeley County, Virginia, where she and Baldwin lived and were ultimately buried. Six of her children were by her 13-year marriage to her first husband; the last four were by Baldwin who bestowed a tract of land to each of his children with Charity Baldwin. The lands warranted to the three sisters ran from north to south along the Monongahela River in the order of Lydia, Rebecca, and Elizabeth Baldwin.[1] The sisters were:

i. Rebecca Baldwin (1749-1799) married Aaron Jenkins Sr (1743-1807) in 1769, and had surveyed to her under the name Content on November 1, 1770, a tract of land situated between her sisters Lydia and Elizabeth's tracts. It was later patented to Lewis Williams, but Aaron Jenkins Sr had bought other tracts in the vicinity, including one at Pierceville, where he maintained a fort during the Revolution. Aaron Jenkins Sr and his wife, Rebecca, sold their land in Washington County after they moved to Monongahela County, Virginia. Later, he moved to Murfreesboro, Cumberland Valley, Tennessee, and settled there.

ii. Elizabeth Baldwin (1747-1830) died in Greene County, Pennsylvania (Greene was formed out of Washington County in 1796). She and her husband, Elias Stone (1740-1823), were buried in present day Greensboro. As Elizabeth Baldwin she had warranted to her on April 3, 1769, on a Virginia Certificate a tract of land next south of her sister, Rebecca Jenkins. This was surveyed to her on November 1, 1770, and then on

September 25, 1787, it was patented to Elias and Elizabeth Stone. On this tract was later laid out a part of the Town of Greensboro. Elias Stone was also a member of Captain John Guthery's Militia Company during this time.

iii. Lydia Baldwin, wife of Captain John Guthery, had surveyed to her as Lydia Baldwin on November 1, 1770, a tract of land under the title Lydia's Bottom. This tract was then patented to John Guthery and Lydia on April 17, 1792. It was situated between the lands of her sisters, Sarah and Rebecca. By deeds recorded in Washington County, John and Lydia Guthery disposed of their land and moved to Pike County, Ohio, where John Guthery at the age of 90 drew a pension on an application dated July 3, 1823, and where he died on March 1, 1824.

Thomas Provins sold to Aaron Jenkins Sr the land that later held the site of Fort Jenkins, previously known as Fort Hudson, by a deed recorded May 8, 1782. Provins, James Bell, Joshua Hudson, and John Long Sr were early settlers in Washington County and appeared on the Tax List for 1772 as shown in the Washington County Deed Book 1A, page 200. Jenkin's Fort was built two miles south of Carmichael Town and one mile southeast of Baily's Schoolhouse on the old Whitehill farm. The Indian chiefs Logan and Snake were at this fort the evening before they massacred the Spicer family.[2]

Aaron Jenkins Sr was included in the 1773 Assessment Roll of Springhill Township, Bedford County, Pennsylvania. On November 7 of that year the Goshen Baptist Church was founded at Garard's Fort with Reverends Isaac Sutton and Daniel Fristoe officiating. Aaron's wife, Rebecca Jenkins, was one its 30 original members. They apparently moved from Bedford County to Garard's Fort during that year.

One day in 1777 William Crawford, a Justice of the Peace and associate of Pastor John Corbly who was also a Justice of the Peace at Garard's Fort, was mowing his land with James Mundle who was worried about something. When Crawford asked what was troubling him James Mundle hesitated, but finally said that Aaron Jenkins Sr and others had designs on Crawford's life. He added that there was a scheme to dispatch not only Crawford, but also John Minor and John Corbly, the leading Patriots in the Garard's Fort settlement. He said he was afraid to reveal these happenings because Jenkins and some of the others knew that he (Mundle) had overheard them discussing their plot. These victims-to-be were alerted and security was tightened around them. This was but one of the many discovered Tory plots hatched by the scattered

Loyalists around Garard's Fort seeking to overthrow the Patriot's rebellion against the Crown. Jenkins became one of the marked men in the area and was watched closely by the Patriots.[3]

In the 1781 Effective Supply tax Rate Book for Greene Township, Washington County, Aaron Jenkins Sr was taxed $130 for 540 acres of land, three horses, four cows and two sheep.[4]

Aaron Jenkins Sr signed the Petition for a New State of Westsylvania in 1782. That year the First Battalion of the Washington County Militia was recruited from men primarily in Whiteley and Greene Townships with a few from Dunkard Township. He served as a Private 6th Class in Captain John Guthrey's Company which included his neighbors Privates John Long, Jeremiah Long, and Benjamin Sutton.[5]

The Washington County Deed Book 1, page 84, shows a bill of sale from Aaron Jenkins Sr to Samuel Hyde and recites that "Aaron Jenkins of Washington County, Pennsylvania, for £300 in gold & silver by Sam'l Hyde of said state and County sells the parcel of land that Jenkins bought of Thomas Provens on the west side of the Monongahela River and joining on Big Whiteley Creek from the mouth up said creek to James Bellshe's line and John Long's lines." It was dated July 26, 1783, and was signed by Aaron Jenkins. Witnessed by James Carmichael and Robert Hamilton, it was acknowledged in Greene County, Pennsylvania, on March 27, 1797, by Aaron Jenkins Sr before John Badolett, Associate Judge and recorded on April 3, 1797, by John Boreman, Recorder.

On November 24, 1786, Aaron Jenkins bought 250 acres of land he called Gregg's Residence in Greene County. It was surveyed October 2, 1802, patented on February 17, 1804, to John Gregg, and recorded in the Greene County Patent Book P54, pages 1 and 192. It recited "Aaron Jenkins of Greene Tp Green Co Pa (formerly Washington County) Commonwealth on Nov 24, 1786 granted to me 300 acres on big Whiteley Creek adjoining lands of Lambert heirs, Andrew Lantz, John Shriver & Richard Hall, aforesaid dated Oct 12, 1796. Signed Aaron Jenkins. Witnesses: David Vail, Joseph Underwood. Ack. Sept 30, 1797 before Sam'l Hyde J.P. & recorded Oct 2, 1797 by John Boreman Rec."

Aaron Jenkins was included in the 1789 Tax List of Greene Township, Washington County Persons Exonerated for being distressed by the Incursions and Depredations of the Indians. He was listed on the 1790 census for Greene Township, Washington County, Pennsylvania, as head of household with his wife, five males under 16 years of age, and two females.

In the 1797 Greene County Tax Book made by Joseph Willford, Assessor, assisted by Elias Stone and Stephen Gapen, Aaron Jenkins was assessed for 590 acres of land at $960, 90 acres of cleared land at $90, one house at $5, two barns at $15, three horses at $40, five cows at $30, one lot at $5, and another house at $10. The next year he was assessed for 500 acres of land at $1000, 100 acres of cleared land at $100, 1½ lots in Greeneburgh at $15, two houses at $12, one barn at $10, one horse at $10, six cows at $36, and ground rents on lots at $7.

The Greene County Deed Book 1, page 491, recorded a deed wherein Aaron Jenkins Sr, late of Greene County, Pennsylvania, conveyed to Aaron Springer of Union Township, Fayette County, Pennsylvania, dated January 1, 1801, for 5s., a lot adjoining the plan of Greensburg, Greene County, Pennsylvania. (Signed) Aaron Jenkins Sr. Witnessed by James Hyde, Benjamin Miller. Acknowledged January 12, 1801, before Samuel Hyde, J.P.

The Greene County Deed Book 1, Page 518 recorded a transaction between Aaron Jenkins and Elias Stone, dated April 27, 1801. It stated that all parties lived in Greene County, Pennsylvania, and recited that "the Commonwealth, by patent dated September 25, 1787, granted to Elias Stone and Elizabeth, his wife, a tract called Delight containing 362 acres which said Elias and Elizabeth laid out in lots in town called Greensburgh" and recited that "Elias and Elizabeth and Aaron Jenkins Sr and his then wife Rebecca conveyed by deed dated September 4, 1795, all of said lots except No 1 and 22 acres adjoining to Albert Gallatin which is recorded in Washington County, Pennsylvania. Now said Aaron and Charity (married by 1801) for $1,425 convey their balance to said Stones. (Signed) Aaron Jenkins, Charity Jenkins. Witnesses:...Jones, Acknowledged both April 29, 1801, before Samuel Hyde, JP. Recorded...1801, John Boreman, Recorder."

In a transaction with Thomas Grayham, Aaron Jenkins and Charity, his second wife, of the Northwest Territory, Ohio State, sold to Thomas Grayham of New Geneva, Fayette County, Pennsylvania, dated September 30, 1803, for $6,371.90, the tract of land called Pleasants Nest on the waters of Big and Little Whiteley Creeks in Greene Township, Greene County, Pennsylvania, patented to the said Aaron Jenkins on March 27, 1799, by the Commonwealth of Pennsylvania. Beginning at a White Oak and by lands of Elias Stone and by lands of Aaron Jenkins Jr and by lands of George Evans and Dorcas Blake containing 398 acres and 39 perches and allowance of 6 percent for roads. Aaron Jenkins, Charity Jenkins (seal). Witnesses: Stephen Gapen, John Caldwell. Acknowledged in Greene County, September 30, 1803, by Aaron and Charity who personally appeared before me, James Black, J. P. Recorded Sept 15, 1806 in Greene County Deed Book 2, page 203.

The Greene County, Pennsylvania, Deed Book 2, page 310, recorded that Aaron Jenkins Sr and his wife Rebecca "Betsy" of the one part, and

Samuel Huston of the other part, all of the Township of Greene, Greene County, Pennsylvania, dated September 1, 1807, "for $2,350 conveys a tract of land called Hawk's Nest on the waters of Little Whiteley Creek in the Township and County aforesaid. Beginning at a stone thence by lands claimed by Elias Stone and by lands of Samuel Hyde, David Evans, and lands of Aaron Jenkins Sr 324 perches to place of beginning containing 235 rods and 9 perches and allowance of 6 percent for roads which tract was surveyed in pursuance of a warrant dated March 29, 1785, granted to the said Aaron Jenkins." (Signed) Aaron Jenkins, Betty Jenkins. Witnesses: John Flenniken, James Seaton. Acknowledged September 1807 before John Flenniken, Associate Judge and recorded March 5, 1808, by John Boreman.[6]

By this time, Aaron and his family had moved from Greene County, Pennsylvania, to Monongahela County, Virginia. Later, they moved to the Cumberland Valley in Tennessee and settled near Murfreesboro. His wife died on the way and was buried at Crab Orchard, Kentucky.

JOHN GREGG

William Gregg, an emigrant, settled on a tract of land known as Rockland Manor in Christiana Hundred, New Castle County, Delaware, in 1682. His son, John Gregg Sr (1669-1738), was born in Waterford County, Ireland, and in 1694 married Elizabeth Cooke. John Gregg Sr owned three square miles of land along the Brandywine River in New Castle County. In February, March, and December of 1733, 1735, and 1735 respectively, John Gregg Sr warranted 218, 177, and 250 acres of land to himself in Newcastle County. John Gregg Sr and Elizabeth Cooke had a son, Samuel (1710-1767), who married in 1737 to Ann Robinson (1717-1774). Both left Wills in New Castle County.

Samuel and Ann Robinson had a son John Gregg (1755-1835)[7] who served in the Revolutionary War as a Second Lieutenant in 1777 in Captain William Crawford's Militia Company in Colonel Walter Stewart's Regiment of the Pennsylvania Line.[8] He also served as an Ensign in Captain Abner Howell's Third Company in Lieutenant Colonel David Williamson's Third Battalion of the Pennsylvania Militia. Private 4th Class John Gregg served in Captain Crawford's Company of the Washington County Militia in the district of the Monongalia River between Whiteley and Muddy Creeks in October 1781.

About 1782 John Gregg signed the petition to form a few state of Westsylvania to put an end the constant fighting between Pennsylvania and Virginia over the ownership of the southwestern lands then known as Pittsylvania Country.[9] John Gregg married Orpha Stubbs (1766-1838), daughter of Daniel and Ruth (Gilpin) Stubbs, in Chester County, Pennsylvania. Their son, Joseph Gregg (1783-1868), married on September 6, 1810, to Cassandra Corbly (1791-1869), daughter of Pastor John Corbly and Nancy Ann Lynn Corbly. Joseph and Cassandra lived on their farm about two miles from Garard's Fort at what was then called Willow Tree and had 12 children.[10]

John Gregg was listed on the 1784 Assessment Roll of Amwell Township, Washington County, Pennsylvania. John Hughes purchased a warrant for a tract of land on October 18, 1784, from Albert Simonson on what was known as the Hughes' branch of Ten Mile Creek adjoining James Tucker. This was surveyed to him as Green Spring on March 2, 1785. He kept an account book from October 13, 1784, to 1816. In 1784 and 1785 it listed the names of John Gregg and several settlers who lived on or near the waters of Ten Mile Creek.[11]

On February 9, 1775, Reuben Haines warranted 260 acres of land in Bedford County, Pennsylvania, to John Gregg which was called Vinyard No. One. The patent was recorded in the Bedford County Patent Book AA, page 15.

John Gregg bought 427 acres of land called Elenore Green on April 4, 1785, surveyed it on June 28, 1785, patented it on July 19, 1786, and recorded it in the Washington County Patent Book P6, page 364.

Aaron Jenkins Jr of Greene Township, Washington County, of the Commonwealth owned the patent dated November 24, 1786. On October 12, 1796, for £700, he granted to John Gregg 250 acres on Big Whiteley Creek adjoining the lands of the Lamberts, Andrew Lantz, John Shriver, and Richard Hall. John Gregg received his patent dated February 17, 1804, and recorded it in the Greene County Patent Book P54, page 1. Signed: Aaron Jenkins. Witnesses: David Vail, Joseph Underwood. Acknowledge September 30, 1797, before Samuel Hyde J.P. Recorded October 2, 1797, by John Boreman, Recorder."

John Gregg was listed in the Greene County Tax Book in 1797 made by Joseph Willford, Assessor, assisted by Elias Stone and Stephen Gapen. He was assessed for 300 acres of land at $360, 65 acres of cleared land at $65, two houses at $10, one horse at $20, six cows at $36, and one gristmill at $150. In 1800 he was taxed for 304 acres of land at $304, 70 acres of cleared land at $70, one house at $6, one cabin at $1, three horses at $42, seven cows at $42, one gristmill at $100, and one sawmill at $50.

John Gregg was also the collector of road taxes in Greene Township, Greene County. Nancy Corbly's Administration Account of the Last Will and Testament of her husband, John Corbly, recorded that the estate paid $3.52 for road tax to John Gregg. It was recorded in Estate Book No. 6 in

168

the Greene County Courthouse, Waynesburg, Pennsylvania, 1827. He was also one of the two Burgesses in Washington, Pennsylvania, from 1819 to 1822. He was the treasurer there from 1820 to 1835 and was one of the two Trustees in 1824 overseeing Mrs. Harriet Lafoucherie's school in Washington Borough where she charged each student $1.50 for three month's tuition.[12]

He enlisted in March 1776 and served as a Private and Sergeant in Captain Albright's Company in Colonel Miles' Rifle Regiment of the Pennsylvania Line in 1777. On April 21, 1777, he was placed on the list of those who wanted an officer's commissions in the Pennsylvania Regiment of Foot, according the Pennsylvania War Office. Ensign John Gregg enlisted January 6, 1777, in Captain James F. Moore's Company in Major Lewis Farmer's Pennsylvania Regiment of Foot which mustered at Red Bank on May 9, 1777. The Battle of Red Bank was on the Delaware River below Camden near the site of Fort Mercer. Major Farmer's much smaller unit defeated a larger Hessian force which had attempted to take Fort Mercer. That same year he was commissioned a Second Lieutenant in Captain Moore's Company in Colonel Stewart's Regiment of the Pennsylvania Line.

He left the service in 1782 because of ill health and was on leave until 1783 when the Army disbanded. He lived in York County, Pennsylvania, and about 1784 moved to Kentucky. He was allowed pension No. 4970 on his application executed April 30, 1838, at age 74 and also received 200 acres of Donation Land. He lived out his life in Xenis Township, Greene County, Ohio, where he died in June 1835.[13]

He had filed his Will in the Greene County Will Book in Volume 1, page 69.

[1] Leckey, Howard. *Tenmile Country and its Pioneer Families.* Rpt, (Closson Press, Apollo, PA. 2007) 608, 609.
[2] Evans, L. K. *Pioneer History of Greene County, Pennsylvania.* (Waynesburg, Republican Press, Waynesburg, PA, 1941) 150, 151.
[3] Corbly, Don. *Pastor John Corbly.* (Lulu Press, Raleigh, NC, 2008) 126.
[4] Pennsylvania Archives, Series 3, Volume XXII, page 699.
[5] Pennsylvania Archives, Series 3, Volume II, pages 18, 19, 271.
[6] Pennsylvania Archives, Series 2, Volume IX.
[7] Leckey, 534.
[8] Pennsylvania Archives, Series 5, Volume II, page 530.
[9] Continental Congress papers, No. 48, Folios 251-256, pages 89-96.
[10] Fordyce, Nannie L. *The Life and Times of Reverend John Corbly...1953.* (Rpt, Revised second edition by Murphy, Leola
[11] Crumrine, Boyd. *History of Washington County, Pennsylvania with Biographical Sketches of Many of Its Pioneers and Prominent Men.* (L. H.

Leverts & Co., Philadelphia, 1882) 652-672.
[12] Crumrine, Boyd. 476-564.
[13] Pennsylvania Archives, Series 1, Volume V, page 318.

ANDREW LANTZ SR

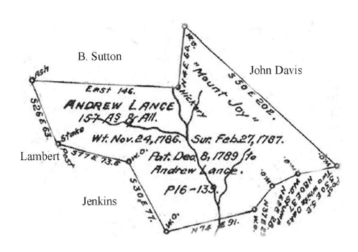

Andrew Lantz Sr[1] and his brother John were descended from Hans George Lantz (-1778) who, with his wife, Catherine, and son, Hans George Lantz II (-1793), came to America from Germany about 1747.

The records of St. Michael's Evangelical church stated, "Hans George Lantz, being a single young man, in good standing, living in the house of Wilhelm Wagner, married this day, December 12, 1752, Maria Margaretha Benderin, a young woman, single and of the reformed religion, having worked her indenture to Richard Wahl of Whitemarsh, was free to marry." Maria had come to America with her mother, Maria Johanna Benderin, a widow, and two sisters. Hans George and Maria wed and moved from Pennsylvania to Shenandoah County, Virginia, about 1754. The children of Hans George Lantz and Maria Margaretha Benderin were:

    i. Margaretha (-1793).
    ii. Johannes "John" (1749-1817).
    iii. Germinia (1754-).

iv. Jacob (1759-1837).

v. George Eurid (1776-1850).

vi. Andrew (1755-1824) married, probably in Frederick County, Virginia, about 1771 to Barbara Lemley (1760-1843). He was born by the Monococy River in Maryland and died at his farm on Whiteley Creek, Greene County, Pennsylvania.

His son, Andrew Jr (1773-1859), was born in the Shenandoah Valley and came to Greene County with his parents where he married Mary Soonover (1775-1851), a daughter of Henry and Catherine (Boos) Soonover. He served in the War of 1812, and died in Greene County. The children of Andrew Lantz Jr and Mary Soonover were:

i. John (-1876) married Jane Boos. The Honorable Andrew Lantz was their only child.

ii. Henry married Elizabeth Hoge (1803-1851), a daughter of Thomas and Ann (Clark) Hoge.

iii. Andrew III (1803-1862) married in 1832 to Mary Baily (1808-1880). Both are buried at Morrisville, Greene County, Pennsylvania.. She was a daughter of Joah and Jane (Mundle) Baily.

During the Revolutionary War in 1782 Andrew Sr served in Captain Henry Kuster's Company in the Fifth Battalion of the Lancaster County Militia, but his record showed that he absented himself for an unknown length of time, according to the Pennsylvania State Archives, Revolutionary War Military Abstract File.

Andrew Sr (1755-1824) and Barbara moved to the Ten Mile Country and secured a warrant on November 24, 1786, for 157 acres of land close to his brother John Lantz's tract of land.

In 1789 John and Andrew Lantz were included on the Tax List of Persons Exonerated on the Frontiers of Washington County for being distressed by the Incursions and Depredations of the Indians. Andrew was listed in the 1790 Census of Greene Township, Washington County, as head of household with seven males under 16 years of age and three females.

In the 1797 Greene Township Tax Book made by Joseph Willford, Assessor, and assisted by Elias Stone and Stephen Gapen, Andrew Lantz Sr was assessed for 170 acres of land at $200, 50 acres of cleared land at $50, one cabin at $1, one barn at $2, three horses at $45, and three cows at $18. The following year he was assessed for 171 acres of land at $210, 50 acres of cleared land at $40, one house at $6, two cabins at $2, one barn at $2, four horses at $45, and five cows at $30. Two years later he was assessed for 171 acres of land at $138, 60 acres of cleared land at $60, one house at $6, one stable at $4, two cabins at $2, three horses at $55, and three cows at $18.

On July 8, 1803, Andrew Lantz Sr and Hugh Stephenson appraised the personal estate of Pastor John Corbly, lately deceased,

A Deed[3] made in 1817 between Thomas Lemonion and Andrew Lantz Sr read:

> This Indenture made this twenty-sixth day of August in the year of our Lord one thousand eight hundred and seventeen, between Thomas Lemonion of the Township of Whitely, County of Greene & State of Pennsylvania and Deborough, his wife of the one County and Andrew Lantz of the Township, County, and State afforesaid of the other part, Witnessneth: That the said Thomas Lemonion & Deborough his wife, for their consideration of the sum of six hundred Dollars, lawful money of the United States, to them in hand paid at and before and delivering of their presents, the receipt whereof is hereby acknowledged having and sold, and by their presents doth grant, bargain and sell unto this said Andrew Lantz and to his heirs & assigns all that tract of land which said Lemonion purchased of Jonathan Hall...bounded as follows viz. a certain piece of land situate on the Waters of Big Whiteley, a part of tract of land called Falsehood, beginning at a Black oak on corner of Edward Hutchins running thence North forty-five degrees West one hundred and thirty five perches to a post, South three degrees East one hundred and fifty perches to a white oak, South sixty five degrees East ninety five perches to a Stake, North two degrees & one half East ninety eight perches to the place of Beginning, computed to be sixty nine acres; together with all and singular the rights, privileges, hereditaments & opportunities that unto belonging & all the Estate, intact which the said Thomas Lemonion....(The transaction was recorded in the Greene Township, Greene County Patent Book.)

Andrew Jr was bequeathed 100 acres of land on Duck Creek, Ohio, in 1817 in his father's Will. Andrew Lantz Sr filed his Will in the Greene County Will Book, Volume 1, page 274. In it he distributed the bulk of his estate among the children of his foster son, Lot Lantz, who was not a relative, but an illegitimate child raised by Andrew Lantz Sr. The Will

172

was contested by his natural children. Andrew and Barbara are buried in the Garard's Fort, Cemetery.

[1] http://johnteets.com/index.htm?ssmain=p305.htm.
[2] Leckey, Howard. *Tenmile Country and its Pioneer Families.* Rpt, (Closson Press, Apollo, PA. 2007) 635.
[3] http://wc.rootsweb.ancestry.com/cgi-bin/igm.cgi?op=GET&db=loisebranch &id=I03333.

JEREMIAH AND JOHN LONG JR

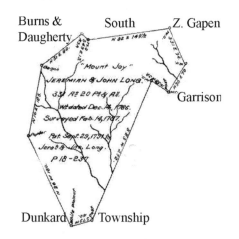

John Long Sr (1722-1785) was born in Queen Anne's County, Maryland, and died in Greene County, Pennsylvania. He married Ann Herrington in 1744 in St Luke's Episcopal Parish, daughter of David Herrington and Rebecca....Their children were:[1]

    i. Jeremiah (1745-1820), born in Queen Anne's County, Maryland, died on Dunkard Creek, Greene County, Pennsylvania. He married (1) Mary Ivers, daughter of Richard Ivers and Mary Hudson, and (2) Jane Jones (1788-1857). Mary Ivers was excommunicated from the Goshen Baptist Church at Garard's Fort. They were buried in the Garard's Fort Cemetery. Jeremiah and Mary Ivers' children were:

1. Frances Priscilla (1775-1824), born and died in Greene County, Pennsylvania, she married William Burge (1837).

2. David.

3. Elizabeth married Perry Johnson.

4. James (1790-) married (1) Ruth Cillon and (2) Mary Frances Burge.

5. Nathan.

6. William.

7. Priscilla (1759-1848), born in Greene County, Pennsylvania, died in Miami County, Ohio. She married (1) Vincent Dye with whom she had four children. She then married (2) Benjamin Dye, Vincent's brother, both were sons of Andrew and Sarah (Minor) Dye. Priscilla was Benjamin Dye's second wife. Benjamin and Priscilla lived out their lives in Miami County, Ohio.

8. Jeremiah Jr (1780-1858), born and died in Greene County, Pennsylvania, married Cyrene Gwynne (1793- 1874).

9. Richard (1786-1852), born and died in Greene County, Pennsylvania, married (1) Mary Rankin (1781-1829) and (2) Charlotte Adamson. He and Charlotte were buried in the Muddy Creek Cemetery.

ii. David (1746-1828), born in Queen Anne's County, Maryland, died in Butler County, Ohio, married Sarah Gapen (-1780).

iii. John Jr (1750-1838), born in Queen Anne's County, Maryland, died in Greene County, Pennsylvania.

iv. James (1752-1848), born in Queen Anne's County, Maryland, died in Orrville, Ohio, married (1) Mary...and (2) Susannah Knight in 1817.

v. Gideon (1754-1834), born in Queen Anne's County, Maryland, died in Greene County, Pennsylvania, married Hannah Phillips in 1781.

vi. Eliel (1756-1834), born in Queen Anne's County, Maryland, died in Monongalia County, Virginia. After his death his widow, Mary Davis, purportedly the daughter of John and Tabitha Davis, applied for his Revolutionary War pension.

vii. Noah (1760-1814), born in Queen Anne's County, Maryland, died in Butler County, Ohio, married Sarah Gapen

(1766-1850) who was born in New Jersey and died in Butler County, Ohio. Sarah was the daughter of Zachariah Gapen and Ruth Tindall.

viii.   Ann (1762-1828 to 1839), born in Queen Anne's County, Maryland, died in Fayette County, Pennsylvania, married George DeBolt. By 1786 he owned land next to the Longs in present day Monongalia Township, Greene County.

By the Law of Virginia, September 1758, in the 32nd year of the reign of George II, John Long Sr was paid 8s,7d,. for provisions he furnished to the Militia of Augusta County.[2]

In August 1763 John Long Sr was one of the 14 settlers "residing betwixt Fort Ligonier and Fort Pitt whose houses and furniture were burned and crops destroyed by the Indians." He signed a petition sent to the Army at Carlisle, Pennsylvania, "take our Distressed Circumstances under your Consideration."[3]

Shortly before 1771 John Long Sr and Ann Herrington, with their seven sons and a daughter, left their home in Maryland and settled on the waters of Whiteley and Dunkard Creeks. They lived for a time in what is now Fayette County, Pennsylvania, where their daughter, Ann, met and married George Debolt.

John Long Sr was listed on the 1773 Assessment Roll for Springhill Township, Bedford County, Pennsylvania.[4] By 1800 John and Ann Long's descendants were divided into two groups: those living in Dunkard Township and those living in present day Monongalia Township. By 1776 they were living on the west side of the Monongahela River where John Long Sr died. His Will was probated in Washington, Pennsylvania, on May 12, 1785, and recorded in the Washington County Will Book 1, page 60.

John Long Sr's Will was devised in 1785 in Washington County, Pennsylvania and read, in part:[5]

> In the name of God Amen. I John Long of the County of Washington and the state of Pennsylvania being weak of body but of sound mind and memory do make and publish this last will and testament in manner following. Viz first and principally recommend my soul to God that gave it and my body to the dust to be buried in a Christian-like manner at the discretion of my executrix. Nothing doubting but that I shall receive the same again at the general resurrection of all flesh at coming to the mighty power of God and as touching my temporal estate

wherewith it hath pleased God to bless me, I will and bequeath it in the following manner.

Imprimus it is my will; and I do hereby allow my executrix to pay all my just debts and also legacies in specie hereafter bequeath.

i. I will and bequeath first unto my son David Long 2s.6d.

ii. Secondly I will and bequeath unto my son John Long 1s.

i. Thirdly I will and bequeath unto my son James Long 1s.

ii. Fourthly I will and bequeath unto my son Gideon Long 1s.

iii. Fifthly I will and bequeath unto my son Jeremiah Long 1s.

v. Sixthly I will and bequeath unto my son Elial Long one half of a tract of land I now live on and the said Elial Long is to take his part where he now lives unto him his heirs and assigns forever. The said Elial Long is to pay one-half of the cost of clearing said land.

iv. Seventhly I will and bequeath unto my son Noah Long the other half of said tract of land which I live on to him his heirs and assigns forever.

v. Eighthly I will and bequeath unto my daughter Ann Debolt…riding horses and one bed and furniture, the bed and furniture after her mother's death.

Ninethly I will and bequeath unto my dear and loveing wife Ann Long for term of life or during her widowhood this house which I now dwell in with the bed and furniture with two cows and one heffer and four sheep and after her death the cows and heffer and sheep go to my son Noah Long and the said Noah Long shall have full power to work and tend or till his half of said land where I now live as he shall think fit with the orchard and meddo and he shall allow his said mother Ann Long a good and sufficient garden for her own use and to furnish her with what is necessary for her to live on comfortably or to support her and lastly I do make and constitute Ann Long my said wife executrix of this my last will and testament dated this twelfth day of May in the year of our Lord one thousand seven hundred eighty five on witness whereof I have hereunto set my hand and affixed my seal signed sealed and acknowledged by the testator as his last will and testament in the presents of us who are subscribing witnesses hereunto: Stephen Gapen, Zachariah Gapen, William Hudson. March 29, 1786

Personally appeared before me Zachariah Gapen and Stephen Gapen after the attestation by law required say that they were personally present and heard and saw John Long sign and acknowledge the annexed will and that they the said Gapens believe at the time of said Long's so doing that he was in his perfect reason. Affirmed before me this day, Thomas Stokeley, Registrar. Signed, Zachariah Gapen, Stephen Gapen. Witnesses: Stephen Gapen, William Hudson and Zacariah Gapen. Filed in Washington.

John Long Jr (1750-1838) was born in Queen Anne's County, Maryland, and died in Greene County, Pennsylvania. He married Grace…and lived in Dunkard Township. Before moving to Dunkard Township he was listed in 1772 on the Rolls of Springhill Township which included present day Greene County and the southern parts of Washington County. (County Will Book 1, page 60.)

John Jr was a Private in Captain Patrick Anderson's Company of Colonel John Bull's Pennsylvania Regiment of Foot in 1776.[6]

In 1781 he was taxed $81 for 300 acres of land, two horses, and two cows in Greene Township, Washington County.[7]

In November 1776 Jeremiah and his brother-in-law, Richard Ivers, marched from Cambridge, Massachusetts, with the Eighth Pennsylvania Regiment to join General Washington's Army in New Jersey and spent the winter of 1777-1778 at Valley Forge. The Eighth Pennsylvania Regiment took part in the Battles of Round Brook, Brandywine, Germantown, and Saratoga under General Morgan before it returned to Fort Pitt in 1778.[8]

Jeremiah was a Private and a Corporal in Captain Haws' Company of Foot in the Second Regiment of the Virginia Line commanded by Colonel Alexander Spotswood in 1777. The Draper Manuscripts disclosed that Jeremiah and his brother Gideon Long (1753-1834) were ordered picked up as deserters about 1778, a term without the stigma that it carries today. After Jeremiah got back to his home on Whiteley Creek he became an Ensign in Captain John Guthery's Company, First Battalion, Washington County Militia, and later was made a Captain in the Frontier Rangers.[9]

Jeremiah was a Private in Captain Thomas Cook's Company in the Eighth Regiment of Foot in the Pennsylvania Line in 1778. He was a Private 1st Class in Captain William Crawford's Company in Lieutenant Colonel Thomas Crooke's Fifth Battalion of the Washington County Militia in the district lying upon the Monongalia River between Whiteley and Muddy Creeks on October 15, 1781.[10]

Jeremiah was a Private in Colonel Aeneas Mackey's Eighth Regiment of the Pennsylvania Line. He served as a Private in the Third Company of the First Battalion of the Washington County Militia in 1781. The next year when he was in the Sixth Company of the First Battalion, the Muster Roll recorded him as "delinquent," (for what reason was not explained), according to the Pennsylvania State Archives, Revolutionary War Military Abstract Card File.

Jeremiah was listed in the 1781 Effective Supply Tax Book of Greene Township, Washington County. He was assessed for two horses and two cows at $24.

Jeremiah served in Captain John Guthery's Company in Lieutenant Colonel John Pomeroy's First Battalion of Associators and Militia, Washington County, Pennsylvania, in 1782.

According to the Pennsylvania Archives, Series 6, Volume 2, pages 18 and 19, all seven Long brothers were in their neighbor Captain John Guthrey's Company in 1782 including Ensign Gideon Long and Private Noah Long.[11]

John Jr was a Private 7th Class substitute on September 21, 1782, in Ensign William Perkins' Company in the Fifth Regiment of Foot of the Pennsylvania Militia. He also served as a Private 4th Class in Captain John Guthery's Company of Washington County Militia. About 1782 he signed the Petition for a new State of Westsylvania to be erected out of Fayette, Washington, and Greene Counties, Pennsylvania, and Ohio and Monongalia Counties, Virginia. He was listed on the 1784 Assessment Roll for Greene Township, Washington County, Pennsylvania.

John Jr and his brother Jeremiah purchased a tract of land on a branch of Dunkard Creek called Mount Joy on a warrant dated December 14, 1786, which they recorded in the Washington County Deed Book 2, page 24. John Long Jr was listed on the 1790 Greene Township Census as head of a household with four males under 16 years of age and four females. Only one of his sons shared in the distribution of his estate which was recorded in O. C. Docket 3, page 164.

Jeremiah, John Jr, Noah, David, Gideon, and Elial, all of Greene Township, were included on the 1789 Tax List of Persons Exonerated on the Frontiers of Washington County for being distressed by the Incursions and Depredations of the Indians.

Jeremiah was an Ensign when he served in the Second Company of Lieutenant Colonel William Crawford's Fourth Battalion of the Washington County Militia, according to the Militia Rolls of 1783-1790. In 1792 he was an Ensign in Major George McCully's First Company of Washington County's Militia.

In the 1797 Greene County Tax Book made by Joseph Willford, Assessor, assisted by Elias Stone and Stephen Gapen, John Long Jr was assessed for 200 acres of land at $240, 30 acres of cleared land at $30, one cabin at $1, one barn at $2, two horses at $20, and two cows at $12. In 1809 he was assessed for 163 acres of land at $570, one barn at $2, one house at $12, two horses at $45, and one cow at $6. He was included in the 1806 Voter List in Dunkard Township, Greene County.[12]

In the 1797 Greene County Tax Book made by Joseph Willford, the Assessor, assisted by Elias Stone and Stephen Gapen, Jeremiah was assessed for 100 acres of land at $120, 45 acres of cleared land at $45, one house at $5, one barn at $2, two horses at $30, and five cows at $30.

After Mary Ivers Long's death, Jeremiah married (2) Jane Jones (1788-1857), daughter of Morgan Jones and Mary Davis, who survived him and was the mother of six of his children. Jane Jones was born in Greene County, Pennsylvania, and died in Silver Hill, Wetzel County, West Virginia. After Jeremiah's death, she married Thomas Rinehart and later...McCormick.

In the 1800 Greene County Census Jeremiah was listed as head of a household with his wife and three boys between 10 and 16 years of age, three boys under 10 years of age, one girl under 10 years of age, and one girl between 10 and 16 years of age.

Jeremiah was an active member of the Goshen Baptist Church. The church's Minute Book contained several entries about him:[13]

> i.. June 27, 1807: Bro Rose to call on Bro Jeremiah Long and Bro Bowen to attend at our next meeting of business....
>
> ii. May 25, 1810: Brother Ross made report that he called on Brother Jeremiah Long to know the reason why he did not attend our meetings and his answer was such the Church think him worthy of censure.
>
> iii. January 25, 1811: Bro Ross to cite Brother Jeremiah Long to attend our next meeting.
>
> iv. March 21, 1811: The business of Brother Jeremiah

Long was investigated himself present and the Church think it proper to suspend him from the privileges of the Church.

v. June 15, 1811: The Church think it their duty to exclude Jeremiah Long....

vi. October 16, 1822: Received Jeremiah Long into full fellowship in the Church by letter....une 21, 1823: The Church met according to app't and after singing and prayer by Brother Jeremiah Long proceeded to business...Heard Brother Jeremiah Long speak and after considering of his gifts agreed they were not such as qualified him to go and preach the gospel. But were willing he might make another trial to improve his gifts before the Church at our meeting of business in August next....

vii. September 27, 1823: Gave liberty to Brother Jeremiah Long to speak in the Church where we met for attending to business.

In 1809 Jeremiah was assessed in Dunkard Twonship for 100 acres of land at $400, one house at $12, one barn at $2, two horses at $50, one cow at $6, and two whiskey stills at $81.

Jeremiah bought several warrantees for land in Greene County; 150 acres were surveyed March 8, 1814, and 265 acres were surveyed on February 12, 1838.[14]

On February 13, 1820, Jeremiah Long, Associate Judge of the Court of Common Pleas in Greene County, Pennsylvania, stated that he was acquainted with Edward Haymore who made a declaration in order to obtain a pension and that he had served with Haymore in the same company of the Eighth Regiment of the Pennsylvania Line of Continental Troops in the Revolutionary War and that he served during the time stated in Haymore's declaration. John Minor, Judge of Greene County, Pennsylvania, certified to Long's deposition on May 11, 1820.

Jeremiah Long died on his farm on July 4, 1820, which was recorded in the Greene County Open Circuit Docket:[15]

18 Sept 1820. On the petition of Jane Long, widow and relict of Jeremiah Long late of Dunkard Township, deceased...the petitioner therefore prays that an inquest may be awarded to make partition to and among the children of said intestate or if such partition cannot be made then to value and appraise the same and make return of their proceedings at the next Orphan's Court for said county. Therefore the Court award

and inquest and that publication be made in the Waynesburg Messenger four weeks preceding the inquest as notice to the heirs living in other states.

At the Orphans Court held at Waynesburg on March 19, 1820, a Writ returned by the Sheriff together with an inquisition thereto assigned in which the Jury state that the Will not admit of a division but that they have appraised the same at Nineteen hundred and eight dollars out of which the widow's dower is estimated at and allotted to be twenty six dollars and sixteen cents. And on 6/21/1821, Waynesburg: Petition of Jane Long...her late husband (Jeremiah Long) died intestate and left a number of children and some real estate and personal estate...during life (of the) intestate considerable advancements were made to some of the children...auditors requested to ascertain such advancements...the Court appointed Robert Maple Esq., Richard Kerwood Esq., and Dr. William Johnson...11/7/1822 report presented: to Nathan Long, $10.00; to Frances Burge, $17.75; to Richard Long, $48.00; to Jeremiah Long, $18.00; to David Long, $40.00; to Elizabeth Johnson, $41.00; to William Long, $70.00; to James Williamson, $42.00; to James Long, $71.00; to John Long, $40.00...3/18/1823 above confirmed except part charged to Richard Long. Objection later waived.

December 18th, 1821. On motion Rule on the time and legal representatives of Jeremiah Long late of Greene County dec'd to appear at the next Court to be held in Waynesburg for the County of Green on the Monday of March next and elect to take or refuse the real estate of the deceased at the valuation, an order that this rule be published four weeks preceding the said Court in the Franklin Gazette or Waynesburg Messenger.

March 18th, 1822. The heirs and representatives of Jeremiah Long decd all called. None answered except Lot Lantz Esq., guardian of the minor children who appeared and refused to accept the land at the appraised value.

June 18, 1822. Rule on the heirs and legal representatives of Jeremiah Long late of Greene County deceased to appear at the Courthouse in Waynesburg on the first day of next term which will be on the 11th day of November next and show cause why the real estate of the intestate shall not be sold. Exit copy of Rule issued 10th August 1822.

November 11th, 1822. The heirs and representatives of Jeremiah long decd being called gave no answer.

January 11, 1823. On motion the Court order that Jane Long administrator of the estate of Jeremiah Long deceased who died intestate sell at public sale or outcry the real estate of the deceased on the premises on the first Monday of March next: One third of the purchase money to be had on the first day of April next when possession is to be given the balance in two equal annual payments. The deed to be made on payment of the whole purchase money. Exit Rule issued Greene County.

To the Honorable Judge of the Orphans Court of Greene County. In pursuance of an order from the Honorable Court for the sale of real estate formerly the property of Jeremiah Long decd in Dunkard Township the said sale was exposed to public sale on Monday the third instant and the said estate was cryed of to Richard Long for the sum of eight hundred and six dollars and fifty cents. The said Richard long being the highest bidder. Jane Long, Administrator.

18th of March On Motion Sale confirmed...1824. Recd June 24 of Wm Hays, Clark, five dollars in part of my dower of the estate of Jeremiah Long decd. Signed, Jane Long.

Received of William T Hays Clk twenty dollars the 9th May 1823. Richard Long paid Richard T--man a Juror on the Inquisition $1.00. Paid Henry Six, a Juror, $1.00. Recd of Clk one dollar my fee as a Juror. Signed, John Gapen. Received of William T Hays Clark of the Orphans Court thirty-five dollars and fifty cents my dividend of the real Estate of Jeremiah Long Oct 8, 1829. Signed, John Long. Received of William T Hays Thirty nine dollars and sixty cents it being the dividend of the real Estate of Jeremiah Long decd allotted to my wife Frances Burge October 26, 1829. Signed, William Burge. Received of William T Hays by the hands of Richard Long Twenty dollars and fifteen cents June 7, 1831 this is my proportion of Frances Burges share of the personal estate. Signed, William Burge. Received of William T Hays clark of the Orphans Court four hundred and fifty three dollars it being the distributive share for Mary Long, Samuel, Ruth, Sarah Ann and Melinda Long minor children of Jeremiah Long, both as to real and personal estate and a calculated up to the 8th September 1829. Signed, Lot Lantz, guardian.

I acknowledge satisfaction in full for the share of Elizabeth Johnson her share having been sold to me on a…to June Term 1821st 18 is far as the sale under her interest in William G Hawkins:
Jeremiah Longs share is $37.60, William Longs share is 5.50, David Long share is 35.50, James Long share is 4.50, Benjamin Dye share is 75.50, Richard Long share is 27.50, all told $186.10.

Recd of William T Hays Clerk of Court the above one hundred and eight six dollars and ten cents as calculated up to the 8th Sept 1829, it being in full of real estate and personal estate Jeremiah it only apply to him as the rest August 29-1832. I also acknowledge the amount of an assignment for Jane Williamson to Jane Rinehart and from her to me. This is to be a credit as the Clerk of Orphans Court. But I have not recd the amount which is $33.50.

There were no records in the Pennsylvania Archives that indicated that John Jr or Jeremiah applied for, or received, pensions for their military service.

[1] http://www.lindapages.com/marshall/dlong.txt.

[2] http://vagenweb.org/hening/vol07-09.htm.

[3] Walkinshaw, Lewis Clark. *Annals of southwestern Pennsylvania, Volume 1.* (Lewis Historical PubliShinng Company, Inc., Baltimore, MD, 1939).

[4] Leckey, Howard. *Tenmile Country and its Pioneer Families.* Rpt, (Closson Press, Apollo, PA. 2007) 127.

[5] Veach, James. *The Monongahela of Old or Historical Sketches of Southwestern Pennsylvania to the Year 1800,* (Kessinger PubliShinng, LLC, Whitefish, MT, 2008).

[6] Pennsylvania Archives, Series 2, Volume X, pages 266, 269, 270.

[7] Pennsylvania Archives, Series 3, Volume XXII, page 699.

[8] Pennsylvania Archives, Series 5, Volume III, page 368, Series 6, Volume II, page 172.

[9] Clark, Homer L. *The Last of the Rangers; Washington County, Pennsylvania, 1794,* (Pub. Washington County Historical Society, Washington, PA, 1906).

[10] Pennsylvania Archives, Series 6, Volume II, page 165.

[11] Pennsylvania Archives, Series 2, Volume X, pages 18 , 19, 671, 678.

[12] http://www.cornerstonegenealogy.com/greene_county_voter_lists_1801.htm.

[13] Corbly, Don. *Pastor John Corbly.* (Lulu Press, Raleigh, North Carolina, 2008).

[14] Pennsylvania Archives, Series 3, Volume XXVI.

[15] http://files.usgwarchives.org/pa/greene/court/long0003.txt.

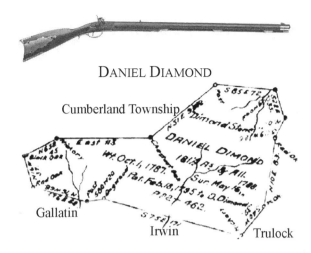

Daniel Diamond (1750-1827) of County Londonderry, Northern Ireland, emigrated to America in the eighteenth century and finally settled in southwest Pennsylvania. He married Christina....[1] He bought 181 acres of land in Washington County and called it Diamond Stone. His warrant was dated October 1, 1787. He had it surveyed on May 16, 1788, but it was not patented to him until February 18, 1795. It was recorded in the Washington County Patent Book P22, page 462.

He was listed in the 1790 Greene Township Census as the head of a household with one male under 16 years of age and two females.

He moved his family to Georges Township, Fayette County, Pennsylvania. In the 1800 census his household consisted of himself and his wife, one male under 10 years of age, another male between 16 and 21 years of age, and two females less than 10 years of age. In 1800 he ran a public tavern, the Black Bear, on the Morgantown Road in Georges Township, Fayette County.

He was a deacon in the old Amish Conemaugh Church in Conemaugh Township which was formed out of Somerset County, Pennsylvania, in February 1801. Conemaugh is an Indian name meaning "long fishing place."[2]

In 1805 the Union Presbyterian Church of Georges Township bought from Daniel Diamond a lot on which to build a church. Their pastor was Ebenezer Jennings who was raised on Dunlap's Creek near New Salem.[3]

By 1810 he had moved his family to Cambria Township, Cambria County, Pennsylvania. His family household consisted of himself and his wife, both over 45 years of age, one male between 16 and 21 years of age, one female under 10 years of age, and one female between 10 and 16 years of age.

184

The 1812 Monongalia County Court records show that Daniel Diamond said John Teste owed him $180 and that Teste had moved from the Commonwealth. On December 11, 1811, he prayed the court to attach Teste's property to satisfy the debt. John Jackson was summoned as garnishee. An Attachment Bond signed by Daniel Diamond was secured by Charles McGill on December 11, 1811. In the February 1812 term, the case was dismissed by Diamond.[4]

On June 5, 1812, Daniel S. Diamond gifted 734 acres in Fayette County to Elizabeth "Betsy" Diamond (1804-1861) who was born in Pennsylvania. She married Ignatius Nathan Cosgray (1801-1880) in Virginia before 1831 in Uniontown, Fayette County, Pennsylvania. Ignatius and Elizabeth's children were: John (1831-1921), Mary Ann (1834-), Catherine (1836-), Christian (1839-), Sarah Margaret (1843-), James (1846-), and David.[5]

The 1860 US Census for Monongalia County, Virginia, listed Ignatius Cosgray, age 59, farmer; spouse Elizabeth, age 56; and children Christian, age 20, Sarah, age 17, and James, age 4.

[1] http://www.familytreedna.com/public/dimond_dymond_dnagenealogy/ default.aspx?section=results.

[2] Blough, Jerome E. *History of the Church of the Brethren of the Western District of Pennsylvania.* (Brethren PubliShinng House, Elgin, IL) 1916.

[3] http://elements.fay-west.com/pdf/fayette/31.pdf.

[4] Zinn, Melba Pender. *Monongalia County, (West) Virginia, Records of the District, Superior and County Courts, 1808-1814.* Rpt. (Heritage Books, Westminster, MD, 2007) Volume 7.

[5] http://freepages.genealogy.rootsweb.ancestry.com/~cosgriff/usa/pa/fayette. htm.

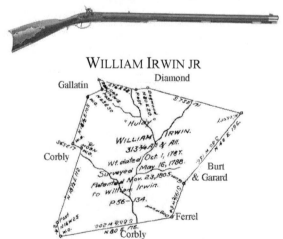

William Irwin Sr (-1748) came to Pennsylvania from Ulster, North Ireland, and died in Pennsboro Township, Lancaster County. His Will, recorded in Carlile, Lancaster County, Pennsylvania, was devised on May 5, 1748, proved the following month, and recorded on February 15, 1763. His wife was Elenor....Their children were:[1]

    i. Alexander (1723-).
    ii. Ann (1726-).
    iii. Francis (1731-1759).
    iv. Mary (1732-).
    v. John (1735-) born in Pennsylvania.
    vi. Margaret (1736-).
    vii. William Jr (1738-1814) born and died in
    Pennsylvania.
    viii. Robert, (1738-) was born in Pennsylvania and died
    near Carlisle.
    ix. Elizabeth (1742-).
    x. Sarah (1744-).
    xi. James (1745-).
    xii. Samuel (1747-).

On May 25, 1762, Martha Finley, widow of John Finley, asked her village Council for the appointment of a guardian for Elizabeth, Michael, John, Andrew, and Samuel Finley, orphan children of her deceased husband. William Irwin Jr (1738-1814) was appointed their guardian except that Elizabeth, over 14 years of age, chose Samuel McClure for her guardian. Justices John Montgomery and Thomas Willson presided over the Orphan's Court.[2]

On May 25, 1763, William Irwin Jr warranted 375 acres in Cumberland County and called it Dryberry. He received his patent on December 30, 1766, and recorded it in the Cumberland County Patent Book on page 146.

He bought several tracts of land between 1755 and 1807. In Cumberland County he bought two tracts totaling 75 acres in 1755, two tracts totaling 275 acres in 1763, and 25 acres in 1765. In 1772 he warranted Lot No. 93 in Cumberland County and recorded the patent for it in the Cumberland County Patent Book AA on page 45. In 1774 he warranted 1,234 acres in Northumberland County called Springfield and recorded the transaction in the Northumberland County Patent Book AA on page 15 (He was referred to as William Irwin "Irish" to distinguish him from another man of the same name). He bought 50 acres in 1786 and 250 acres in 1807 in Cumberland County and in 1787 he bought 350 acres in Washington County and 50 acres in Franklin County.

In June 1778 he was fined 3s. for not complying with a Militia law in the Northeast District of Newcastle Hundred, Delaware. He was a Private in Captain John Winston's Company in Colonel William Davis' 14th Virginia Regiment of Foot in August 1778. He enlisted as a Private in Captain Joseph Pott's Company in Colonel Johnston's Fifth Pennsylvania Regiment of Foot during November and September (when he was hospitalized in West Nantmill, Chester County) in 1778. As active as he was in serving in these various military units, he also served when called upon, in Washington County's Stockley Rangers during the years 1778 to 1783.

On March 9, 1778, courts were held in Buffalo Valley, Washington County, Pennsylvania. John Clark, John Crider, George O'Vermeier, Martin Dreisbach, and William Irwin were appointed "viewers" on a petition to divide Buffalo Township by a line commencing at the mouth of Beaver Run, thence a southwest course to Switzer Run. This was never acted upon.[3]

He was a Private in Captain Jacob Piatt's Company in Colonel Mathis Ogden's Fifth New Jersey Regiment of Foot in Elizabeth Town, Virginia, in May 1779. He was a Private in Captain Nathaniel Bowman's Company in Colonel Israel Shreve's Second Regiment of New Jersey Foot in March and April 1779 and received $33.50 for two month's service and subsistence. He served again in this Company and Regiment for one month in 1780 and again in January and October 1782 when the Regiment was commanded by Colonel Elias Dayton.[4]

He was a Private in Captain John Cotton's Company in Lieutenant Colonel David Williamson's infamous Expedition again the Moravian Indians at the town of Gnadenhutten on the Muskingum River in March 1782. The Expedition consisted of 160 men from the Fourth Battalion of the Washington County Militia. Williamson may have been the only ranking officer in the Fourth Battalion who was immediately available to lead the expedition. The authority to call out the Militia had been delegated to the commanding officers in the field by the Supreme Council of Pennsylvania. History has stated that the raid was in retaliation for frequent Indian attacks by the Moravian Indians, so called because they had been converted by Moravian missionaries to Christianity. On the other hand, it has been called wanton murder of innocent Indians. Many of the men had recently lost relations at the hands of the savages. During the raid several of them reportedly found articles which had been plundered from their own houses, or those of their relatives, in the houses of the Moravians Indians.[5]

From 1778 to 1783 William Irwin was called to duty with Gideon Long's Ranger Company in Westmoreland County and with Stockley's

Rangers in Washington County.[6]

The 1781 Effective Supply Tax Rate Book for Greene Township, Washington County, showed he was taxed $48 for 200 acres of land and two horses.[7]

He was on the 1784 Assessment Roll for Greene Township and was one of the three Justices of the Peace in Washington County in 1785. In 1784 he received four pay certificates for a total of £17.3s for service in Washington County's Militia according to the Pennsylvania State Archives, Revolutionary War Military Files.

He warranted 313 acres in Washington County called Huldy on October 1, 1787. It was surveyed on May 16, 1788, patented on November 23, 1805, and recorded in the Washington County Patent Book P56 on page 134.

In 1791 he was again commissioned a Justice of the Peace as well as one of the three Assessors in Washington County. In the 1798 Greene County Tax Book made by Joseph Willford, Assessor, assisted by Elias Stone and Stephen Gapen, William was assessed for 200 acres of land at $160, 35 acres of cleared land at $30, one house at $5, and four cows at $24. In the 1799 Greene County Tax Book he was assessed for 225 acres of land at $180, 50 acres of cleared land at $50, one house at $5, and five cows at $30.

No authentic record of whom he married could be found. In the 1790 Census for Greene Township, Washington County, he was listed as the head of a household with one male over 16 years of age, two males under 16 years of age, and three females. In the 1800 Census of that township he was listed as head of a household with his wife, one male between 16-26 years of age, one female between 10-16 years of age, and one female between 16-26 years of age.

On February 22, 1802, an Act of the Legislature incorporated the Borough of Canonsburg, Washington County. William Irwin was in its first list of taxables.[8]

No record of his application for a pension for Revolutionary War service could be found. He was living in Cumberland Township when he filed his Will in the Greene County, Pennsylvania, Recorder's Office in File 221, Book 1, page 136. It recorded his death on August 31, 1814.

[1] Logan, John H. *A History of the Upper Country of South Carolina from the Earliest Periods to the Close of the War of Independence.* (The Reprint Company, Spartanburg, SC, 1960).

[2] Pennsylvania Archives, Cumberland County, Volume 2, page15.

[3] Linn, John. *Annals of Buffalo Valley, Pennsylvania, 1755-1855.* (Lane S. Hart, Printer, 1877).

[4] Pennsylvania Archives, Series 5, Volume V.

[5] Pennsylvania Archives, Series 6, Volume II, pages 257, 258.

[6] Pennsylvania Archives, Series 3, Vol. XXIII, pages 198-220.

[7] Pennsylvania Archives, Series 3, Volume XXII, page 699.

[8] Crumrine, Boyd. *History of Washington County, Pennsylvania with Biographical Sketches of Many of Its Pioneers and Prominent Men,* (Philadelphia: L. H. Leverts & Co., 1882), 601.

BENJAMIN SUTTON SR

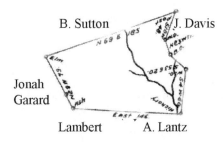

Benjamin Sutton Sr (1722-1806) was born in Middlesex County, New Jersey, the son of Judah Sutton and Emma Canter. He married Mary Jennings Branch (1730-) before 1758 at New Jersey. He is buried in the Garard's Fort Cemetery, Greene County, Pennsylvania. The children of Benjamin Sutton Sr and Mary Jennings Branch were all born in Somerset County, New Jersey:[1]

i. Stephen (1760-1846) died in Mount Washington, Hamilton County, Ohio.

ii. Ebenezer (1740-) married (1) Margaret, and (2) Margaret.

iii. Eunice (1740-) married William McDermont of Somerset County, New Jersey, in 1781.

iv. Mary (1740-) married Thomas Lucas.

v. Nathan (1740-) married Patty Woodruff of Clermont County, Ohio, in 1815,

vi. Sarah (Aft. 1740-) married John Porter.

vii. Benjamin Jr (1759-1841) died in Decatur, Brown County, Ohio. He married (1) Sarah Robe, then (2) Sarah Tingley (1765-1784). Benjamin Jr and Sarah Tingley were buried in the Decatur Cemetery, Byrd Township, Brown County, Ohio. He served as a Private from Greene County in 1777-1778 in the Pennsylvania Militia. He was included on the Pension Roll in Brown County, Ohio, Number S.16266, in 1833. The children of Benjamin Sutton and Sarah Tingley were:

1. Tingley (1782-1843) died in Brown County, Ohio, and married Elizabeth Morrow (1790-) who was born in Virginia.
2. Sarah (1780-1841) married Nathaniel Beasley.
3. Ortho (1784-1845) was born and died in Brown County, Ohio.

The Meeting held at the Mount Bethel Church in Bernard Township, Somerset County, New Jersey, on November 11, 1767, opened with a prayer by Reverend Mr. Crosley. Benjamin Sutton Sr was chosen as Moderator; Abner Sutton was chosen to keep books, and Benjamin Sutton Sr was the reading clerk. It was agreed that they would send for David Sutton Sr at Piscataway, New Jersey, to join them.[2]

In early 1768 Pastor John Corbly set out for the Western District of Augusta County with the Sutton brothers, Reverends John, James, Isaac, and Benjamin Sutton, in a small group of travelers in one of the many wagon trains departing from Winchester, Virginia. They encamped temporarily on Simpson's Creek (at present day Bridgeport, Pennsylvania) before pushing on farther south to Whiteley Creek.[3]

During the Revolutionary War the settlers on Tubmill Creek, a large stream between Chestnut and Laurel Hill Ridges near Bolivar, Westmoreland County, Pennsylvania, built a formidable blockhouse on what was then called the Indian Farm. The blockhouse got its name, Inyard's Blockhouse, from David Inyard who first improved it. The settlers who built the blockhouse were, in part, David Inyard, Benjamin Sutton Sr, James Clark, William Wood, William Ilettnett. Archibald McGuire, Neil Dougherty, David Lakens, and James Galhraith.[4]

Ensign Benjamin Sutton Sr served in Lieutenant Colonel Henry Enoch's First Battalion of Washington County Militia. He also served in Stockley's Rangers of the Washington County Militia on the Four Mile Run near Fort Williams in Donegal Township between Donegal and Stahlstown, Pennsylvania, in 1778. Fort Williams was the home of Colonel David Williamson who led raids against the Indians on the Tuscurawas River.[5]

In 1782 Captain John Guthrey commanded a Company in the First Battalion of the Washington County Militia. The men were largely recruited near Fort Lindley in Whiteley, Greene, and Dunkard

Townships. Among the Privates were John Long, Jeremiah Long, Aaron Jenkins, and Benjamin Sutton Sr.[6]

On January 29, 1780, the Minute Book of the Goshen Baptist Church at Garard's Fort recorded that the "Church met according to appointment. First agreed by the voice of the Church unanimously that Brother Benjamin Sutton be laid under censure for taking of hogs that was none of his property."[7]

In the 1781 Effective Supply Tax Rates for Washington County, Benjamin Sutton Sr of Greene Township was assessed for two horses and three cows valued at $27.[8]

Ebenezer, Henry, Nathan, Benjamin, and Stephen Sutton, sons of Benjamin Sutton and Mary Jennings Branch, were listed as single freemen in the 1784 Assessment Roll for Greene Township, Washington County, Pennsylvania.[9]

Benjamin Sutton Sr bought 100 acres called Sutwell on a warrant dated November 20, 1787. It was surveyed on April 22, 1788, patented on April 23, 1793, and recorded in the Washington County Patent Book P19, page 284.

He also served in the Westmoreland County Militia in March 1786 and received pay of £1.11s. according to the Pennsylvania State Archives, Revolutionary War Military Abstract Card File.

On October 29, 1787, Benjamin Sutton and his daughter, Sarah, sold to John Boyle and George Baker Lot No.83 in Morgantown, Virginia, for £15. The transaction included an annual quit rent of 5s.6d. paid to Zack Morgan, his heirs, and assigns. Signed: Benjamin Sutton Sr, Sarah Sutton. Witnesses: none. Acknowledged in court, October 1787. Recorded: OS 2:411.

On October 24, 1788, Josiah and Moses Lambert paid £7.9s.2d. for 221 acres called The Lamb on Big Whiteley Creek in Washington County next to Jonah Garard, Benjamin Sutton Sr, Andrew Lantz, Aaron Jenkins, Richard Hall, Robert Crosley, and Joseph Frazer. It was recorded in the Washington County Patent Book 16, page 138.

Benjamin Sutton Sr was listed in the 1790 Greene Township Census as head of household with one male under 16 years of age and three females.

In the 1797 Greene County Tax Book made by Joseph Willford, Assessor, assisted by Elias Stone and Stephen Gapen, Benjamin Sutton Sr was assessed for 50 acres of land at $80, 25 acres of cleared land at $25, one house at $5, one barn at $2, two horses at $30, and two cows at $12. Two years later he was assessed for 50 acres land at $50, 20 acres of cleared land at $20, one house at $5, one cabin at $1, one horse at $15, and two cows at $12.

Benjamin and Mary appeared in the 1800 Greene Township, Greene County Census as one male and one female, both over 45 years of age.

Benjamin Sutton Sr was on the List of Voters Names residing in the Township of Greene, Greene County, who voted in the annual election held at the house of John Burley on October 13, 1801.[10]

Benjamin died at his home, Sutwell, in Greene County, Pennsylvania, and was buried in the Garard's Fort Cemetery. He was a veteran of the Revolutionary War.

[1] http://www.dragonbbs.com/members/ww8566/SuttonRobertAmbrose Genealogy.html.
[2] http://www.angelfire.com/my/crosleyconnect/master2.html.
[3] Corbly, Don. *Pastor John Corbly.* (Lulu Press, Raleigh, NC, 2008) 73.
[4] Albert, George D. *The Frontier Forts of Western Pennsylvania,* (C. M. Busch, state printer, Harrisburg, PA, 1896) 448.
[5] Walkinshaw, Lewis C. *Annals of southwestern Pennsylvania, Vol. 2,* (Lewis Historical Pub. Co., Inc., New York,1939) 242.
[6] Pennsylvania Archives, Series 6, Volume II, pages 18, 19, 271.
[7] Corbly, 278.
[8] Pennsylvania Archives, Series 3, Volume XXII, page 699.
[9] Leckey, Howard. *Tenmile Country and its Pioneer Families.* Rpt, (Closson Press, Apollo, PA. 2007) 136.
[10] http://www.cornerstonegenealogy.com/greene_county_voter_lists_1801.htm.

EBENEZER SUTTON

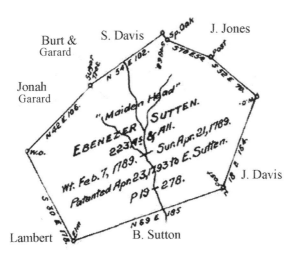

The Sutton family originated in England. At least two names in the family were found in later generations in America. The namesake of Ebenezer Sutton, the present subject, was found in this excerpt from *Ipswich Village and the Old Rowley Road.* [1]

> A wedge-shaped lot between Rowley Road and the road to Muddy River in the village of Ipswich in the town of Suffolk, England, was owned in 1653 by Daniel Bosworth, a cowherd. Every morning he gathered a herd of cows at Mr. Paine's farm and he and his helpers drove the herd up High street and out into the great Cow Commons where they watched them all day, and at sunset they brought them home again. His two daughters were summoned to court in 1675 for wearing finery beyond their father's station in life. After his death his widow, Abigail Bosworth, sold her dwelling and about an acre of land to William Baker in 1702. It was later bought back by Richard Sutton. Except for that brief change of ownership, the Sutton family possessed the land continuously until 1794 when Ebenezer Sutton sold the buildings and the two-acre lot to Jeremiah Day.

The children of Benjamin Sutton Sr and Mary Jennings were born in Somerset County, New Jersey. Their son, Ebenezer (1740-), married (1) Margaret...and (2) Margaret....[2] Not much is known about Ebenezer whereas his brother, Benjamin, left more of a historical trail.

The Effective Supply Tax Rate for Greene Township, Washington County, in 1781 taxed Ebenezer Sutton $45 for 300 acres of land.[3]

Moses Lambert mentioned in his Will, which was signed February 28, 1782, that his land on Big Whiteley Creek was situated next to Ebenezer Sutton, Joseph Frazer, Jonah Garard, Tentha Dudgless, and Francis Baldwin.

Ebenezer, Henry, Nathan, Benjamin, and Stephen Sutton, sons of Benjamin Sutton and Mary Jennings Branch were listed as single freeman in the 1784 Assessment Roll for Greene Township, Washington County, Pennsylvania.[4]

In the Washington County Tax Lists for 1787-1789 Ebenezer Sutton was included in the List of Persons Exonerated on the Frontiers of Washington County for being distressed by the Incursions and Depredations of the Indians.[5]

Ebenezer bought 223 acres called Maiden Head on a warrant dated February 7, 1789. It was surveyed April 21, 1789, patented on April 23, 1793, and recorded in the Washington County Patent

Book P19, page 278.

In the 1790 Greene Township Census Ebenezer Sutton was listed as head of household with two males under 16 years of age and two females. On December 28, 1796, Ebenezer witnessed a land transaction between Elisha and Mary Boyd of Berkeley County to Lewis Wolf which was recorded in the Monongalia Deed Book, Sutton, page 78.

[1] Ipswich Historical Society, *Ipswich Village and the Old Rowley Road.* (Newcomb & Gause, Printers, Salem, MA, 1914).
[2] http://www.dragonbbs.com/members/ww8566/SuttonRobertAmbrose Genealogy.html.
[3] Pennsylvania Archives, Series 3, Volume XXII, page 699.
[4] Leckey, Howard. *Tenmile Country and its Pioneer Families.* Rpt, (Closson Press, Apollo, PA. 2007) 136.
[5] http://archiver.rootsweb.ancestry.com/thread/PAGREENE/199907/093115824

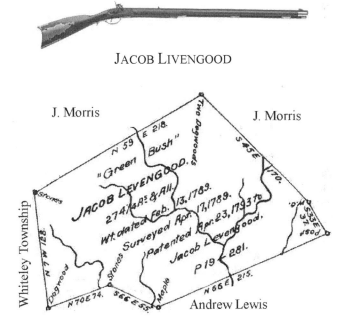

JACOB LIVENGOOD

Peter Livengood (Leibundguth) (1731-1827), the pioneer of an Amish family in America, was born in Switzerland. He emigrated to America about 1750 and lived in Berks or Lancaster County until 1775 when he moved to Elk Lick Township, Somerset County, Pennsylvania. He married in Berks County, Pennsylvania, to Barbara Nafziger. He and a number of other Amish folks united with the Brethren soon after 1783 after which he was called to the ministry. He was for many years a minister of the Elk Lick congregation except that he was a "silent preacher" as he never preached, but always sat in the pulpit and assisted with the services by Scripture reading and prayer. He was a very just and pious man and was noted for his charity and other good qualities that endeared him to his neighbors. He and Barbara were buried on their farm near Elk Lick, (present day Salisbury) Maryland.

One of their sons, Jacob (-1849), owned 25 acres of land in Berks County, Pennsylvania, that was surveyed on February 26, 1759. He later found his way to Washington County. Jacob was a Private for ten months in 1776 in Captain Kuhn's Company in Colonel Kuhn's Battalion of Northampton County Militia of the Pennsylvania Line. He was wounded in his right shoulder by a musket ball during the Battle of Brandywine. He served four tours of two months each in other units. He served his fifth tour in place of his father, again under Captain Kuhn. He served in the Northumberland County Rangers on the Frontier during 1778-1783.

In 1781 Joseph Gwyne, Collector of Taxes in Cumberland Township, Washington County received a notice that read, "You are hereby authorized and required to notify every person in your respective township what their taxes is either personally or in writing as expressed in your duplicate at least five days before the appeal which will be held at the home of Henry VanMetre Esq., Friday 16th of May." Jacob Livengood was one of the persons so notified.

In 1785, as a civilian in Berks County, he received £54.18s.7d. for provisions he supplied to the military.

Jacob was listed in the 1788 Assessment Roll for Cumberland Township, Washington County, Pennsylvania.[1]

He and his wife, Catherine…, were warrantees of 274 acres of land called Greene Bush on February 13, 1789. It was surveyed on April 17, 1789, but was not patented until April 23, 1793. It was recorded in the Washington County Patent Book P19, page 281. They sold it in 1806 and disappeared from the local county records. Their daughter, Catherine Livengood, married James Lucas, a neighbor who lived on a branch of Big Whiteley Creek.

In the 1790 Census for Cumberland Township, Washington County, Jacob Livengood was listed as head of a household with two males under 16 years of age and four females.

(Benjamin Livengood, living in the same neighborhood, was listed as head of household with two males under 16 and one female. He may have been a son of Jacob and Catherine.)

The Nicholas Livengood family tradition says that this Jacob Livengood was a brother of their common ancestor, Phillip (1708-1761).[2]

Jacob was listed on the 1793 Greene Township, Washington County

Tax List.

In 1794 he was listed as a Sergeant in the Muster Roll of Captain William Hill's Company in Colonel George Hutcheson's Fourth Regiment of Westmoreland County Militia which was called out for duty on the frontiers of Westmoreland County.[3]

Jacob had a run-in with the law:

On January 12, 1796, Governor Thomas Mifflin, under the Constitution of 1790, this day granted a Pardon to Jacob Livengood, who was convicted of Forgery in the County of Berks in the Month of May, one thousand seven hundred and ninety one, and sentenced by the Court of General Quarter Sessions to pay a fine of Fifty pounds, one half to the Commonwealth and one half to the party injured—to a servitude of one year at hard labor, fined security for good behavior.

In the 1799 Greene County Tax Book made by Joseph Willford, Assessor, assisted by Elias Stone and Jonathan Black, Jacob Livengood was assessed for 120 acres of land at $95 and three acres of cleared land at $3. In 1800 he was assessed for 60 acres of land at $60 and 30 acres of cleared land at $30.

He was listed in the 1800 Greene County Census as head of a household with his wife, both over 45 years of age, one male between 16-26 years of age, one male between 26-45 years of age, and two females between 10-16 years of age.

He was married to Margaret Chambers in 1803.

Jacob received a pension for his service during the Revolutionary War beginning in 1843 at $33 per year. He died in Conemaugh Township, Indiana County, Pennsylvania. After his death she lived in Indiana County, Pennsylvania, and received his pension.

---

[1] Leckey, Howard. *Tenmile Country and its Pioneer Families.* Rpt, (Closson Press, Apollo, PA. 2007) 134.
[2] Leckey, 432.
[3] Pennsylvania Archives, Westmoreland County Militia, 1790-1800, Series 6. Volume V, page 786.
[4] MacKinney, Gertrude. *Pennsylvania Archives, Ninth Series, 1796.*

THOMAS WRIGHT

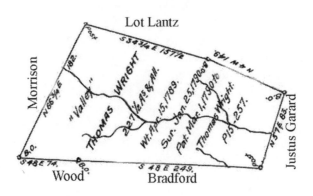

Thomas Wright (1762-1853) was a Private for one month in Captain John Patterson's Company in Colonel James Irvine's Second Pennsylvania Regiment of Foot and received £2.1s. pay. In March 1777 during another enlistment in Captain John Patterson's Company he was paid £1.17s.6d. Shortly afterward, Thomas Wright served as a Private 7th Class in Captain Robert Sweeney's Sixth Company in Lieutenant Colonel Thomas Crooke's Fifth Pennsylvania Battalion.[1]

Thomas Wright married in Philadelphia in 1788 to Elizabeth Northrup (1763-1852). He was then a clerk at No. 142 Market Street. Three days after they married they received their church letter from the Church of Christ at Lower Dublin, known then as Pennepack, in Philadelphia County. They traveled to the Garard's Fort area in Washington County, Pennsylvania, and united by letter with the Goshen Baptist Church. Three of their children were:[2]

    i. Justus Wright (1789-1873) married Rachel Morris (1790-1914), daughter of George Morris and Margaret Corbly, a daughter of John Corbly and Abigail Kirk, his first wife.
    ii. John Foster Wright (1792-1880) married Sarah Corbly (1793-1814), daughter of John Corbly and Nancy Ann Lynn, his third wife.
    iii. Amos Wright (1795-1871) married Amelia Corbly (1796-1855), daughter of John Corbly and Nancy Ann Lynn.
    iv. Elizabeth Wright... m. Henry Morris.

Thomas bought 227 acres called Valley on a warrant dated April 15, 1789. It was surveyed January 25, 1790, patented on March 1, 1790, and recorded in the Washington County Patent Book P15, page 257.

On June 18, 1794, Thomas Wright bought 184 acres called Shewmaker in Washington County from Richard Hall who had originally warranted it on July 31, 1786. It was patented to Thomas Wright who called it Richborough and recorded it in the Washington County Patent Book P22, page 108.

In the 1797 Greene County Tax Book made by Joseph Willford, Assessor, assisted by Elias Stone and Stephen Gapen, he was assessed for 411 acres land at $200, 40 acres of cleared land at $40, three cabins at $3, one barn at $2, one horse at $45, and two cows at $12. By 1800 he was assessed for 327 acres of land at $327, 50 acres of cleared land at $50, one house at $10, one horse at $15, and five cows at $30.

Thomas and Elizabeth were active in the Goshen Baptist Church. Among the entries in the church's Minute Book were:[3]

i. February 24, 1798. Met at Thomas Wright after singing and prayer proceeded to business. Jonathan Morris reported he had talked with Bro John Guthery and rec'd no satisfaction therefore the Church agreed to lay him under censure. After Bro Morris reported he had talked with David Long he confessed his conduct was unbecoming and would attend next meeting but he neglected. Bro Taylor and Bro Mundle appointed to talk with him and cite him to next meeting.

iii. March 30, 1798. Met at Thomas Wrights and after singing and prayer proceeded to business. Abia and Margaret Minor were received by a letter of dismission from Highestown, New Jersey.

iv. February 4, 1802. Church met sung and prayed when Bro Morris layd on a charge against Wright for speaking reproachfully of him to more members seen at last meeting postponed til next meeting.

v. March 27, 1802. Met according to appt and after singing and prayer proceeded to business. The former charge against Bro Wright by Bro Morris brought and Bro Wright could not make good his charge, together for his conduct towards the Church at different times, with that of certificate from Mr Hesten. The Church did unanimously lay him under suspension.

vi. January 4, 1802. Met according to appointment and after singing and prayer proceeded to business. Bro Wright when laying in his charges against Bro Jonathan Morris respecting some dealings between them, the Church upon the whole on both sides unanimously was of the opinion there was nothing in Bro Morris's conduct that ought to break Bro

Wright's fellowship with him, agreed that Bro Morris take his place.

vii. March 24, 1804. The Church met and business between Jonathan Morris and Thomas Wright and left unsettled.

Thomas Wright was on the List of voters of Greene Township who voted at the house of John Campbell on October 14, 1806.[4]

Thomas and Elizabeth Wright were buried in the Garard's Fort Cemetery.

[1] Pennsylvania Archives, Revolutionary War Rolls, Pennsylvania, 2nd Regiment, 1777-1778.
[2] Fordyce, Nannie L. *The Life and Times of Reverend John Corbly. 1953.* (2nd ed., Leola Wright Murphy. Knightstown, Indiana: Mayhill Publications, 1970) 227, 228.
[3] Corbly, Don. *Pastor John Corbly.* (Lulu Press, Raleigh, NC, 2008) App. F, page 273.
[4] http://www.cornerstonegenealogy.com/greene_county_voter_lists_1801.htm.
[5] Fordyce, 228.

MICHAEL BURNS AND ELIZABETH DAUGHERTY

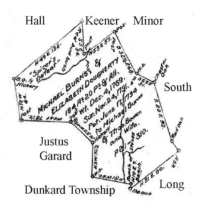

Michael Burns (1754-1808) was born in Pennsylvania and died in what became Sainte Genevieve, Missouri. He married Mary Spicer (1751-1834), daughter of William Spicer and Lydia Johnson, about 1776 in Washington, Pennsylvania. Mary died in what became Bois Brule, Perry, Missouri. Michael and Mary had a son, James, and a daughter, Elizabeth.

Michael enlisted in the Continental Army for the duration of the Revolutionary War and became a Sergeant in Captains Augustin Loseau and Peter Van Rensselaer's Companies in Colonel Livingston's Battalion of Continental Troops during two tours in 1777 and 1778. He received five pay certificates totaling $320 for his service during 1780 through 1783 and served in Washington County's Rangers through 1783.

The 1781 Effective Supply Tax for Greene Township, Washington County, showed that Michael Burns was taxed $69 for 300 acres, two horses, and two cattle.[1]

At the end of his first enlistment he reenlisted as a Private in the First Pennsylvania Regiment of Foot in the Pennsylvania Line and was subsequently transferred to the Third Pennsylvania Regiment of Foot during 1780 to 1783. He received five military pay certificates in 1784 in the total amount of $388. He also served briefly in the Fifth Maryland Regiment of Continental Troops.[2]

Michael Burns was listed in the Assessment Roll in Greene Township, Washington County, Pennsylvania, in 1784. The Greene Township, Washington County, 1789 Tax List of Persons Exonerated on the Frontiers of Washington County for being distressed by the Incursions and Depredations of the Indians included Elizabeth Daugherty and Michael Burns.[3]

Because he had enlisted for the duration of the Revolutionary War, Michael Burns received 200 acres of Donation Land on April 6, 1794.[4] He applied for a pension on January 16, 1832, in Virginia. He said that he had enlisted in Washington County, Virginia. His Pay Voucher showed that he was a Private in Captain Bradly's Company in Colonel Slaughter's Virginia Regiment for nine months which met the minimum six-month requirement. He received a pension from Virginia for $30 per year beginning March 1834 on a Certificate issued in March 1833.[5]

BURNS, BOWEN AND WIFE

William Spicer and Lydia Johnson had four children: Mary (1751-1834), Jobe (1759-1773), Elizabeth (1761-1854), and William Jr (1763-). In June 1773 seemingly friendly Indians massacred the parents, William and Lydia. Mary was not at home and thus escaped death to marry Michael Burns in 1776. Elizabeth and William Jr were taken captive. Elizabeth Spicer was held captive by the Seneca Indians from June 4, 1773, until December 25, 1774. A treaty in 1774 required the Indians to return all captives. Elizabeth was returned to the Garard's Fort settlement on Christmas Day in 1774. William Jr chose to remain with the Seneca Indians and eventually became a tribal chieftain. A few years later

Elizabeth married William Daugherty (-bef1790)[6] and two children were born, Elizabeth Burge and Lydia Hubbs.

The 1789 Greene Township, Washington County Tax List of Persons Exonerated on the Frontiers of Washington County for being distressed by the Incursions and Depredations of the Indians included the widow Elizabeth Daugherty.

Thomas Bowen (1747-1832) came from Parish Llangennech, Carmarthenshire, Wales. He married March 22, 1768, to (1) Agness Crea of Muddy Creek, Greene County, Pennsylvania. They had six children:

    i. George (1769-).
    ii. Robert (1770-).
    iii. Sarah (1771-).
    iv. Elizabeth (1778-).
    v. Alexander (1780-).
    vi. Isaiah (1784-).

Following Agness Crea's death, Thomas Bowen married on October 16, 1791, (2) Elizabeth Spicer Daugherty. They raised their family at Davistown, Washington County, Pennsylvania, on a farm on the west branch of Meadow Run. Elizabeth Spicer Daugherty Bowen and Thomas Bowen were buried on their family farm at Davistown, Greene County, Pennsylvania. Their children were:

    vii. Spicer (1792-).
    viii.Corbly (1794-).
    ix. Mary (1796-).
    x. William (1798-).
    xi. Thomas Jr (1800-).
    xii. Agness (1802-).

Michael Burns, Elizabeth's uncle, retained an interest in the Spicer farm, Spicer's Defeat. Elizabeth then lived with her sister Mary and Michael Burns who became her guardian. The naming of the farm, Spicer's Defeat, indicates that she returned from Indian captivity as a minor of 12 years of age and later gained title to the land (naming it Spicer's Defeat) in 1789 (date of the warrant).

Elizabeth Spicer Daugherty was widowed by the death of her first husband, William Daugherty, who served as the Fife Major in 1777 in Captain John Wendell's Company in the First Regiment of the New York Line during the Revolutionary War.[7] The warrant to Spicer's Defeat was changed into her married name, along with Michael Burns. Then, in 1794, three years after her marriage to Thomas Bowen, the land was patented to "Michael Burns & Thomas Bowen and wife," she being that wife. Changing the title into her husband's name was in keeping with the laws of the time that made a husband the legal owner of all property within a marriage. Michael Burns remained on the title, indicating his interest in the land.

[1] Washington County Supply Tax, 1781, pages 736-740.

[2] Washington County Tax Lists for 1787-1789.

[3] Pennsylvania Archives, Series 2, Volume V.

[4] Pennsylvania Archives, Series 3, Volume VII, Chapter; Donation Lands granted Soldiers of the Pennsylvania Line.
Leckey, Howard. *Tenmile Country and its Pioneer Families.* Rpt, (Closson Press, Apollo, PA. 2007) 35.

[5] Pennsylvania Archives, Series 2, Volume V.

[6] http://familytreemaker.genealogy.com/users/s/u/p/Jim-A-Supan-VA/BOOK -0001/0009-0002.html.

[7] DePeyster,John W. *New York Historical Society, 1915*, (Printed for the Society, NY).

FREDERICK GARRISON JR AND LEONARD GARRISON

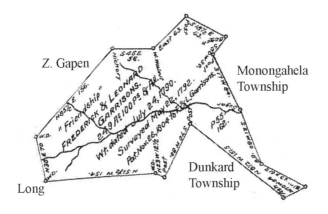

Frederick Garrison Jr (1733-1813) was born in Germany and died in Greene County, Pennsylvania. His Will was probated on June 17, 1813. His parents were Frederick Sr and Elizabeth...Garrison. He married Margaret...(-1813) who died in Greene County, Pennsylvania. Their children were:[1]

i. George (1759-1843) was born in Maryland and died in Greene County, Pennsylvania. He married Elizabeth Long.

ii. Leonard (1760-1819) was born at Frederick, Maryland, and died in Greene County, Pennsylvania.

iii. Jacob (1762-1846) died in Greene County, Pennsylvania.

iv. Barbara (1764-1850 married James Stone. Her death was recorded in the Goshen Baptist Church Minute Book in 1857. She was mentioned as Barbara Stone in her father Frederick's Will found in the Greene County Will Book 1, pages 113-114.

v. Rebecca (1764-1813) married...Foreman.

vi. Dolly (1768-1813) married...Clawson.

vii. Elizabeth (1770-1850) married David Dunham.

In November 1754 Frederick Garrison Jr was appointed an overseer of a road that was planned to extend from the top of Kittocton (Catoctin) Mountain, south of the Potomac River in Frederick County, Virginia, to the Shenandoah Mountain peak in northern Loudoun County, Virginia.[2]

Frederick Jr and his son, Leonard Garrison (1760-1836), lived on Stony Creek near Strasburg in Shenandoah County, Virginia, before settling in Washington County, Pennsylvania. They were among the earliest settlers on Dunkard Creek in present day Greene County, having arrived there from Maryland. Frederick Jr was listed as the head of household on the tax list for Springhill Township, Bedford County, Pennsylvania, in 1772 in what is present day Perry Township, Greene County. He was listed on the 1773 Assessment Roll for Springhill Township, Bedford County, Pennsylvania, and was taxed £2.[3]

In 1784 Frederick and Leonard Garrison were on a Deed (Washington Abstracts, Volume K, pages 5-6) dated September 9, 1785, wherein Joseph Wolford, a farmer in Greene Township, Washington County, Pennsylvania, warranted to Frederick and Leonard Garrison of the same place a tract of land of 318 acres where said Garrisons lived on the waters of Dunkard Creek in Greene Township, Washington County, near the lands of Zachariah Gapen, John Long Jr, Lewis Luther, and Henry Sykes except for 3.5 acres which were cleared by Henry Sykes. Witnessed by Stephen Gapen, Zachariah Gapen and signed by Joseph Willford. Of the original 318 acres, 69 acres were sold.

On July 24, 1790, the remaining 249 acres were again warranted to Frederick and Leonard Garrison and they called it Friendship. It was surveyed on May 22, 1792, patented to them on November 26, 1804, and recorded in the Greene County Patent Book P55, page 162.

Frederick was in the 1789 Greene Township, Washington County, List of Persons Exonerated on the Frontiers of Washington County for being distressed by the Incursions and Depredations of the Indians. In the 1790 Greene County Census Frederick was listed as the head of household with one male under 16 years of age and three females.[4]

In the 1797 Greene Township Tax Book made by Joseph Willford, Assessor, and assisted by Elias Stone and Stephen Gapen, he was assessed for 150 acres of land at $180, 40 acres of cleared land at $40, one cabin at $1, one barn at $2, one horse at $20, and three cows at $18. The next year he was assessed for 150 acres of land at $180, 30 acres of cleared land at $24, one cabin at $1, one barn at $2, two horses at $30, and two cows at $12. He was listed in the 1809 Dunkard Township Tax Book and assessed for 140 acres land at $560, one house and barn at $12, one horse at $20, and two cows at $12.

When Frederick Garrison died in 1813 he left a wife, Margaret, three sons and three daughters whom he named in his Will that was recorded in the Greene County Will Book 6, page 92. The Will was probated June 17, 1813.

LEONARD GARRISON

Leonard Garrison (1760-1819) was born at Frederick, Maryland, and died in Greene County, Pennsylvania. He married about 1785 to (1) Rebecca Gray (1774-). Their children included:[5]

i. Barbara (1775-1816,) married John Nicely.

ii. Elizabeth married George Hoover and moved to Ohio County, Kentucky.

iii. Jonathan (1775-1842) was born in Western Augusta District, Virginia, and died in Butler County, Ohio. He married Mary Sykes, daughter of Conrad Sykes. They moved to Butler County, Ohio about 1803.

iv. Rebecca (1783-1859) was born in Fayette County, Pennsylvania, and died in Hocking County, Ohio. She married George Glosser.

He next married about 1800 in Greene County Rebecca's sister, (2) Elizabeth Gray (1761-1851). Their children were:

v. Lawrence (abt 1803-) was born in Dunkard Township, Greene County, Pennsylvania.

vi. David (1807-1878) was born in Dunkard Township, Greene County, Pennsylvania, and died in Monongalia County, West Virginia.

vii. Daniel (abt 1809-) was born in Greene County, Pennsylvania.

viii. Leonard Jr (abt 1810-1819) was born and died in Dunkard Township, Greene County, Pennsylvania.

ix. Reason (abt 1813-1820) was born and died in Dunkard Township, Greene County, Pennsylvania.

In 1782 Leonard was listed as paying taxes in Springhill Township, Bedford County, Pennsylvania, with two horses and two cattle.[6] That year Leonard Garrison signed the Petition for a New State of Westsylvania to be formed from the present counties of Fayette, Washington, and Greene, Pennsylvania, and Ohio and Monongalia Counties, Virginia.[7]

He was listed in the 1783 Springhill Township Tax Roll, Westmoreland County, Pennsylvania, and was taxed for two horses and two cows.[8]

Leonard was on the 1784 Assessment Roll for Greene Township, Washington County, Pennsylvania.

He was named in the 1789 List of Persons Exonerated on the Frontiers of Washington County for being distressed by the Incursions and Depredations of the Indians.

He was listed in the 1790 Washington County, Pennsylvania, Census as the head of a household with one male over 16 years of age, one male under 16 years of age, and two females.

Leonard Garrison was listed on the 1793 Tax Roll of Washington County, Pennsylvania. In 1797 he was listed as paying taxes in Dunkard Township, Greene County, Pennsylvania. In the 1797 Greene County Tax Book made by Joseph Willford, Assessor, assisted by Elias Stone and Stephen Gapen, he was assessed for 150 acres of land at $240, 45 acres of cleared land at $45, two cabins at $2, one double barn at $2, two horses at $35, and three cows at $18. In 1798 he was assessed for 150 acres of land at $240, 40 acres of cleared land at $30, one cabin at $1, one barn at $2, three horses at $30, and three cows at $18. He acquired land in Dunkard Township and in 1809 was assessed for 100 acres of land at $200, one cabin at $1, two horses at $30, and two cows at $12. In Dunkard Township the following year he was assessed for 140 acres of land at $700, one house and barn at $4, three horses at $50, and one cow at $6.

In 1816 his Will was devised and recorded in the Greene County Will Book 1, pages 208-209. The Will was not probated until March 3, 1821, in Greene County, Pennsylvania, with David Dunham, Frederick's son-in-law, as administrator replacing Leonard's wife, Elizabeth. Leonard's Will was filed March 3, 1821, listing his wife Elizabeth and their children.[9]

In the name of God Amen, I Leonard Garrison of Dunkard Township in the county of Greene in the state of Pennsylvania yeoman being sick and weak in body but of sound mind, memory and understanding...give and dispose...in the following manner to wit;

Item I give and devise unto my son Jonathan One hundred dollars,

Item 2d I give and devise unto my daughter Barbara Nicely Seventy five dollars,

Item 3d I give and devise unto my daughter Elizabeth Hoover Seventy five dollars Item

4th I give and devise unto my daughter Rebecca Blaser one hundred dollars

Item 5th My will further is that all the above gifts and bequests shall not be given paid or become due until my son Reason arrives to the age of twenty-one years or within one year afterwards.

And as touching all the rest residue and remainder of my estate real and personal...I give and devise the same unto my dear wife Elizabeth to be under her orders and control...until my son Reason arrives to be sixteen years old...the profits and produce of my lands and the use of my horses Cows sheep and swine with what money I now have...keep and support maintain cloath, board and lodge and wash for and Sufficiently educate all and every one of my five sons to wit, Lot, David, Daniel, Leonard, and Reason...further that after Reason shall arrive to be Sixteen years old I give and devise unto my five children Lot, David Daniel Leonard Reason...all my estate real and personal...except one third part of my household furniture which I give and devise unto my loving wife and the money which shall be got for the residue of my personal and real estate to be equally divided between my five sons to wit, Lot, David, Daniel, Leonard, and Reason after they arrive to be twenty one years old, and it is my will further that my five sons Lot David Daniel Leonard and Reason [sic] shall be bound apprentices to good trades....

And lastly I nominate constitute and appoint my trusty friends George Garrison and James Williamson both of Dunkard township...executors of this my will ...In witness whereof I have hereunto set my hand and seal this twenty fifth day of March in the year of Our Lord Anno Domini

one thousand eight hundred and sixteen. Leonard Garrison
Signed sealed published pronounced and declared by the
said Testator as his last will and testament in the presence of
us, Jacob Garrison, David Jones, and Matthew Campbell.

When he applied for a Revolutionary War Pension for his service in the
Pennsylvania Militia the Military Records of Leonard Garrison included
this Declaration:[10]

On the 17th day of September 1833 personally appeared in
open court before the Judges of the court of common pleas of
said county now sitting Leonard Garrison aged seventy-three
years who being duly sworn &c. depose and say on oath to
the following declaration in order to obtain the benefit of the
act of congress passed the 7th of June 1832.

That he entered the service of the United States under the
following named officers and served as follows viz: That he
first entered the services of the United States in as a drafted
militiaman at a place called Garrard Fort in Greene County,
Penn, under command of Samuel Swingler in July 1777 for
two months which he served out in guarding defending the
frontier against the Savages in Greene and the adjacent parts
of Virginia and Pennsylvania that a few days after his return
home there was an alarm of Indians and he was called out
again and went under command of Stephen Gapen who left
them shortly after they started and he continued under
subordinate officers to serve against the Indians for
something more than a month say six weeks when they
returned that the next Spring 1778 in May he was drafted to
go to Hannah's town in Westmoreland County under
command of Lieut. Henry Myers that they marched into
Fayette County to a place called Union town here he was
detailed to go with Col. Alexander McClean on to the
Virginia line between Monongalia and Fayette Counties near
the Ohio river that he was out on this service two months
that the next time he went out for any length of time was in
the fall of the year 1778 in September he went out in a party
of which George Garrison had the command and they were
out about six weeks. That after these tours which amount
together to about seven months besides then he was
appointed and selected as a Minute man to be ready at a
moments warning on the frontiers when the savages were
very troublesome constantly lurking about committing

murders and robberies in the settlement that in this capacity he was called out and went on short tours sometimes a week or two and some times a day or two without any particular officers as scouts and as spies it is therefore impossible to Enumerate each tour or the number of them or times of each then he continued to…in the frontier and to serve in the character of a scout or Spy and minute man to the end of the war a space of five years and upwards and he states that upon a…estimate he would be safe in saying that the whole time he served as above mentioned in short tours would amount at least to one year.

i. That he has no documentary Evidence nor does he know of any which to prove his services.

ii. That he relinquishes all claims to any other pension or annuity whatsoever except the present…declares that his name is not on the rolls of the agency of any state.

iii. That he was born in Frederick county Maryland the 5 day of May 1760.

iv. That he has no record of his age it having been destroyed.

v. That he went out as a drafted militia man as a volunteer spy and scout against the Indians.

vi. That his officers were Swingler, Gapen, Myers, McClean, Col McFarland.

vii. That he resided when he went out in Greene County Penna then claimed by Virginia now in Pennsylvania not far from the Ohio where he still resides.

viii. That he has no written discharge.

ix. That the Reverend John Fordyce and John Niceley his neighbors will prove his reputation as a soldier.

His Leonard (LG) Garrison mark.

Sworn & Subscribed in open court Sept 17 1833. E. Hook, Prothonotary.

Leonard Garrison's pension claim number was W.7503. He was placed on the pension roll on December 30, 1833, after his death. His widow, Rebecca, was allowed his pension in June 1839 while she was living in Aleppo Township, Greene County, Pennsylvania. She received $40 per year on Certificate S.5015 beginning March 1848 until her death.[11]

He was living in Dunkard Township when he filed his Will in the Greene County Will Book, Volume 1, page 113.

Leonard Garrison was buried on the Schuyler Garrison Farm in Monongahela Township, Greene County.[12]

[1] http://home.granderiver.net/~rlblack/black1/d920.htm#P2541.

[2] http://archiver.rootsweb.ancestry.com/th/read/GARRISON/199900916963527.

[3] Leckey, Howard. *Tenmile Country and its Pioneer Families.* Rpt, (Closson Press, Apollo, PA. 2007) 127.

[4] Leckey, 159.

[5] *Biographical and Portrait Cyclopedia of Monongalia, Marion and Taylor Counties, West Virginia.* (Rush, West & Company, Phil, PA, 1895)134-136.

[6] Pennsylvania Archives, Series 3, Volume XXII, page 41.

[7] Continental Congress papers, No. 48, Folios 251-256, pages 89-96.

[8] Pennsylvania Archives, 422.

[9] http://listsearches.rootsweb.com/th/read/GARRISON/2007-01/1168230218.

[10] http://files.usgwarchives.org/pa/greene/military/revwar/pensions/garris01.txt.

[11] Revolutionary War, Pensioners, 1835, Greene County, Pennsylvania.

[12] http://www.easternusresearch.com/easternusresearch/cemet/revwarcem2.html.

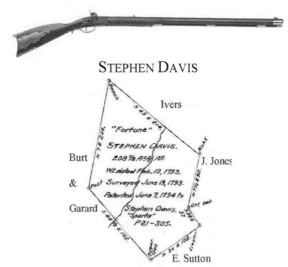

STEPHEN DAVIS

Stephen Davis (1771-1846) emigrated to America during the 1750s. He first lived in Connecticut and then moved to Saratoga County, New York.[1] He married Elizabeth...(-1844) who was born in Horse Neck, Connecticut, and died at Danby, New York. She was a daughter of ...Davis and Elizabeth Thatcher.[2]

About 1782 Stephen Davis signed the Petition for a new state of Westsylvania to be formed from the lands that later became Fayette, Washington, and Greene Counties, Pennsylvania.

Mr Joseph Gwyne, Collector of the Taxes of Cumberland County for 1788, received this notice, "You are hereby authorized and required to notify every person in your township what their taxes is either personally or in writing as expressed in your duplicate at least five days before the appeal which will be held at Henry VanMetre Esq, Friday 16th of May." Among those notified were Robert Crosley, John Daugherty, John Davis, Azariah Davis, and Stephen Davis.[3]

The 1790 Cumberland Township census listed Stephen Davis as the head of a household that included three males under 16 years of age and two females.

He received a patent on April 23, 1793, from William Burt and Isaac Garard for 433 acres called Gath. The warrant was dated November 24, 1786; the survey was performed on February 5, 1787. The transaction was recorded in the Washington County Patent Book P13, page 283.

Stephen Davis warranted 208 acres of land on February 19, 1793, and called it Fortune. On June 19, 1793, he had it surveyed. The patent was awarded to him on June 7, 1794, and was recorded in the Washington County Patent Book P19, page 283.

Azariah Davis and Elizabeth Davis became members of the Goshen Baptist Church in 1801.[4] In 1790 John Corbly Jr, Joseph Martin, John and Jonah Garard, Elias Garard, and Joseph Frazer, departed Goshen Baptist Church at Garard's Fort, Washington County, on two flatboats with their families and livestock and traveled via the Ohio River and the Little Miami River to settle near Cincinnati, Ohio. They founded the Garard-Martin Station in Anderson Township, Virginia Military District. Before 1800 other early migrants to Anderson Township from Garard's Fort included Captain James Flinn, Stephen Betts, Joseph Williamson, Stephen Davis, Richard Hall, and Jacob Bachofen.[5]

On March 29, 1810, Stephen Davis and John K. Day were witnesses to the signing of the Will of George Richter, a farmer in Roxborough, Philadelphia County, (Wills: Abstracts, Book 3: 1809-1811).

He served as a Private in Captain William Stilson's Company in Colonel Wyman's Regiment of the New Hampshire Militia. On July 1776 he was paid £10.6s.6d. He was a drummer in Captains David Smith and Theophilus Monson's Companies in Colonel John Chandler's Eighth Regiment of Connecticut Militia in 1777 and received $7.30/90ths pay.

He enlisted in Captain Benton's Sixth Company of Colonel Zebulon Butler's First Connecticut Regiment of Militia in 1783. He was discharged in May 1783 and received $28.80/90ths pay. He served nine months in the Second and Third Companies of Foot in Lieutenant Colonel Olney's Regiment of Rhode Island Militia during 1782-1783 and was discharged in December 1783.

No records were found to show that he applied for or received a pension for his Revolutionary War service, but he served more than the required six months to qualify.

[1] http://www.hopefarm.com/ulstnew3.htm.
[2] http://www.archive.org/stream/bennettbentlybee00benn/bennettbentlybee00 benn_djvu.txt.
[3] http://www.lindamclark.net/genealogy/familytrees/clark_william_gr.pdf.
[4] Leckey, Howard. *Tenmile Country and its Pioneer Families.* Rpt, (Closson Press, Apollo, PA, 2007) 578.
[5] Corbly, Don. *Pastor John Corbly.* (Lulu Press, Raleigh, NC, 2008) 161.

SEBASTIAN "BOSTON" KEENER

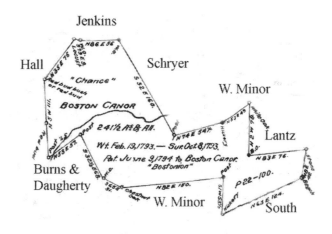

Ulrich Keener, a native of Germany, came to America on the ship Goodwill that arrived at Philadelphia on September 27, 1727. Ulrich took the Oath of Allegiance to the British Crown and moved to the Shenandoah Valley where on February 19, 1746, his petition to "build a water grist mill on ye Narrow Passage Creek near his house" was rejected.[1] Soon after 1773 he left his home in the Shenandoah Valley and bought a tract of land in German Township, Fayette County, Pennsylvania, near the headwaters of Brown's Run.

Ulrich Keener married Elizabeth Ehrehart, but he did not mention her in his Will. He did name in his Will, however, a granddaughter Elizabeth, daughter of his son, John. Ulrich and Elizabeth's children were:

i. Samuel, whose daughter, Elizabeth 1755-1830) was born in Millersville, Virginia, near the Shenandoah River. She married (1) Peter Miller and (2) John Dobbins. She was buried in the Keener Cemetery near Lantz's Meadow in Dunkard Township, Greene County, Pennsylvania, on land that was the original homestead of her brother, Sebastian Keener.

ii. Ulrich Jr (1745-1830) was born in Lancaster County, Pennsylvania, and died in Washington County, Tennessee.

i.   Peter (1750-1837) was born in Lancaster County, Pennsylvania, and died in Knox County, Tennessee

ii.   David (1751-) was born in Shenandoah County, Pennsylvania, and died in Sevier County, Tennessee.

iii.   Barbary.

iv.   John.

v.   Elizabeth "Tacy" Keener Miller.

viii.. Sebastian "Boston" (1755-1826) was born near Narrow Passage, Frederick (present day Shenandoah) County, Virginia, and was buried with his wife, Margaret, in the Keener Cemetery in Willow Tree, Dunkard Township, Greene County, Pennsylvania.[2] Sebastian married Margaret Gilleland (1758-1831), a daughter of John Gilleland. She was born in Fayette County, Pennsylvania, and died in Greene Township, Greene County. She is mentioned in her father's Will of March 21, 1820, and in the Will of her sister, Elizabeth Gilleland. Margaret's children were named in the Will of her sister, Letty Gilleland, who died in Fayette County about 1838. She is buried with Sebastian on their original tract of land. Their children were:

1. David Keener (-1843) who died in Greene County. He married Margaret Long; Margaret Keener; and Peter.

2. Keener who died in Greene County, Pennsylvania.[3]

3. John (-1774).

4. Margaret Jane.

5. Peter.

6. James.

7. Benjamin.

8. Elizabeth.
9. Joseph.
10. William
11. Charles.
12. Robert B.

Just before moving into the Shenandoah Valley, John Keener (1774) one day found himself in trouble at a Council held at Philadelphia on November 23, 1772.[4] Present were The Honorable Richard Penn, Esquire, Lieutenant Governnor; Benjamin Chew, and James Tilghman.

Then was read the Transcript of a Record of the last Court of Oyer and Terminer held in New Castle County, by which it appears that John Keener was tryed for and convicted of Felony and Burglary, and hath received Sentence of Death for the same; but the Governor of the said Court having recommended him to the Governor for Mercy, His Honor, with the advice of the Board, was pleased to order a Pardon to be made out for him also, under the Great Seal of the Province.

The years 1773-1774 did not bode well for John. He escaped the death sentence of the year before only to be killed near the close of Dunmore's War in 1774 by a party of Indians led by Chief Logan and his sub-chief, Snake. George Morris had just returned from that war to Garard's Fort to farm and function as a scout in the surrounding area. While scouting on the day of the Spicer Massacre he, Richard Hall, and John Keener were fired upon by Indians concealed in a thicket. John Keener was killed, but Morris, slightly wounded, and Hall escaped to the fort. They had killed an Indian who was found scalped the next day by Henry Sykes.[5]

John Keener was buried on John Lantz's meadow on Big Whiteley Creek east of Sebastian Keener's farm. In a letter to the Pennsylvania Assembly dated June 10, 1774, Deveraux Smith referred to the Spicer Massacre on June 5 and said that "word has just been received that two men were killed the same day (of the Spicer Massacre) at the site of a fort just lately built on Dunkard Creek." (Garard's Fort on Big Whiteley Creek.) The Spicer farm was located in a valley between Keener's Knob and the ridge between Whiteley and Dunkard Creeks, about two miles east of Garard's Fort and one mile south of Willow Tree.[6]

John Keener's daughter, Elizabeth, married Joseph Price probably in present day Greene or Fayette County, Pennsylvania, since her family was in that area in the 1770s and Joseph and Elizabeth were listed in the 1790 Census of Washington County, Pennsylvania.

The Muster Roll of Lieutenant William Cress' Company under Colonel Zackwell Morgan was found among the General Edward Hand papers in the Draper Manuscripts[7] which proved that Sebastian Keener of Whiteley Creek, Greene Township, Washington County, was enlisted in the Militia of Monongalia County on September 2, 1777, and was in the military service at Fort Pitt on October 1, 1777.[8]

In October 1782 Ulrich Keener of Monongahela County, Virginia, sold some land situated on the North Branch of the Shenandoah River by the Great Wagon Road. The tract contained 300 acres and in addition to the cash involved required the yearly payment of one peppercorn, as was usually stated in a quitclaim, lease, and release deed. This deed, recorded in the Shenandoah County Deed Book D, pages 34 and 35, was witnessed by three of his sons who signed their names Ulrich, David, and Boston Caner. No wife joined the deed; she may have died.

On April 9, 1784, Ulrich Keener made his Will in present day Fayette County, Pennsylvania. The Will, in German script, was witnessed by John and Valentine Overturf, and John Gilleland. It was probated September 13, 1784. The date of this Will dispels the mistaken notion that it was he, not his son John, who was the man later killed on Whiteley Creek in 1774 by the Indians. It was recorded in the Fayette County Will Book No. 1, pages 11, 12. Sebastian Keener and Ehrhart Keener, his mother, received a Bill of Sale for her homestead. He and his brother, Samuel, were executors of their father's Will.

Sebastian was listed in the 1784 Greene Township, Washington County, Tax List as "lives out of the Township," (he had just received the home farm in Fayette County, Pennsylvania). He was taxed in German Township, Fayette County, in 1785 and was included in the 1789 Greene Township List of Persons Exonerated on the Frontiers of Washington County for being distressed by the Incursions and Depredations of the Indians.

In the Washington County Deed Book No.1, page 559, a deed dated December 29, 1792, recorded the transaction from John and Mary Bradford of 98.5 acres of land at a price of £20, it being part of a tract patented to Bradford under the title of Deer Park. The purchasers were Joseph Price and Hannah Keener. Elizabeth and Hannah, John Keener's daughters, in settling their father's business affairs, made a deal for their father's unpaid claim in the land patented to Bradford and arrived at a settlement which gave them a profit. Hannah made her mark on the deed. Elizabeth, the eldest daughter, received £15.2s.2d. On November 16, 1795, Joseph Price joined by his wife, Elizabeth, and her sister, Hannah, sold that land to Michael McCarty for £53. Hannah Keener married Henry Jackson Jr, bore eight children, and died at about 30 years of age.[9]

214

Sebastian Keener bought 241 acres of land in Washington County called Chance. The warrant was dated February 19, 1793. It was surveyed on October 8, 1793, and patented on June 9, 1794. He changed the tract's name to Bostorion and recorded it in the Washington County Patent Book P22, page 100. About this time he added to his land holdings with the purchase of a tract of land from William Minor.

In the 1797 Greene County Tax Book made by Joseph Willford, Assessor, assisted by Elias Stone and Stephen Gapen, Sebastian Keener was assessed for 220 acres of land at $260, 35 acres of cleared land at $35, one house at $5, one barn at $2, two horses at $20, and four cows at $24. The next year he was assessed for 170 acres of land at $200, 35 acres of cleared land at $30, one house at $6, one cabin at $1, two horses at $20, and three cows at $18. In 1800 he was assessed for 170 acres of land at $170, 40 acres of cleared land at $40, one house at $8, one cabin at $1, one horse at $15, and three cows at $18.

Sebastian Keener was buried in the Keener Cemetery, Greene County, Pennsylvania.

[1] Chalkley, Lyman. *Records of Augusta County, Virginia, Original Petition and Papers in Court 1745-1748, Vol.1*. Rpt. (Genealogical PubliShinng Co, Baltimore, MD,1965).
[2] http://www.easternusresearch.com/easternusresearch/cemet/revwarcem2.html.
[3] Leckey, Howard. *Tenmile Country and its Pioneer Families*. Rpt, (Closson Press, Apollo, PA. 2007) 651.
[4] Hazard, Samuel. *Colonial Records of Pennsylvania, Volume 10*, (General Books LLC, 2010).
[5] Evans, L. K. *Pioneer History of Greene County*. Rpt. (Greene County Historical Society, Waynesburg, PA, 1941. Rpt. 2000). 128-129.
[6] Corbly, Don. *Pastor John Corbly*. (Lulu Press, Raleigh, NC, 2008) 100.
[7] Draper, Lyman Copeland. *Draper Manuscripts,* (Wisconsin Historical Society).
[8] Leckey, 28.
[9] Leckey, 649.

THOMAS MILLER

Cumberland Township

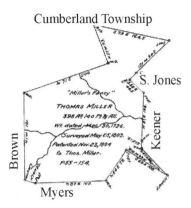

S. Jones

Myers

On April 29, 1763, John Hughes[1] and Thomas Miller[2] (1749-1819), a tavern keeper, both of Baltimore County, Maryland, sold to Reuben Perkins of the same county for £637 part of Miller's Gain which was called Boothy. This transaction, and others to come involving these parties, was recorded in the Maryland Land Records, Volume AL, No. G, page 262.[3] All parts of the sold land were on or near Rock Run Creek "adjacent of the land Thomas Miller is to convey to Kent Mitchel." Margery, wife of Miller, and Jemima, wife of Hughes, relinquished their dower rights. (Margery and Jemima reportedly were sisters).

That sale of land marked the approximate date the Miller and Hughes families departed for Pennsylvania. They first spent some time in western Maryland, from 1763 to about 1768, before joining a group which migrated into the Ten Mile County, that area drained by the Ten Mile Creek, a tributary of the Monongahela River. With others they settled on or near Muddy Creek, a branch of Ten Mile Creek in present day Greene County, but which was then organized as both Monongalia County, Virginia, and Washington County, Pennsylvania. The claims by both Virginia and Pennsylvania caused the settlers living there to refer to the disputed land as Pittsylvania Country.

The lure of Ten Mile Creek was too irresistible for Reubin Perkins. On May 20, 1774, he entered into a Lease Agreement described in the Harford County Maryland Land Record AL, No. 1, Folios 39 and 40, as follows:

Reubin Perkins of Ten Mile Creek and James Horner, Harford Co, MD, lease all that Tract of Land now belonging to him, Reubin Perkins, purchased from Thomas Miller whereon Robert Boner now livith, lease for 12 years commencing April next which will be in

1775, £20 to be paid to Perkins every year until the said 12 years shall be expired. Horner to plant apple trees to number 100 at the expiration of 12 years. Plantation to be delivered up to Perkins at the end of 12 years in as good shape as it was delivered to Horner. Horner to have the bargain til such times as said Perkin's son Ruben comes of full age of 21 if he is not of age at the end of the 12 years. Witnesses: Sam'l Kimble and Sam'l M Fader. Recorded 21 May 1774.

That agreement of May 20 was followed the next day by this agreement:
Rubin Perkins late of Harford Co, MD, on one part and John Hughes, son of William of Harford Co, the other part. Rubin Perkins received £162.10s. paid by John Hughes. Perkins purchased the tract from Thomas Miller, whereon the tavern stands. Miller kept part of the tract by Henry Stump's land and purchased of Thomas Miller to Edward Mitchell's corner also purchased from Thomas Miller. Kent Mitchell purchased of Thomas Miller laid out for 81 ¼ acres. Witnesses: Sam'l Kimble, Ja's Horner, John Ellis. Proven 21 May 1774. Reuben Perkins examined and Sarah wife of Reuben released dower rights. This transaction was recorded in the Harford County Land Record AL, No. 1, Folios 27, 28, 29 and 30.

On July 27, 1774, the Harford County Land Record AL No. 1, Folios 69, 70, 71, and 72 recorded the following:
Conveyance of 198 ¾ acres, part of Harmon's Addition. Reubin Perkins late of Harford Co, MD of the first part and James Horner of Harford Co of the second part. Reubin rec'd £450 for land in Harford Co whereon the Tavern now stands that Thomas Miller formerly did keep which Reuben Perkins did lately purchase of said Miller, land Perkins sold to John Hughs and land he now sells to James Horner. Kent Mitchell purchased of Thomas Miller laid out to be 198 ¾ acres. Witnesses: Sam'l Kimble and Robert Boner. Proven 27 Jul 1774. Rec'd £450 Pennsylvania currency. Came Sarah Perkins wife of said Rubin surrendered her Right of Dower.

Miller served in Washington County's Stockley Rangers during the years 1778 to 1783. In July 1779 he was a Private in Captain Gamble's

Company of the Seventh Virginia Regiment which captured the British fort on the Hudson River at Stoney Point, New York.[4]

He was a drummer in Captain John Ten Broeck's Company in the First Regiment of the New York Line in 1781.[5] Private 8th Class Thomas Miller served in Captain James Munn's Company of the Washington County Militia when it was ordered to rendezvous on June 14, 1782. He received two pay certificates totaling £15.15s. for those tours of duty.

In the 1781 Effective Supply Tax Book for Peters Township, Washington County, Thomas Miller was taxed $118 for 200 acres of land, three horses, three cows, and two sheep.[6]

When he was 70 years of age he said that he did not serve in the Revolutionary War, but did serve out a three-year enlistment as a militiaman with Washington County's Stockley Rangers on the frontiers during 1778 to 1783. He was a Private 1st Class in Captain John Wall's Company in Lieutenant Colonel George Vallandigham's Second Battalion of Washington County Militia that was ordered to rendezvous on March 4, 1782. For some reason he changed his mind about going to the rendezvous. The records revealed that he paid a substitute to go in his place, which was a common occurrence at the time.

> I do hereby Certify that Thomas Sweet hath served as a substitute in the Room of Thomas Miller, the said Miller being in the first Class of Capt. Wright's Company, thirty Days under my Command, Two Days before the Day of General Rendevous Included, said Sweet found himself in provision, and is Intitled to the Militia State accordingly. Given under my hand Camp near Baker's Fort, March 30th, 1782. David Reed, Captain, for Lieutenant Colonel John Marshal's Fourth Battalion.[7]

Thomas Miller bought 325 acres of land on May 7, 1787, in Washington County.[8]

According to Creigh's *History of Washington County, 1870, page 155,* Thomas Miller was among the 18 prisoners sent to Philadelphia on November 24, 1794, during the Whiskey Insurrection. They were held in jail for six months, tried, and subsequently released.[9]

Thomas Miller bought 398 acres in Greene County called Miller's Fancy on a warrant dated March 30, 1796. It was surveyed May 25, 1803, patented on November 23, 1804, and recorded in the Greene County Patent Book P55, page 154.

He was a member of the Quaker Church on Muddy Creek in 1804 and was assessed for one whiskey distillery, one horse, and one cow at $241. Two years later he was assessed with the same, less the horse and cow, at $160.

Henry Rankin was one of the earliest settlers of Smith Township, Washington County, Pennsylvania. On June 15, 1778, he and Alexander McBride purchased from George McCormick 564 acres of land. Rankin sold a small portion of this tract to Thomas Miller on August 9, 1805.[10]

When the War of 1812 was declared Washington County held meetings in the courthouse and when Detroit was surrendered to the British the citizens were spurred to action. The Washington Infantry and Williamsport (Monongahela) Rangers were formed. The Ten Mile Rangers from both Washington and Greene Counties were also organized. Four other companies were recruited in Washington County and Brigade Inspector James Dunlap gave orders for the battalion, composed of the companies of Captains William Sample, Thomas Miller, Edward Thomas, James Warne, and David Buchanan, to march to Niagara where they participated in the battles along Lake Erie.[11]

On June 10, 1819, Thomas Miller stated that John Miller, William Miller, and Guyon McKee enlisted on August 13, 1776, at Peter's Creek near Redstone by Pittsburgh. He was sure of the date because his son John was born the following summer and recorded in the family bible as born on June 17, 1777. He said that he was not himself in the public service, but did serve out his three-year enlistment as a militiaman.

Thomas Miller was in Burgettstown, west of Pittsburg, Pennsylvania, before 1810 where he kept a tavern and where, in 1811, he became its first postmaster. He was also a drover. In 1819, when returning home from Philadelphia where he had been with a drove of cattle, he was taken sick and died. He had resided for at time in Hickory, Washington County.[12]

[1] http://www.ourfamilyhistories.com/hsdurbin/hugh/rowland.html.

[2] http://www.chartiers.com/beers-project/articles/miller-1461.html.

[3] http://littlecalamity.tripod.com/Genealogy/Perkins1.html,

[4] Waddell, Joseph. *Augusta County, Virginia, from 11736 to 1871. 2nd Ed.,* (Caldwell Pub., Staunton, VA, 1902), 267.

[5] DePeyster,John W. *New York Historical Society, 1915*, (Printed for the Society, NY.).

[6] Pennsylvania Archives, Series 3, Volume XXII, page 699,

[7] Pennsylvania Archives, Third Series, Vol. XXIII, pages 198-220. Series 6, vol ii, page 32, 33, 29, and 140.

[8] Egle, William Henry. *Warrantees of Land in the Several Counties of the State of Pennsylvania, 1730-1898, Volume III.* (William S. Ray, State Printer of Pennsylvania, 1899).

[9] Creigh, Alfred. *History of Washington County: From its first Settlement to the Present Time, 1870.* Rpt.(Nabu Press, Charleston, SC, 2010), 155.

[10] http://www.chartiers.com/crumrine/twp-smith.html.

[11] Walkinshaw, Lewis C. *Annals of Southwestern Pennsylvania, Volume 3,* (Lewis Historical PubliShinng Co., NY, 1939).

[12] http://www.chartiers.com/crumrine/twp-smith.html.

STEPHEN GAPEN AND WILLIAM ROBERTS

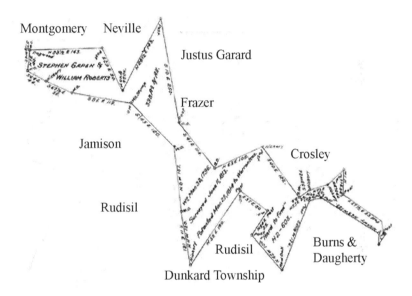

Zachariah Gapen (1733-) married Ruth Tindall (1740-). Their son, Stephen (1761-1838), was born near the Monocacy River in Virginia, a tributary of the Potomac River which empties into the Chesapeake Bay. The river's name comes from the Shawnee name, Monnockkesey, or the "river with many bends."

In 1778 Stephen married Rebecca Snider (1788-) of Washington County, Pennsylvania. They lived in Dunkard Township, Washington County, Pennsylvania, not far from John Snider's farm, Rebecca's family home.[1] In October 1777, a year before marrying Rebecca Snider, Stephen Gapen and his neighbor Private Sebastian Keener, enlisted as Privates in Major James Chew's command at Fort Pitt.[2] Many years later Stephen became a friend to Albert Gallatin, Secretary of the U. S. Treasury under Presidents Jefferson and Monroe, whose home, Friendship Hill, on the

Monongahela River, Fayette County, was a few miles southeast from the Gapen farms.

In 1778 the Fort Martin Methodist Church was organized in a log cabin on land donated by John Snider (1743-1830), Stephen Gapen's neighbor and father-in-law. Bishop Francis Asbury preached there in 1786 and 1788. In a trip to the area in 1804 Asbury stayed at Stephen and Rebecca's home.

In 1782 Stephen Gapen, Josiah Prickett, John Guthery, John Knotts, Jeremiah Williams, and two others were hired as Indian spies in a company of soldiers to work the area around Big Whiteley Creek near Garard's Fort. Another company of soldiers was hired by Colonel William Minor to spy on the Indians on Dunkard's Creek. On one of the scouting trips William Hanna was killed, Amos Morris was wounded, and Richard Hall barely escaped with his life. Major James Carmichael was their Commanding Officer.

In 1785 Stephen and Zachariah Gapen were witnesses at the signing of their neighbor John Long's Will in Washington County, Pennsylvania.

The records of the Supreme Executive Council of the State of Pennsylvania show that on November 2, 1787, Lieutenant Frederick Crow of Washington County was ordered to pay £27.2s.6d to Stephen Gapen, Frederick Crow, William Crawford, Jesse VanMeter, Peter Clawson, and others for their services in spying on the Indians and protecting the frontiers in 1782.[3]

In 1789 Stephen Gapen was included in the Greene Township, Washington County, Tax List of Persons Exonerated for being distressed by the Incursions and Depredations of the Indians. He was listed in the 1790 census for Greene Township as the head of a family of two males under 16 years of age and two females.[4]

On September 13, 1790, Stephen Gapen and Pastor John Corbly witnessed the sale of 250 acres of land on Buffalo Creek by Dorsey Pentecost and Reubin Kemp of the Counties of Washington and Fayette, respectively, for the sum of £200 to Robert Mays of Jefferson County, Virginia.[5]

A tract of land patented by Stephen Gapen on January 6, 1792, as Ripley Valley was conveyed to Zachariah Piles on November 30, 1803. It was recorded in the Greene County Deed Book 4, page 595.

Stephen Gapen, an aspiring landowner, acquired 2,490 acres of land between 1784 and 1795 in Washington County and 400 acres in 1796 in the first year of existence of Greene County, Pennsylvania.[6]

He was a witness to the signing of his neighbor Richard Ivers' Will on January 6, 1793, in Washington County, Pennsylvania. He was also the first Surveyor of Washington County, Pennsylvania. One of his earliest surveys involved the Depreciation Lands which were a large tract of lands appropriated by the Act of Assembly of March 12, 1783, for the redemption of depreciation certificates issued in lieu of pay (merchants would not accept the Continental Dollars) to soldiers during the Revolutionary War. In 1793 and 1794 Surveyor Stephen Gapen made a map of the connected surveys in the territory around the Allegheny River and below the dividing line between the Donation Lands and the Depreciation Lands in Washington County and the adjoining territory in Butler County, being then in his Eighth Surveyor District.[7]

Stephen was one of the most active of the Revolutionary patriots in Washington County. The pension applications of several members of the Revolutionary War mentioned serving with him when their militia units were sent out to intercept the Indians. Along with Colonel John Minor he took an active part in the formation of Greene County and served as one of the commissioners to select a site and lay out the County Seat after which he served a term as the County Surveyor.

On February 9, 1796, a bill passed by the Legislature organized Greene County out of Washington County into a "free and independent county." At Colonel Minor's suggestion, Governor Mifflin appointed Stephen Gapen, David Grey, Isaac Jenkinson, William Meetkirk, and James Seals as Commissioners to procure up to 500 acres of land within five miles of the center of the county, to survey and lay out the same into town lots and sell them, which, together with certain taxes, would enable them to construct a Court House and a prison. Until those conditions were met, the county courts were held at the house of Jacob Kline on Muddy Creek.[8]

Stephen Gapen and William Roberts bought 398 acres of land in Greene Township called Hard to Find. The warrant was dated March 30, 1796. It was surveyed June 11, 1813, patented on March 29, 1814, and recorded in the Greene County Patent Book H2, page 603.

The Greene Township Tax Book of 1797 was made by Joseph Willford, Assessor, assisted by Elias Stone and Stephen Gapen. Stephen was assessed for 4,000 acres of land at $850, 50 acres of cleared land at $50, one house at $10, five horses at $70, and five cows at $30. The following year he was assessed for 4,100 acres of land at $1,100, one hundred acres of cleared land at $80, one house at $6, two cabins at $2, four horses at $40, seven cows at $42, and one sawmill at $20.

He lived in Greene Township, but owned lands inside and outside of Greene Township. On March 10, 1788, he bought 231 acres in Dunkard Township called Hardy. It was surveyed on June 21, 1788, patented on December 22, 1789, and recorded in the Washington County Patent Book P15, page 244. He bought 52 acres of land on November 3, 1789, in Monongahela Township called Cove Point. It was surveyed on June 3, 1790, patented on July 13, 1790, and recorded in the Washington County Patent Book P16, page 344. He obtained another warrant on March 30, 1794, for 263 acres called Thompson. It was surveyed on August 16, 1810, patented June 18, 1816 to George Reynolds, and recorded in the Greene County Patent Book H13, page 684

Benjamin Dye (1752-1788) died in Greene County, Pennsylvania, leaving a wife, Sarah Elizabeth Lemley Dye, and three minor children including a son, James, for whom Stephen Gapen was appointed guardian by the Greene County Orphan's Court on September 12, 1799. All three children migrated to Morgan County and Noble County, Ohio, in the early 1800s.[9]

Stephen was on the list of Voters of Dunkard Township, Greene County, in 1806. The Dunkard Township Tax Book of 1809 showed that he was assessed for 200 acres of land at $800, one house at $20, three horses at $36, and two cows at $12. In 1810 the Census of white households on Dunkard Creek, Greene County, listed Stephen Gapen owning two slaves.[10]

By the time of the advent of the American Industrialization era in the early 1800s, disputes among the pioneers of southwestern Pennsylvania were seldom settled over opposing gun barrels. The courts had taken their place, but were almost overwhelmed by the volume of disputes among the population. One of the leading chroniclers of the court cases was Melba Pender Zinn[11] who wrote about a typical case:

> In 1811 the Monongalia County Court heard the case of Colonel Charles Martin's estate papers, with Executors Major Stephen Gapen and Presley Martin. Among many receipts for various debts against the estate, Gapen signed a receipt for one day of surveying dated August 1800. Another receipt was signed by Gapen for $25 for attending to the estate for 25 days on August 24, 1810. "I hereby certify that I gave Stephen Gapen, executor of the estate of my grandfather, Charles Martin, deceased, a receipt for the sum of $82 which he the said Gapen paid to my father, Jesse Martin deceased. And as said Gapen tells me he has lost the receipt, I hope these lines to have the affect of the aforesaid receipt," undated, signed by Charles Martin.

> William Martin was summoned to answer a Bill in Chancery exhibited against him by Stephen Gapen and Presley Martin, executors of Colonel Charles Martin, deceased, on September 18, 1800. Gapen's complaint was that in 1800, shortly after William Martin returned from

Cumberland River, he asked William what he had done with the notes of Henry Martin and the property that his father sent by him down the river. William said he sold part of the property and left the rest and that Gapen and Presley might go and hunt it, that he would never look after it anymore. He said Gapen and Presley might go and hunt the notes where they pleased. Gapen told William that he expected a receipt from the persons where he left the property and William said "you may go and hunt them," on April 12, 1803. William Martin's answer: Sometime between the years…he rendered sundry services to his father, Colonel Charles Martin. At two different times his father employed him to go to Richmond to pay money into the treasurer as Sheriff of Monongalia County and he found his own horse and provisions both times. This took him eight days in going and eight days to return both times and he was detained five days doing business. He said he did not keep account of his expenses, but considered $2.50 per day for his expenses and $1 per day for labor and horse. Because he had business of his own in Richmond, he believed he should share the costs at one-half value. Sometime in 179…he was employed by his father to collect the land tax and to act for him as Deputy Sheriff and he was still owed $38 for this employment. He continued with a list of monies due him which were listed as being allowed or disallowed.

In the disallowed part of the bill was a total of £1,480 for sundry sums of money and shoes for $45.33); 14.5 pounds of iron for $1.20; and an obligation on Harry Martin which the defendant acknowledged the receipt of in his answer, but didn't state the sun due thereon. Also disallowed was the traveling to Richmond and expenses of $74; one gelding $100; one mare $50; one cow $12; services as Sheriff $38.33; part of the price of Gifford's land $150 and half of Johanna's $24. William Laughlin for making one pair of shoes 5s. and to cash 7s. Martin signed a statement that he would pay the cost of the suit brought by Charles Martin's executors against William Martin and to dismiss and take the suit out of court on 28 September 1810. Presley Martin agreed to dismiss according to the conditions that on March 11, 1800 he received of William Martin by the hands of Presley Martin $383, it being in full for debt and costs on an attachment Bartholomew Clark against William Martin, signed by Arthur Wilson. In addition, the cost of Richard Harrison's three pair of millstones to be converted to the use of Charles Martin on April 27, 1793 signed by William Martin in the presence of George Martin. On April 27, 1799 John Clark sent a note to William Martin saying he could not get any iron, but had pot metal at Geneva and would be in Geneva that evening or next morning and would see him on that occasion. He said he had Gillispie's obligation from Charles Martin. William wrote back and said he would accept the pot metal.

Commissioner William McCleery, appointed by the court, examined the bill and answered the evidence and depositions and determined the following: "William Martin to Stephen Gapen and Presley Martin, executors. To 400 Ibs. pot metal received from William John $5 per $20; to a quantity of ditto rec'd from J. Gillispie $23.33; to one pair of millstones $30; to the amount of an obligation due by Harry Martin and delivered to you to collect $123.17; interest thereon then due $10.24; to your assumption for Rich'd Harrison and to be paid out of the price of his millstones $48; to a quantity of rye for which you gave your note $2; by a note of 15 pounds part of Gifford's land - $50; total $261.74."

In another Monongalia Superior Court case in 1814, John Snider and Stephen Gapen were summoned to answer Michael Core, assignee of Daniel Rick, in a plea of debt for $150.03 with interest and $50 damage on February 10, 1814. A two-month note signed by John Snider to Michael Core for $150.03 with interest dated February 1, 1811, was co-signed by Stephen Gapen and witnessed by J. Martin and W. Ayers. An Appearance Bond was signed by Gapen and secured by James Scott on March 28, 1814. In the September 1814 term, a judgment was entered against Snider and Gapen.

An Act of the Assembly on June 11, 1832, provided relief for John Rau and Stephen Gapen, soldiers of the Revolutionary War. It authorized the State Treasurer to pay each of them $40 dollars immediately and an annuity of $40 payable half yearly to commence on January 1, 1832.[12]

The Declaration of Stephen Gapen, PA S-8545, pursuant to obtaining a Revolutionary War Pension and Bounty Land in the County of Monongalia, State of Virginia, follows:[13]

On this 27th day of August, in the year 1832 personally appeared before the County court of Monongalia aforesaid, Stephen Gapen, a resident of said county, aged seventy-one years, who being first duly sworn, according to law, doth, on his oath, make the following declaration, in order to obtain the benefit of the provision made by the act of Congress, passed June 7th 1832. That he enlisted in the army of the United States in the year 1777 at Minors fort on Big Whitely creek now in Green county Pennsylvania, with Capt. John Minor for the term of six months.

That Capt. Minor, Capt. Pigman, and two other captains were commissioned at the request of General Hand, commander of the army at Fort Pitt, he raise four companies in this part of Virginia and Pennsylvania, that he supposes these companies were called Pennsylvania troops, that he believes that it was in the early part of summer that he marched to Fort Pitt under the command of Capt. Pigman and encamped on Grants hill where we remained a few weeks and then went into the barracks; that he believes that it was in September that an express arrived at Fort Pitt; that Capt. Foreman of the south branch of the Potomac, his son, and 19 others were killed by the Indians about eight miles below Wheeling on the Ohio river. That upon receiving intelligence, he with about 200 of the troops volunteered to go and bury Foreman and his men and we accordingly descended the Ohio in two boats under the command of Major Chew and buried the dead. We then returned to Wheeling where we remained (being sick with measels) about a month, from thence he returned to Fort Pitt where he remained until the end of his term and was discharged. That during the years 1778 and 1779 he frequently turned out as a spy and scout in pursuit of the Indians and was employed in this service at least six months.

That he believes that it was in March 1779 he turned out as a volunteer under the command of Capt. Philips to guard provisions out to Fort Lawrence [Laurens] to feed the men that were suffering there and returned in about one month. That in the spring of 1781 he turned out as a volunteer for six months, at the request of the county Lieutenant James Marshall of Washington county Pennsylvania for the purpose of guarding the frontiers and acting as spies back of the settlements; that he continued in this service six months and two days and returned home, the said Marshall making out our pay roll for which service he received a certificate which he believes he gave to his father. That he thinks it was in 1782 he again went out as a volunteer for three months as a spy in Washington County, Pennsylvania, and served out his time for which he received no pay and furnished his own provisions. That he is confident if he could recollect dates and circumstances more particularly, that he was in the service between two and three years. Tho. P. Ray

I, George Garrison of the county aforesaid being duly affirmed deposes & says that Stephen Gapen & this deponent volunteered for three months & served together & afterwards were scouting together & following the Indians. George Garrison, Affirmed & Subscribed before me 14th May AD 1832, Jas. Garrison.

I, Jonathan Morris of the County aforesaid being duly sworn deposes and says that Stephen Gapen and this deponent volunteered and went to Fort Lawrence on the Tuscarawas River and guarded provisions to the men in the fort who where starving. This was in the month of March the spring after General McIntosh's campaign the year this deponent Cannot now Recollect and they Returned together to fort McIntosh. General Mackintosh Commanded & Col. Broadhead. His (Jonathan X Morris) Mark. Sworn and subscribed before me the 19th day of May AD 1832, David Taylor

Stephen Gapen's pension application was approved on August 27, 1832, and he was awarded a $73.33 annual allowance while he was residing in Monongalia County, Virginia. He died on December 26, 1838, leaving a widow. He was buried in the Martin Church Cemetery in Monongahela Township, Greene County, Pennsylvania. His widow, Rebecca, received his war service pension upon his death.[14]

WILLIAM ROBERTS

Isaac Roberts (1741-) married Agnes Harper (1743-1814), daughter of Robert Harper and Sarah Buzby. Their son, Captain William Roberts (1832),[15] in December 1776 marched his Company of Militia from New Britain, Connecticut, to Philadelphia to receive arms. From there he moved his unit to Trenton, New Jersey, where it joined Colonel Joseph Hart's Regiment of Militia from the County of Bucks, Pennsylvania, and engaged in battle. During that year Captain William Roberts also commanded a company in Colonel McMasters' Regiment in the Pennsylvania Line and marched it from New Britain Township to Amboy, New Jersey. Roberts was commissioned a Colonel in command of the Fourth Battalion of Pennsylvania Militia in Bucks County in May 1777. In 1780 he commanded the Third Company of the Third Battalion of the Bucks County Militia. In 1795 William Roberts was a County Commissioner in Fayette County, Pennsylvania. In 1808 he was a Justice of the Peace in Fayette County.

On March 30, 1796, Stephen Gapen and Roberts warranted 398 acres in Greene County called Hard to Find. It was surveyed on June 11, 1813, patented to them on March 28, 1814, and recorded in the Greene County Patent Book H2, page 603.

In an attempt to prevent the Federal Army from arresting certain Rebels during the Whiskey Insurrection, William Roberts co-signed with Albert Gallatin and others a petition letter to General Washington's representatives in 1794 certifying that the inhabitants of Fayette County would abide by the laws of the state and government.

William was a member of the Hopewell Methodist Episcopal Church about 1830. Two years later he joined the Hopewell Cumberland Presbyterian Church.

After the Revolutionary War Colonel William Roberts migrated from Bucks County to southwest Pennsylvania and settled on a 300-acre farm known as Searight's on the National Road, five miles west of Uniontown in Fayette County. It became a famous stagecoach and freighter wagon station. He was Justice of the Peace for 25 years and died in Menallen Township, Fayette County, Pennsylvania.

[1] http://www.ingenweb.org/intippecanoe/tbios.html.
[2] Leckey, Howard. *Tenmile Country and its Pioneer Families.* Rpt, (Closson Press, Apollo, PA, 2007) 28.
[3] Evans, L. K. Pioneer History of Greene County, Pennsylvania. (Waynesburg, Republican Press, Waynesburg, PA, 1941) 86.
[4] Leckey, 159.
[5] Wheeling Area Genealogical Society, Abstracts of Deed Book No. 1, 1777-1789, (Wheeling Area Genealogical Society, Ohio County, VA. 1789) 23.
[6] Ray, William Stanley. *Warrantees of Land in the Several Counties of the State of Pennsylvania, 1730-1898.* (State Printer, Phil, PA, 1899) 560-562, 631.
[7] Smith, Robert Walker. *History of Armstrong County, Pennsylvania,* (Waterman, Watkins & Co., Chicago, IL, 1883) 429-455.
[8] Evans, 26.
[9] http://www.uh.edu/~jbutler/gean/andrewdye.html.
[10] Waychoff, Andrew J. *Local History of Greene County and Southwestern*

228

Pennsylvania. (Pub, Greene County Historical Society, Waynesburg, PA, 1975).

[11] Zinn, Melba P. *Monongalia County, (West) Virginia, Records of the District, Superior, and County Courts, 1811-1812 and 1814-1820, Volume 8.* Rpt (Heritage Books Inc., Westminster, MD, 2007).
[12] The Statues at Large of Pennsylvania, Laws passed Session 1831-1832, Harrisburg, PA, George Wolf, Governor, 1911.
[13] Pension File of Gapen, Stephen PA S-8,545. Revolutionary War Pension and Bounty Land Warrant Application Files.
[14] *Report from the Secretary of War In relation to the Pension Establishment Of the United States 1835. Pension File of Gapen, Stephen PA S-8545.* Revolutionary War Pension and Bounty Land Warrant Application Files, Virginia Pension Roll of 1835.
[15] Ellis, Franklin. History of Fayette County, Pennsylvania, with biographical sketches of many of its pioneers and prominent men. (L.H. Everts &Co., Philadelphia, PA) 1882.

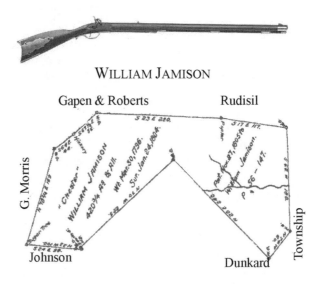

WILLIAM JAMISON

Henry Jamison Sr[1] was born in Midlothian, Scotland, and moved to the Province of Ulster, Ireland, in 1685. He came to Bucks County, Pennsylvania, about 1720 with his sons Henry Jr, Robert, and Alexander. They settled in Warrington, Bucks County, about 1720 and became large landholders and prominent citizens. In 1724 Henry Sr purchased 1,000 acres in what later became Northampton and Warwick Townships and was one of the founders of the Neshaminy Church in 1727. They lived in Warwick Township and in 1734 Henry Sr conveyed the greater part of his real estate to his sons and returned to Ireland where he died.

His son, Henry Jr (1698-) was one of the original trustees of the "New Lights" of the Neshaminy Church in 1743 in the Scotch-Irish settlement on the Neshaminy River. Henry Jr, about 1720, married Mary Stewart (1705-), who was from a large and influential family of early settlers in Warwick, New Britain, Warrington, Plumstead, and Tinicum Townships of Buck County, Pennsylvania. He sailed for Florida in 1765 and was never heard of afterwards. Henry and Mary's children were born in Bucks County:

i. Isabel (1730-) married Tristram Davis.

ii. Alexander (1734-1812) born in Bucks County, died in Greene County, Pennsylvania.

iii. John (1735-) married Agnes Darroch, sister of Captain Henry Darroch.

iv. William (1737-1819) born in Bucks, Pennsylvania, died in Dunkard Township, Greene County, Pennsylvania. He married in 1782 Nancy...who was born (1741-) in Bucks County, Pennsylvania. Their son, John (1783-1861), was born in Greene County and died in Dunkard Township, Greene County, Pennsylvania. William and Nancy are buried in the Robert Cemetery, Dunkard Township, Greene County.[2]

v. Jean (1738-) married Captain Thomas Craig.

vi. Ann (1740-) married Captain Henry Darroch in 1760. Their children were James, who married...Shaw; Margaret, who married William Hewitt; William (1767-1838; John, and George, the last two died young.

vi. Margaret (1742-).

vii. Robert (1748-) married Jean Blackburn.

William Jamison (1737-1819) was one of the witnesses to a land transaction between Samuel NcNabb and Jacob Gabhart wherein on April 6, 1768, NcNabb paid to Gabhart 10s. for 225 acres of land, a part of a larger tract surveyed for Thomas Percy in Beverley Manor, Augusta County, Virginia (present day Greene County, Pennsylvania). Registrar, Jacob Gabhart, Augusta Court, 1769.[3]

He was a Private in 1775 in Captain John London's Company in Colonel William Thompson's Rifle Battalion of the Pennsylvania Line. He was a Private in Captain McMyer's Company in the First Regiment of New Jersey Militia commanded by Right Honorable Earl of Stirling from 1775 to 1776. He served as a Private 8th Class substitute in 1777 in the Second Battalion of Cumberland County Militia, receiving pay of £37.10s. In 1778 he served in Captain McKee's Company of the Third

Battalion and in Captain George McMillan's Company in 1782 in the Lancaster County Militia, according to the Pennsylvania State Archives, Revolutionary War Military Abstract File.[4]

He was listed in the 1781 Effective Supply Tax Roll of Cumberland Township, Washington County, as owning 100 acres of land, three horses, and one cow, all valued at $113.[5]

On May 1786 page 21 of the records of the First Court of Franklin County, Virginia, read:

> Ordered that Robert Sherwood, William Jamison, James Majors & James Beavers, or any three of them, are App'd to view a Road from the County Road leading to Henry C House the Nearest & best Way to David Stewarts on Chestnut Creek & Make Rept to the Court." On page 34 the record read, "A Report of a View of a Road from the County Road leading towards Henry Courthouse & from thence to David Stewart Ret & OR. And that James Beavers & a Gang belonging to his Road Clear the Road from the Road that leads to Henry Courthouse to William Jamison.

William Jamison was listed on the 1790 Washington County Census as the head of a household containing two males over 16 years of age, one male under 16 years of age, and two females.

In May 1790 William Jamison, a Sergeant, drew pay of $6.80 for one month on the Pay Roll of a Detachment of Westmoreland County Militia while employed as a Ranger under the command of Captain Hugh Hammill. At one time he was a Private in Captain Hugh Hammill's party of men of the Third Battalion of the Westmoreland County Militia who reconnoitered the frontiers of the county during May 11 to 15, 1791. For that special duty he was paid $1.80. He drew $8.67 pay from Charles Campbell, Lieutenant of Westmoreland County, for a tour of Militia duty under Captain Andrew Findley in August and September 1792.[6]

In 1796 he bought 420 acres of land adjoining Ligonier's land in Greene County and called it Chester. The warrant was dated March 30, 1796. It was surveyed January 24, 1804, patented November 27, 1805, and recorded in the Greene County Patent Book P56, page 147.

He was listed as a cooper (barrel maker) in the 1797 Dunkard Township, Greene County Tax Book made by Joseph Willford, Assessor, assisted by Elias Stone and Stephen Gapen. He was assessed for 100 acres of land at $20, 10 acres of cleared land at $10, one cabin at $1, one horse at $20, and one cow at $6. The following year he was assessed for 200 acres of land at $40, 15 acres of cleared land at $12, two cabins at $2, one horse at $10, and two cows at $12. William Jamison, of Dunkard

Township, Greene County, was listed in the Will Testators Register in the Greene County Testator Book PA, page188.

The 1800 Greene Township, Greene County Census listed William Jamison as a head of household with one male 16 to 26 years of age, three females under 10 years of age, one female between 10 and 16 years of age, and one female aged 26 to 45.

William and Nancy were buried in the Robert Cemetery, Dunkard Township, Greene County, Pennsylvania.

[1] Davis, William W. *A Genealogical and Personal History of Bucks County, Pennsylvania, Vol.1,* 2nd ed. (Genealogical Pub. Co., Baltimore, MD, 1999).
[2] http://www.familysearch.org/eng/search/frameset_search.asp?PAGE=/eng/ search/ancestorsearchresults.asp.
[3] Chalkley, Lyman. *Chronicles of the Scotch-Irish Settlement in Virginia, Extracted from the Original Court Records of Augusta County, 1745-1800.* (Genealogical Pub. Company, Baltimore, MD, 1999) Volume 3. pages 470-479.
[4] http://www.rootsweb.ancestry.com/~ohross/Military%20Files/charter_members _ofthe_national.htm.
[5] Pennsylvania Archives, Series 6, vol v, page 653, 654, 676.
[6] Pennsylvania Archives, Series 3, Volume XXII, page 698.

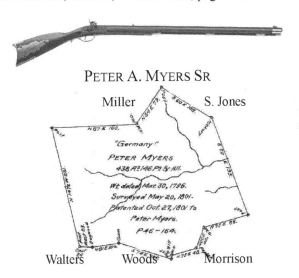

PETER A. MYERS SR

On September 18, 1743, in Bucks County, Pennsylvania, the emigrant Jacob Myers took the oath to become a naturalized subject of Great Britain. The Myers in this sketch descend from him. He was listed in the 1755 Assessment List for Lebanon Township, Lancaster County, Pennsylvania.[1] On January 11, 1777, the Council of Safety in

Philadelphia directed Mr. Nesbitt to pay Jacob Myers £4.15s for his work and drayage for the Continental Troops of the Pennsylvania Line

Jacob Hibbs (1735-1796) was the son of Joseph Hibbs (1688-1762) and Rachel Waring Hibbs. He was born in Byberry Township, Pennsylvania, and died in Greene County, Pennsylvania. In 1760 in Bucks County, Pennsylvania, he married Elizabeth Lacy (1738-) who was born there. Their daughter, Mary Lacy Hibbs Myers (1762-1826), married Peter A. Myers Sr (1760-1820) who was born in the Jersey Colony.[2]

Peter Sr was a wagon master and team clerk in Pittstown, New Jersey, in 1779. In 1780 he served in Captain John McCall's Company in Colonel Benjamin Eyre's Second Regiment of Foot in the Philadelphia County Militia.[3] Sergeant Peter Myers Sr served in Captain Manus Yost's Company in Colonel John Keller's First Regiment of Foot, Bucks County Militia of Pennsylvania, in 1781. For that service in 1781 he was paid $65.60/90 on Certificate 72665A. For service in that unit in 1782 he was awarded $88 on Certificate 72841; both awards were paid on October 15, 1784. Peter A. Myers Sr also served as a Private in the German Battalion of the First Pennsylvania Regiment of Foot of the Continental Troops in 1783.

He came to Greene County about 1784 and became a member of the Goshen Baptist Church at Garard's Fort. The following entries were made in the church's Minute Book.[4]

> i. September 10, 1791: Met at Whiteley to unite again on former order and not admit any member by other order and no member to commune with any other order. Rec'd Peter Myers for baptism.
>
> ii. 1793: Met at Muddy Creek. Trouble between Brother Myers and Jonathan Morris. Bros Henry Crosley, Harrod, Jones, Davis and Charles Anderson heard matter between Myers and Morris.
>
> iii. November, 1793. Met at Muddy Creek Bro Gustin and Banajah Gustin cited Peter Myers worthy of censure.
>
> iv. February 25, 1804: The Church met after prayer and then proceeded to business. The following persons should be excluded: Elijah Moore, Henry Johnson, Jonathan Mundle, Peter Myers, Benassah Guston, Jeremiah Gusten, John Guthrey, David Long. Peter Myers was Excommunicated.

Peter was included on the Assessment Roll for Cumberland Township, Washington County, Pennsylvania, for the years 1784 and 1788.[5]

He bought 49 acres called The Top in Whiteley Township on a warrant dated February 23, 1790. It was surveyed on June 17, 1790, patented on January 6, 1792, to James Flyen and recorded in the Washington County Patent Book P18, page 315. On March 30, 1796, he bought 438 acres of land called Germany at the head of a branch of the South Fork on Muddy Creek in Greene County. It was surveyed on May 20, 1801, patented on October 27, 1801, and recorded in the Greene County Patent Book P46, page 164.

Jonah Garard was an ensign in Captain John Huston's Company in the First Battalion of Washington County Militia in February 1782. He was out on a scouting party on the Crawford Expedition when he was killed. He left a Will which was filed in Washington County on July 2, 1782. Garard's Fort had been built on his land which was warranted October 28, 1785, under the title Garard's Fort. He had applied for the warrant prior to his death or it was taken out by his estate. It was later patented to Peter A. Myers Sr.[6]

Peter was very well off financially and owned thousands of acres in Pennsylvania and Ohio. His holdings in Greene County were over 1,770 acres. Three of his children married Reverend John Corbly's children which suggests a strong relationship between these prominent men.

In Orphans Court Proceedings in 1806 Peter A, Myers Sr and his wife, Mary Hibbs, asked for a partition of Jacob Hibbs' land. It was recorded in the Open Court Docket 1, page 88. Jacob and Mary Hibbs were buried in Greene County. The children of Mary Hibbs and Peter A. Myers Sr were:[7]

i. Jacob (1780-1862), who died in Savannah, Ohio. In 1800 he married Mary Corbly (1785-1864), first child of Pastor John Corbly and Nancy Ann Lynn. He became a Baptist minister in Greene County, Pennsylvania, and then moved from Garard's Fort to Savannah, Ohio, in 1829 where they raised eight children.

ii. Sarah (1786-1808) married William Bailey.

iii. Peter A. Myers Jr (1787-1880) was born in Greene County, Pennsylvania. In 1805 he married Pleasant Corbly (1789-1860), third child of Pastor John Corbly and Nancy Ann Lynn, and they raised 14 children, 11 of whom lived to adult age. They lived and raised their children on the Jonah Garard farm his father had bought.

iv. Phoebe Myers (1794-1890) born in Greene County, Pennsylvania, died in Preston County, Wyoming. She married Charles Boyles.

v. John Myers (1795-1865), born in Greene County,

Pennsylvania, in 1865 married Orpha Gregg (1780-1869).

vi. Mary Myers (1796-1870) born in Greene County, Pennsylvania, married Justus Eakin (1784-1869). They had 10 children. Justus was a cooper by trade. They moved to the farm at Jollytown at the age of 50 to land inherited from his wife's father, Peter Myers. He was buried in Gilmore Township, Greene County, in the Eakin Cemetery He was a veteran of the War of 1812.

vii. Joseph (1797-1878), born in Greene County, Pennsylvania, married (1) Mary Gregg who died at Garard's Fort and (2) Ester Bennett. He is buried in the Riverside Cemetery at Riverside, Ohio.

viii. Elizabeth (1798-) born in Greene County, Pennsylvania, married Andrew Corbly, son of Pastor John Corbly and Nancy Ann Lynn. They moved to Tyler County, West Virginia.

In 1803 John Corbly died. Peter A. Myers Sr's bill for 24 days spent in administering his estate was $24. Other legacies were:

Sarah Corbly her legacy	$80
Joseph Gregg & Cassandra his wife	$80
Peter A. Myers Jr and Pleasant his wife	$80
Amos Wright and Amelia his wife	$80
Jacob Myers and Mary his wife	$80

Shares of books to Justice Garard & Jacob Myers were not valued.

Peter A. Myers Jr was included on the list of voters of Greene Township who voted at the house of John Campbell on October 14, 1806. He received warrants for 20 acres of land surveyed in 1820 and 180 acres surveyed in 1827.[8]

He was living in Morgan Township when he filed his Will in the Greene County Will Book, Volume 1, page 379.

[1] Egle, William H. *History of the counties of Dauphin and Lebanon, in the Commonwealth of Pennsylvania.* (Unigraphic, Inc., Woburn, MA, 1977).

[2] Fordyce, Nannie L. *The Life and Times of Reverend John Corbly.* 1953. 2nd ed., (Leola Wright Murphy. Knightstown, Indiana: Mayhill Publications, 1970). Pennsylvania Archives, Series 6, Volume I, page 154.

[3] Pennsylvania Archives, Series 6, Volume I, page 154.

[4] Corbly, Don. *Pastor John Corbly.* (Lulu Press, Raleigh, North Carolina, 2008) Appendix F, page 273.

[5] Leckey, Howard. *Tenmile Country and its Pioneer Families.* Rpt, (Closson Press, Apollo, PA. 2007) 132, 134.
[6] Leckey, 642.
[7] Fordyce, 174.
[8] Pennsylvania Archives, Series 3, Volume XXVI.

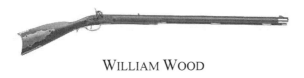

WILLIAM WOOD

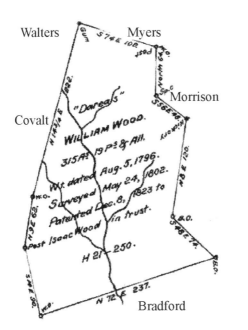

William Wood (1754-1801) married Dorcas…(1749-1821) in Washington County, Pennsylvania. A soldier in the Revolutionary War, he settled on the Mount Morris road about six miles south of Waynesburg in 1775 and became prominent in the early history of Greene County. William and Dorcas were buried in the Garard's Fort Cemetery in Green County, Pennsylvania. Their children were:[1]

i. Isaac (1785-) married Elizabeth….
ii. Eleanor married William Morris and moved to Indiana.
iii. Nancy married…Brown and moved to Muskingham County, Ohio.

iv. Rachel (1792-) married before 1824 to Henry Jacobs and lived in Greene County, Pennsylvania. They were buried in the Jacobs Cemetery in the Smith Creek-Fairhall area of Greene County.

v. Susannah married Nathan Veach and moved to Knox County, Ohio.

vi. Elizabeth married Samuel McCarty and moved to Muskingham County, Ohio.

vi. William Jr (1796-) married Mary Bowen.

vii. Daniel (1790/1794-) married Rebecca...

viii. John (1797-1868), born and died in Greene County, Pennsylvania, married Sarah Jane Hunt (1801-1883

John Corbly and William Wood were close friends and associates in the Goshen Baptist Church at Garard's Fort and in the Redstone Baptist Association which was organized at the Redstone Fort in present day Brownsville, Pennsylvania. It was the first Baptist Association west of the Allegheny Mountains. Pastor John Corbly, generally recognized as the founder of the Redstone Baptist Association, was elected its moderator at its first meeting and William Wood was elected clerk. Fourteen messengers representing their churches met at the Goshen Baptist Church in Garard's Fort on October 7, 1776, to inaugurate this new Association and establish its rules. Six churches were represented at this meeting of the Redstone Association. Among them were Pike Run in the township of that name, but now extinct, represented by William Wood and David Ruple.

The Association's first meeting was held at the Goshen Baptist Church five years before the Redstone Presbytery of the Presbyterians held its first meeting at Pigeon Creek. Two of the six churches west of the Monongahela River in then Washington County were the Goshen Baptist Church at Garard's Fort represented by Pastor John Corbly, John Garard, and Jacob VanMeter; and the Forks of Yough Baptist Church at Peters Creek in present day Library, Allegheny County, represented by Samuel Luellen and John McFarland.

They traveled together when preaching in the outlying areas around Garard's Fort. Preacher William Wood was said to have been the god-father for Isaiah, John's son with his second wife, Betsey.[2]

In 1775 Reverend William Wood was licensed to preach. He replaced Reverend James Sutton Jr as pastor of the North Ten Mile Baptist Church which was located 24 miles north of Garard's Fort. His first recorded baptism was early in 1776. Reverend James Sutton Jr was the subject in February of this significant entry in the church's Minute Book: "After divine service James Sutton Jr was excommunicated, his crime being drunkenness and profane swearing." The North Ten Mile Baptist Church was the first of any denomination organized in Washington County. It became in 1776 one of the constituent members of the Redstone Baptist Association. The minutes of that body read:[3]

> 1st. The introductory sermon was preached by Mr. James Sutton from these words, "The Angel of the Church," wherein the duty of the messenger was clearly exhibited.
>
> 2d. Proceeded to business. Brother John Corbly was chosen moderator and William Wood clerk.
>
> 3d. A request from Cross Creek for the constitution of a church granted and Brothers John Corbly and William Wood appointed to officiate in constituting the said church.

In the 20 years leading up to the Revolutionary War, Virginia and Pennsylvania increasingly fought over the ownership of the land west of the Allegheny Mountains. Pennsylvania believed that Virginia was encroaching on lands given to William Penn in his charter. Virginia claimed that their charter, awarded a hundred years earlier, included the lands Pennsylvania claimed. The settlers who lived in this contested land wanted resolution and petitioned to have this land, previously referred to as Pittsylvania Country, made into a new Colony of Westsylvania. In 1776, after land speculators had greatly increased the price of land in the proposed new state of Westsylvania, William Wood added his name to the list of petitioners who wanted to remain in the Colony of Virginia.[4]

The Redstone Baptist Association records stated that the Cross Creek Baptist Church in present day Brooke County, West Virginia, 60 miles northwest of Garard's Fort, was organized by Pastor John Corbly and his close friend and neighbor, Pastor William Wood, in 1776. Each of them preached there shortly after its founding.

The Redstone Baptist Association records show that in 1778 it met at the Goshen Baptist Church. Pastor Corbly, his church's messenger, was chosen to be the clerk of the annual Association meeting. At the meeting John Corbly, William Wood, and John Whittaker of the Goshen Baptist Church were chosen by the Association to "examine" William Taylor, an aspiring minister of the Cross Creek Baptist Church, to determine whether his talents to become the pastor over that church warranted him being ordained to preach.[5]

In 1780 the Shirtee (Chartier) congregation requested from the Redstone Baptist Association that a constitution be devised for a Baptist Church in their community. The Association resolved that Elders William Wood and John Corbly attend there the Saturday before the fourth Sabbath in October and comply with their request. Shirtee (Chartiers Township, but pronounced "Shirtee" by the locals) was 12 miles north of Garard's Fort.[6]

William Wood was listed in the 1781 Effective Supply Tax Book for Greene Township, Washington County, and was assessed for 300 acres of land valued at $15. He also was taxed $22 for two horses, three cows, and four sheep in Fallowfield Township, Washington County.[7]

William Wood was a Private 6th Class in Captain Joseph Cisnas' Fifth Company in Lieutenant Colonel Vallandigham's Second Battalion of the Washington County Militia when it was ordered to rendezvous on June 14 and September 16, 1782.[8]

On October 2, 1784, the Redstone Baptist Association met at Muddy Creek. Among the churches represented was the Pigeon Creek Baptist Church pastored by Reverend William Wood. He was included on the Assessment Roll for Greene Township, Washington County, Pennsylvania in 1784.[9] He was on the 1789 Greene Township List of Persons Exonerated on the Frontiers of Washington County for being distressed by the Incursions and Depredations of the Indians.

William Wood obtained a grant of 315 acres of land from the State of Pennsylvania in the Whiteley Creek area in Washington County, Pennsylvania. The land grant was called Dorcas and was warranted on August 5, 1796. It was surveyed May 24, 1802, patented on December 8, 1823, in trust to his son, Isaac Wood, and was recorded in the Greene County Patent Book H21, page 250.

In the 1797 Greene County Tax Book made by Joseph Willford, Assessor, assisted by Elias Stone and Stephen Gapen, William Wood was assessed for 400 acres of land at $400, 35 acres of cleared land at $35, one house at $10, one barn at $2, one horse at $15, and two cows at $12. The next year he was assessed for 300 acres of land at $50, 20 acres of cleared land at $16, one cabin at $1, and six cows at $36. In 1799 his assessment was for 300 acres of land at $120, 20 acres of cleared land at $20, one cabin at $1, and five cows at $30.In 1800 he was assessed for 300 acres of land at $240, 40 acres of cleared land at $40, one cabin at $1, and five cows at $30.

William Wood's Will was filed in the 1801 Greene County Will Book, Volume 1, page 58. He died on December 2, 1801. John Corbly and Jonathan Morris appraised his estate at a value of $376.35. After the deaths of John Corbly and William Wood, his son William Jr, ministered at the Goshen Baptist Church and the Muddy Creek Baptist Church in the early 1800s. Dorcas died on October 12, 1821. They were buried in the Garard's Fort Cemetery.[10]

[1] http://www.ourfamilyhistories.com/hsdurbin/huffman/wood2Outline.html.
[2] Corbly, Don. *Pastor John Corbly.* (Lulu Press, Raleigh, NC, 2008) 116, 121.
[3] Crumrine, Boyd. *History of Washington County, Pennsylvania* …(L.H. Everts, Pub., Chicago, Philadelphia, 1882) 652-672.
[4] Leckey, Howard. *Tenmile Country and its Pioneer Families.* Rpt, (Closson Press, Apollo, PA. 2007) 164.
[5] Corbly, 122, 134.
[6] Corbly, 138.
[7] Pennsylvania Archives, Series 3, Volume XXII, page 699.
[8] Pennsylvania Archives, Series 6, Volume II, page 69.
[9] Leckey, 136.
[10] http://www.findagrave.com.

JOHN WALTER

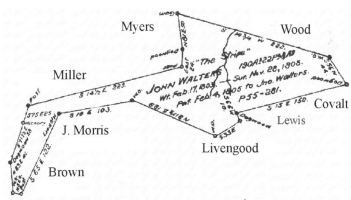

JOHN WALTER TO OWEN BIDDLE, 1777.[1]

Sr.,

I have a quantity of Crude Sulpher to refine for y[e] Hon. Councile of Safety; under a notion that y[c] price of Wood woud fall, I did not lay in a sufficient quantity; owing to the unexpected distraction of the times there is none now to be purchasst at any price; unless I can get a supply 1 must stop my Work. There is a Wood near iny House

that supplys the Barracks, and where I am inform'd I may supply myself, provided I have an Order from the Councile of Safety for that purpose. I beg you will furnish me -with such an order; my own Servants will cutt it down and I am willing to pay any reasonable price for the Wood. I am, S^r, Your most Humble Serv, JOHN WALTER.
Spring Gardens, 14th Jan., 1777.
To Mr Owen Biddle, Prest.

In 1781 the Effective Supply Tax Rates for Cumberland Township, Washington County, assessed John Walter, a single man, $10 for one horse.[2] Private John Walter served in Captain Hugh McAlister's Company (Flying Camp), Cumberland County Militia, from August to October 1781.[3]

In 1782 at Fort Pitt, General Irvine advised the Council of Safety in Philadelphia by letter that he was "raising a volunteer expedition to move against the Indian settlement at Sandusky to atone for their savagery at Muskingum against the Moravians." Most volunteers came from Uniontown and Georges Creek in Westmoreland County and from Redstone in Washington County. The Washington County contingent met at Redstone Old Fort and proceeded northwesterly adding to their numbers by more volunteers from the settlements at Ten Mile and Catfish (present day Washington). The expedition reached its rendezvous point on the east side of the Ohio River opposite of the town of Mingo Bottom. It then numbered 480 armed men including John Walter. Colonel Crawford was its commander. The force was ultimately defeated and Colonel Crawford was burned at the stake.[4]

Henry and Catherine Stotler's daughter, Catherine, married John Walter (1764-1830) in 1792.[5] Their children were:

i. Elizabeth (1793-) married John Rodney.
ii. George (1795-).
iii. Barbara (1797-) married James Jones.
iv. John (1801-).
v. Mary (1803-) married ...Reed.
vi. Philip (1807-).

In the 1797 Greene County Tax Book made by Joseph Willford, Assessor, assisted by Elias Stone and Stephen Gapen, John Walter was assessed for 150 acres of land at $100, 30 acres of cleared land at $30, one house at $5, one barn at $2, one horse at $10, and three cows at $18. In the 1800 Tax Book he was assessed for 130 acres of land at $120, 40 acres of cleared land at $40, one house at $10, two cabins at $2, one horse at $15, and three cows at $18.

John Walter bought 190 acres called The Stripe on a warrant dated February 17, 1803. It was surveyed November 28, 1803, patented on February 4, 1805, and recorded in the Greene County Patent Book P55, page 281. On February 4, 1805, the Commonwealth of Pennsylvania granted 90 acres of land in Greene County, to John Walter who then granted it by deed to Nicholas Livengood on April 4, 1807. The transaction was recorded in the Greene County Deed Book 8, page 558.

In his application for a pension John Walter submitted a Declaration.[6] In it he stated, "he was married to Catharine. He enlisted in 1782 in Captain Parker's Company of the Fourth Pennsylvania Regiment commanded by Colonel Butler. He was later transferred to the Third Regiment under another Colonel Butler (a brother) from which he was discharged in 1783." He was living in Westland Township, Guernsey County, Ohio, when he applied for the pension. He listed property valued at $3,555.56. The law governing a citizen of Ohio required that the applicant could have no property for support and that he be aged in years. He received 200 acres of Donation Land for his service as a Private in the First Pennsylvania Regiment during the Revolutionary War.

The Pension Board's record for John Walter stated that he was born in Berks County, Pennsylvania, the son of Anthony Walter. He enlisted in Bedford, Pennsylvania, in 1780 and served nine months as a Private in Captain Joseph Erwin's Company in Colonel Broadhead's Pennsylvania Regiment which fought in the campaign against the Muncy Indians and also participated in a battle near Hickory Town. After his service he lived with his father near Hannastown, Pennsylvania, until he married Catherine...in September 1792 and moved to Washington County, Pennsylvania, where he remained two years. Then he moved to Allegheny County, Pennsylvania, living there eight years in St. Clair Township, then in Pine Township, both in Allegheny County.

He was allowed a pension of $96 per annum on an application submitted April 2, 1833, when he resided in Pine Township at age 75. After his death in Allegheny County on March 30, 1830, his widow, Catherine, applied for a widow's pension based on his service. She was allowed a pension of $40 per year on her application dated October 18, 1839, when she was living in Adams Township, Coshocton County, Ohio. She stated that without his pension she would live out her years in "wretched poverty." She said that they married in 1792 and their first child was born in 1793. In 1839 she lived in Adams Township, Coshocton County; in 1843 she lived in Newcomerstown, Tuscarawas County, Ohio. She stated that their children were Elizabeth, George, Barbara, John, Mary, and Philip.

[1] Pennsylvania Archives, Series 1, Volume V, 1777, page 182.

[2] Pennsylvania Archives, Series 3, Volume XXII, page 699.

[3] Pennsylvania Archives, Series 3, Volume XXIII.

[4] Ellis, Franklin. *History of Fayette County, Pennsylvania...1882.* (L.H. Everts & Co., Philadelphia).

[5] Jordan, John W. Genealogical and personal history of western Pennsylvania Vol. 3. (Lewis Historical Pub. Co., New York, 1915.).

[6] Pennsylvania Archives, Revolutionary War Pensions, John Walter.

On Thursday, June 9, 1803, at the age of seventy years, three months, and twelve days, Pastor John Corbly was at home preparing to attend the next Redstone Baptist Association's meeting. A sudden sickness overwhelmed him and he became violently ill. There is no mention in existing records that he had a recurring illness; on the contrary, records indicated that he was in robust health throughout his life.

The sudden sickness was very severe, unexpected, and of short duration. Nancy Ann was at his side and his near-by children Margaret, Rachel, Andrew, Pleasant, Cassandra, Sarah, Amelia, and William were quickly summoned. Word was sent to Garard's Fort and his brethren hurried to his home. Sensing that his end was nearing, he spoke to them from his bed of the Lord's work as he was able and asked for his hymnbook. He read a verse and tried to sing, but he suddenly expired as if he had been summoned.

It was said at the time of his death that "Elder Corbly died in the prime of life and apparent usefulness. He was much esteemed as a man and a preacher. In person he was a large and fine looking man, with a countenance expressive of great amiability."

As was the custom, his body was most certainly prepared by Nancy Ann and her oldest daughters for viewing at the home on Friday and Saturday.

Word of John's death spread rapidly throughout Greene County and the adjacent counties. Riders were dispatched to many of the churches where he had so often preached and where he had so many old friends.

The funeral ceremony was held on the following Sunday at the Goshen Baptist Church. By one account the service had to be conducted outside to accommodate the over-flow crowd. Reverend Edgar David Phillips, pastor of the Peter's Creek Baptist Church, based his funeral sermon on Revelations XIV, 13: *Blessed are the dead which die in the Lord from henceforth: Yea, saith the Spirit, that they may rest from their labours; and their works do follow them.*

Pastor Corbly's burial was attended by a large assembly of saddened relatives and sorrowing followers mourning their irreplaceable loss. Led by the Reverend Phillips the cortege followed the wagon carrying John to the adjacent cemetery. His immediate family was followed by many of the church members he had ministered to for so many years. Several of the preachers and elders of the many churches he had organized over the years completed the long line of mourners.

The epitaph on his tombstone expressed most vividly his ultimate triumph over the inevitable enemy: *Oh death, thou has conquered me, I by thy darts am slain. Jesus Christ will conquer thee, Then, I shall rise again.*

Pastor Corbly's body lies near the entrance at the west end of Garard's Fort Cemetery between his second wife, Elizabeth (Tyler) with their massacred children, and his third wife, Nancy Ann (Lynn) who died August 1, 1826.

Nancy Ann lived her remaining 23 years in their home with her children. Andrew Lynn was the oldest at 16 years of age and in five years would marry Elizabeth Myers. Pleasant was then 14 years of age and would marry Peter A. Myers Jr in two more years. Cassandra was 12 years old and would marry Joseph Gregg in 1810. Sarah was 10 years old and would marry John Foster Wright in 1813. Amelia was seven years old and would marry Amos Wright, John Foster's brother, in 1814. Nancy, born in 1798, died suddenly in an accident at the family home the same year her father died, in 1803. That must have been doubly hard on Nancy Ann, her mother. William was the baby of the family, then only two years old. In 1823 he would marry Rebecca Stephens.

In the 1810 United States Census, Nancy was listed as head of the family along with one male aged under 10 (William, 9), one female aged between 10-16 (Amelia, 14), two females between 16-25 (Sarah, 17, and Cassandra, 19), one female between 26-45 (Mary or Pleasant may have been visiting), and one female over 45 (Nancy, 49). Nancy had her hands full raising these children for the next several years. The last one, William, did not marry until 20 years after his father died. Nancy was then 61 years of age and lived but three more years before she died in 1826.

After Nancy's death, William sold the family home at Garard's Fort and moved to Athens County, Ohio, in 1837.

Nancy Ann probably would have known these families who bought land warrants in Greene Township after John's death.

WILLIAM BROWN JR

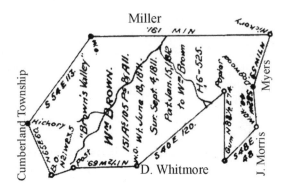

William Brown Sr (1725-1781) was born in Scotland and died in Greene County, Pennsylvania. He married Mary Daily (1730-) and they came to Pennsylvania when he was 18 years old along with his brother, Mathew. William and Mary settled on land where present day West Waynesburg now stands. William Brown Sr was buried in the Green Mount Cemetery at Waynesburg, Greene County, Pennsylvania. Mary was buried in Ohio. William and Mary's children were: [1]

i. Mary.

ii. James.

iii. Catherine married Asa McClelland in Pennsylvania. Their six children were born in Greene County: Nancy, Elizabeth, Mary, Mariah, Dawson, and Asa Jr.

iv. Matthew immigrated with his parents.

v. William Jr (abt 1750 -) was born in Greene County, Pennsylvania, and moved with his family to Ohio about 1817.

vi. John Brown (abt1750-1828) born in Greene County, Pennsylvania, died in Vermillion County, Illinois. He married Jane Hurley and had children Mary, Zachariah, Sarah, Nancy, Nellie, and William.

vi.Vincent_(abt1755-) married in 1775 to Sarah Corbell and had eight children: Hannah, Elizabeth, Martha, Lucy, Peter, Vincent Jr, Molly, and Joanna.

vii. Sarah Elizabeth (1769-) was born in Shippensburg, Pennsylvania. She was 15 years of age when her father was killed by the Indians in 1779. In July 1784 she was married to James Seal, a blacksmith, by Pastor John Corbly. On March 29, 1785, James Seal bought the Brown farm, Brown's Run, from William Brown Jr and Vincent Brown, sons of the deceased William Brown Sr, and recorded the transaction in the Washington County Deed Book 1-B-61-62 and Deed Book 1-1-533. Captain James Seal lived there until he died in 1832. His widow lived there until her estate was settled in 1847. Sarah and James had 13 children: William, James Jr, John, Samuel, Sarah, Charlotte, Martha, Matilda, Mary, Catherine, Joseph, Barbara, and Vincent.

In 1772 William Brown Sr was listed in the Tax Rolls of Spring Hill Township, Washington County.

He served in the Revolutionary War as a Private in the Bedford County's Third Regiment of the Pennsylvania Line. Private 5th Class William Brown served in Captain John Hamilton's Company, a Flying Camp, of the Cumberland County Militia in October 1777. Private 3rd Class William Brown served in Captain James Munn's Company in the Second Battalion of the Washington County Militia when it was ordered to rendezvous on April 18, 1782. He also served with Stockley's Rangers on the frontier during 1778. For his service, he received 200 acres of Donation Lands.[2]

He was listed on the Assessment Roll for Greene Township, Washington County, Pennsylvania, in 1784.

William Brown Sr and his neighbor, Simon Rinehart, agreed to exchange their lands and were killed in an Indian ambush while moving their belongings from one farm to the other. Harrod Newland, one of the men called out to follow the marauding Indians, said that the incident occurred about 1779 and that William Brown Sr, William English, John Owens, and another man were killed at their sugar camp as they were preparing to take their kettles home. Vincent and Mathew, sons of William Brown, escaped to reach home and spread the alarm. The massacre site on William Brown Sr's farm was designated on early maps as "Brown's Run," but later was known as "Bloody Run" or "Toll Gate Run." The transfer of land by William Brown Sr and Simon Rinehart was not achieved by the heirs of William Brown until several years later.[3]

William Brown Jr (abt 1750 -) became a member of the Goshen Baptist Church prior to 1792. The following entries were in the church's Record Book.[4]

i. March 1792, Sat. Met at Muddy Creek. William Brown and

Anna his wife rec'd for baptism. Bro Harrod to cite Sears'
daughter to attend Whitely in April.

ii. September 4, 1792, Met at Whitely. Bros Corbly, Crosley,
Harrod, Jonathan Morris, Jones, William Brown Jr and
Fordyce appt'd messengers to ass'n at George Creek. Bro
Corbly to write letter.

iii. August 22, 1807. The Church met according to
appointment after addressing the throne of grace proceeded
to business. A letter prepared by Brother Hersey to our next
Association was read and approved. Brother Hersey, Abner
Mundle, Levi Harrod, Justus Garard, and William Brown Jr
were appointed Messengers to Association.

Thomas Kent migrated to the Ten Mile County in 1774 and got a warrant
for a tract of land adjoining Thomas Slater's farm which he patented
under the name of Fogaronian. It was situated where West Waynesburg
now stands. He sold part of Fogaronian on February 12, 1791, to Mary
Brown, widow of William Brown Sr, and on the following May he sold
the rest of Fogaronian to James Seal. The transactions were recorded in
the Washington County Deed Books 1-1-92 and 533.[5]

In June 1811 William Brown Jr bought 151 acres in Greene County
that he named Brown's Valley. He had it surveyed in 1811 and patented
to himself in 1812.[6]

[1] http://wc.rootsweb.ancestry.com/cgi-bin/igm.cgi?op=GET&db=bcoll30038&id
=I1050.

[2] Pennsylvania Archives, Series 3, Volume XXIII/ Rangers on the Frontiers,
1778 to 1783 (Flying Camp).

[3] *Portrait and Biographical Album of Stephenson County, Ill.*(Chapman
Brothers, Chicago, 1888. Rpt General Books LLC, Bel Air, CA 2010).

[4] Corbly, Don. *Pastor John Corbly.* (Lulu Press, Raleigh, NC, 2008) Appendix
F, page 273.

[5] Leckey, Howard. *Tenmile Country and its Pioneer Families.* Rpt, (Closson
Press, Apollo, PA. 2007) 424.

[6] Pennsylvania Archives, Series 3, Volume XXVI, page 40. Warrantees of Land
in the County of Greene, 1795.

JOHN JONES

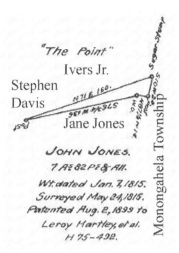

As early as 1733 in Potomac Hundred, Prince George's County, Maryland, John Jones, Robert and William Inghram, John Jackson, John Smith, William Williams, William Brown, and John Gray were among the taxables.[1]

The family of John Jones (1726-1816), (son of the John Jones of Potomac Hundred, but was not given the name John Jr), was found in his Will wherein he named his second wife Hannah Wood (1752-1823) and his children: Cassandra, Mary, Sarah, Elizabeth, Martha, Susannah, Thomas Jr (son of Thomas, deceased), John Jr, Samuel, and Nancy. The first six girls each inherited a tract of 400 acres on Middle Island Creek, Tyler County, West Virginia. Thomas Jr was bequeathed a tract of land called Beach Bottom in Brooke County, Virginia. John Jr received an adjoining tract there. Samuel and Nancy received land in Morgan Township, Greene County, Pennsylvania.

John Jones (1726-1816) signed a petition which was sent to the Assembly of Maryland in 1751 asking for the formation of a new county to be erected out of Frederick and Prince George's Counties. The same session of the Assembly received a petition from Nicholas and Greenberry Ridgely (John's father-in-law from his first marriage) of Maryland to have an entail (a settlement of inherited property so that it remains within a family) removed from tracts of land in Prince George's County known as Lakin's Forest and Ridgely's Addition.[2]

John Jones was listed in the 1773 Assessment Roll for Springhill Township, Bedford County, Pennsylvania. He was paid £2.14s. for furnishing provisions to the Bedford County Militia under the Law of Virginia in the 32d year of the reign of George II of England.[3] In that year he was found among the settlers in Fayette County and contiguous parts of what became Westmoreland, Washington, and Greene Counties according to the Assessment Rolls of Bedford County for 1773.[4] By 1774 he had left Bedford County and bought land on the Ten Mile Creek in Washington County from John Simpson, the original improver.[5]

A husbandman (farmer), he entered the Revolutionary War as a Private 4th Class in Captain William Fife's Company in the Washington County Militia in 1775.[6] He became an Ensign in Captain Singleton's 15th Company of the Second Battalion of Pennsylvania troops under Colonel Burd in 1775-1776 according to Walkinshaw.[7] He also served in Stockley's Rangers in Washington County from 1778 to 1783.

In the 1781 Effective Supply Tax Book for Cumberland Township, Washington County, he was assessed for 50 acres of land, two horses, and two cattle for a total value of $45.

As a Third Sergeant, John Jones served in Captain Thomas Parkeson's Company of Colonel Thomas Crooke's Battalion of Washington County Militia in October 1781. Later in October 1781, Private 7th Class John Jones served in Captain Crawford's Company of Washington County Militia in the district lying upon the Monongalia River between Whiteley and Muddy Creeks. Crawford's company was recruited from men living in the vicinity of Carmichael Town, Washington County. He also served as a Private 5th Class in Captain James Archer's Company in the First Battalion of Washington County Militia when they rendezvoused at Jackson's Fort on May 17, 1782. Private 6th Class John Jones served in Captain Zadok Wright's Company in the Washington County Militia when it was ordered to rendezvous on June 14 and again on September 15, 1782.

He signed the petition for the formation of the new state of Westsylvania about 1782. He was listed in the 1784 and 1788 Assessment Rolls for Cumberland Township, Washington County, Pennsylvania. He was on the 1788 Assessment Roll for Franklin Township, Washington County, Pennsylvania.[8]

On February 13, 1786, John Jones sold to Paul Reed 400 acres along Peter's Creek (which extended 50 miles from Nottingham Township, Washington County, to the Monongahela River at Clairton in Allegheny County). On September 17, 1789, he bought 400 acres on Peter's Creek.

John Jones was one of the earlier settlers in the Ten Mile Country, having arrived there by 1772. He was twice married with no record found of his first wife,...Ridgely, a daughter of Greenberry Ridgely of Maryland. It is not certain that she was the mother of any of the children named in his Will. His second wife was Hannah Wood (1752-1823), widow of Kent Mitchell (-1786). She first married about 1764 to Kent Mitchell who died leaving a number of minor children for whom guardians were appointed as recorded in the Washington County Orphan Docket 1, pages 22-28, February 1786. After the death of Kent Mitchell, Hannah married John Jones and settled near Jackson's Fort on Whiteley Creek.

William Rhodes, a merchant, kept accounts from 1789 to 1794 which included the names of the people who traded with him at Jackson's Fort. During that period John Jones bought goods there which cost £1.1s.[9] About 1790 Richard Jackson, the owner of the land containing Fort Jackson, sold the land to John Jones and moved to Kentucky. In 1799 Captain James Hook bought a tract of land on Richard Jackson' Run known as Sharp's Delight which adjoined land owned by John Jones in present day Franklin Township, Greene County, Pennsylvania.[10]

On April 6, 1794, John Jones received 200 acres of Donation Land for his service in the First Pennsylvania Regiment during the Revolutionary War. There was no record that he applied for, or received, a pension. He was listed in the Warrantees of Land, Greene County, 1795-1894, as owning 10 acres of land which was surveyed on January 7, 1815.[11] It was situated about four miles northeast of Uniontown, Fayette County, Pennsylvania.

He was on the List of Voters residing in Greene Township, Greene County, who voted at the annual election held at the house of John Burley on October 13, 1801. In 1806 John Jones and Hannah were living on the land they had purchased from Richard Jackson. They sold a part of it (154 perches) to the Trustees of the Methodist Episcopal Church who recorded the transaction in the Greene County Deed Book 2, page 197 and later built a church on the property.

On January 7, 1815, John Jones bought seven acres called The Point in Greene County. It was surveyed on May 24, 1815, patented on August 2, 1899, to Leroy Hartley and recorded in the Greene County Patent Book H7a5, page 432.

His Will was filed in the Greene County Will Book 1, page 177 and was probated May 7, 1816. [12]

Soon after his death in 1816, the Jones Town post office in Fallow-field Township, Washington County, Pennsylvania, was named in his honor. He died there at the age of ninety years.

---

[1] Leckey, Howard. *Tenmile Country and its Pioneer Families.* Rpt, (Closson Press, Apollo, PA. 2007) 311.

250

[2] Leckey, 384.

[3] http://vagenweb.org/hening/vol07-10.htm.

[4] Veech, James. *The Monongahela Of Old: Or Historical Sketches Of Southwestern Pennsylvania To The Year 1800.* 1910, Rpt. (Kessinger PubliShinng, LLC, Whitefish, MT, 2008).

[5] Leckey, 450.

[6] Pennsylvania Archives, Associators & Militia, Muster Rolls, 1775-1781. Series 2, Volume XIV, pages 729-752.

[7] Walkinshaw, Lewis Clark. *Annals of southwestern Pennsylvania,* (Lewis Historical Pub. Co, NY, 1939).

[8] Leckey, 132, 133, 136.

[9] Leckey, 382.

[10] Leckey, 333.

[11] Pennsylvania Archives, Series 3, Volume XXVI.

[12] Leckey, 338, 339.

JOHN JOHNSON SR

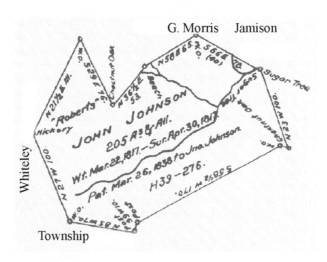

In 1765 on the Great Cacapon River, Hampshire County, Virginia, one of John and Abigail Corbly's closest neighbors was John Johnson Sr (1753-after1833).[1] John Johnson Sr followed the migrant trains westward and settled his family at Muddy Creek in Washington County. Since his name followed that of Nicholas Johnson in the 1790 Census, it is likely that they were brothers. The 1790 census for John Johnson Sr showed there were six males less than 16 years of age in his household.

One of Nicholas Johnson's sons was John; another was Nicholas Jr who was born in Philadelphia and settled in Blackville, Wayne Township, Greene County, as a young man and lived there until his death in 1890. He married Margaret Minor, a granddaughter of Samuel Minor.[2]

John Johnson Sr (1753-after1833) was a private in the Second Battalion, Pennsylvania Rifle Regiment on August 21, 1776, when he was imprisoned for three nights for deserting and selling gun supplies which appeared to have been stolen. In 1777 he enlisted as a Private in Captain James Hook's Calico Hunting Shirt Company which assembled at Fort Redstone and marched to Maryland to join Colonel Morgan's Rifle Company. After they had marched 80 miles an express came to them and part of the Company returned under orders from General Broadhead to relieve the garrison at Wheeling. He was a Private in the Cumberland County Rangers on the Frontier during the years 1778 to 1783.[3]

John Johnson Sr sat with a jury in the case of Crow v. Dye in West Elizabeth, Yohogania County, on March 29, 1780. The court was first held at Augusta Town, present day Washington, and afterwards on the Andrew Heath farm near West Elizabeth during 1776 to1780.[4]

In the 1781 Effective Supply Tax Roll for Hopewell Township, Washington County, John Johnson's assessment was for 200 acres of land, four horses, two cattle, and four sheep, a total of $112.[5]

About 1782 John Johnson Sr signed the petition for a new state to be formed out of present Fayette, Washington, and Greene Counties of Pennsylvania, and Ohio and Monongalia Counties of Virginia.[6]

In the 1797 Greene County Tax Book made by Joseph Willford, Assessor, assisted by Elias Stone and Stephen Gapen, John Johnson was assessed for 100 acres of land at $20, one cabin at $1, and one horse at $10. The next year he was assessed for 100 acres of land at $20, one cabin at $1, and two cows at $12.

On June 27, 1807, the Goshen Baptist Church "met after singing and prayer by Bro Hersey and proceeded to business. Bro Crawford to call on Bro VanMetre, Bro Mundle on Sister Myers, and Sister Corbly call on Sister Write, Bro Hill call on Bro Johnson."

The patriotic citizens of Washington County diligently kept up their military organizations. A subscription of the citizens to equip a company of volunteers to meet the enemy was organized. "We, the subscribers, do promise to pay the sums annexed to our respective names for the purpose of equipping such of the volunteers now about to march on a tour of duty as are unprepared for the expedition. Witness our hands at Washington, October 31st, 1814." John Johnson Sr subscribed $5.[7]

On a March 22, 1817, land warrant John Johnson bought 205 acres in Greene County called Roberts. It was surveyed on April 30, 1817, patented on March 26, 1833, and recorded in the Greene County Patent Book H39, page 276.

John Johnson, a Private in the Virginia Continental Line during the Revolutionary War, received 200 acres of Donation Land. On March 16, 1833, at age 80, he was placed on the pension roll for $80 per year.[8]

[1] Corbly, Don. *Pastor John Corbly.* (Lulu Press, Raleigh, NC, 2008) 57.

[2] Wiley, Samuel B. *History of Monongalia County, West Virginia, from its First Settlements to the Present Time; With Numerous Biographical and Family Sketches.* (Preston Printing Co., Kingwood, WV. 1883).

[3] Leckey, Howard. *Tenmile Country and its Pioneer Families.* Rpt, (Closson Press, Apollo, PA. 2007) 19.

[4] Crumrine, Boyd. *Minute book of the Virginia Court held for Yohogania County, Virginia. County Court (Yohogania), 1838-1916.*

[5] http://files.usgwarchives.net/pa/fayette/history/local/earlysett01.txt.

[6] Continental Congress papers, No. 48, Folios 251-256, pages 89-96.

[7] Creigh, Alfred. *History of Washington County from its First Settlement to the Present Time.* (Nabu Press, Charleston, SC, 2010) 233.

[8] Pennsylvania Archives, Revolutionary War, Pensioners, 1835, Greene County, Pennsylvania.

BENJAMIN SOUTH

Joseph South (abt 1733-abt 1812), son of Thomas South and Dorothy Lippington, was born and died in Middlesex County, New Jersey. Joseph married Sarah Gilpin. One of their sons, Benjamin (1758-1839), was born in Windsor Township, Middlesex County, New Jersey, and married in 1778 in New Jersey to Elizabeth Slack (1755-1848), daughter of Benjamin and Rebecca (Shooley) Slack. Benjamin (1758-1839) was buried in the South Cemetery in Green County, Pennsylvania.[1] Two of their daughters married into the Minor family in Greene County.

i. Sarah Elizabeth (1779-) married Noah Minor (1781-1865), son of Captain William Minor and Ellen Phillips. After the death of Sarah, Noah Minor married Miss Minks.

ii. Rebecca (1783-1876) married) Otho Minor (1776 1831). They are buried near Greensboro, near his father and mother.

iii. Enoch (1787-1863), born in New Jersey, was their only son. He married Ruth Gregg. Their children: Delilah married John F. Gans; Elizabeth married Abner Bailey and died in Greene County, Pennsylvania, leaving five children; Ruth married William Knotts and died in Greene county leaving four children; Sarah married Abijah South and moved to Green County, Wisconsin; Melinda married William Britton and died in Brownsville, Pennsylvania; Maria died of a fall from her horse at the age of 16; Rebecca married Evan Evans and died in Greene County, Pennsylvania; John died in Greene County, Pennsylvania; Benjamin died in Greene County, Pennsylvania, on the homestead settled by his grandfather. Enoch was buried in the South Cemetery.

In the Greene County Tax Book made in 1797 by Joseph Willford, Assessor, assisted by Elias Stone and Stephen Gapen, Benjamin South was assessed for 80 acres of land at $100, 30 acres of cleared land at $30, one cabin at $1, one barn at $2, two horses at $20, and two cows at $12. Two years later he was assessed for 88 acres of land at $70, 30 acres of cleared land at $30, one cabin at $1, one horse at $15, and three cows at $18.

He was included in the List of voters of Greene Township who voted at the house of John Campbell on October 14, 1806.[2]

In 1816 Benjamin South was the postmaster at Canonsburg, Washington County, Pennsylvania.[2]

Benjamin South had 110 acres of land in Greene County surveyed on November 14, 1817.[3] He bought 106 acres called Gapen's Neglect on a warrant dated November 14, 1817. It was surveyed on October 15, 1819, patented on January 28, 1824, and recorded in the Greene County Patent Book H21, page 297.

Benjamin's Declaration when he applied for a pension for service during the Revolutionary War contained the following:[5]

While residing in Windsor TWP, he served as a Private in the NJ Militia. From 1776 he served one month in Capt Barr's Co., Col Soudder's Reg't; one month in Capt Comb's Co.;

two months in Capt Schenck's Co, Col Neilson's Reg't, and was in an engagement on Staten Island for one month; one month in Capt Stout's Co; one month under General Dickinson and one month in Capt James' CO. His application for pension was executed Aug 27, 1832, while a resident of Greene TWP, Greene CO., PA. He married 1778 in Middlesex Co., NJ, Elizabeth Slack who was born Jun 4, 1755. He died May 2, 1839, in Dunkard TWP, Greene CO., PA, and she died there Apr 3, 1846.

Winfield Scott, Commissioner, War Department, Claims during Revolutionary War. IAW law of the US of Jun 7, 1832, Benjamin South who was a soldier in the Army of the Revolution, is entitled to receive $30 per annum during his natural life commencing on Mar 4, 1831 and payable semi-annually on Mar 4 and Sep 4 of each year. Given at the War Office Mar 23, 1833. (No records indicate that his widow filed a claim for his pension.)

Benjamin South's Will was recorded in the Greene County Will Book 2, page 106. It was proved on May 12, 1800. In it he stated he had another plantation in Nottingham which was where his brother, Zedekiah South, was living before he went to New York about 1786. Benjamin's Will was witnessed by James McCabe who was the father of the wives of both Zedekiah and Lippington South. Benjamin's Will states so much was to be given to each of his five children and was stated in such a manner as to indicate that he had previously given moneys to other of his children not mentioned in his Will.

[1] Leckey, Howard. *Tenmile Country and its Pioneer Families.* Rpt, (Closson Press, Apollo, PA. 2007) 662.
[2] http://www.cornerstonegenealogy.com/greene_county_voter_lists_1801.htm
[3] Crumrine, Boyd. *History of Washington County, Pennsylvania with Biographical Sketches of Many of Its Pioneers and Prominent Men*, (L. H. Leverts & Co., Philadelphia, 1882) 601.
[4] Pennsylvania Archives, Series 3, Volume XXVI, 1795-1894.
[5] Pennsylvania Archives, Revolutionary War, Pension Roll Claim R. 993

JEREMIAH GALLATIN JR

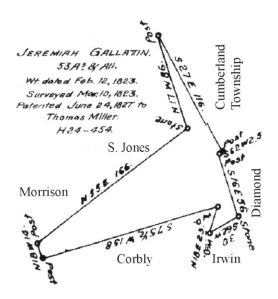

Abraham Gallatin (1762-1836) was born in Bethyl, Lebanon County, Pennsylvania, and died in Houston, Harris County, Texas. He married Eliza Thompson (1785-) about 1808. One of their sons was Jeremiah Sr who married Jerusha Boyce (1790-1859).[1] Jeremiah Sr and Jerusha Boyce's son, Jeremiah Gallatin Jr (1797-1866), was born in Greene County, Pennsylvania, and died in Springhill, Livingston County, Missouri. In 1846 he married (1) Tabitha Winfrey (1829-1863). They had at least eight children including:

  i.   Jerusha Ann (1823-1846) who married William Marquis (1822-1889).
  ii. Francena (1825-) who married ... Wiley. According to her obituary she was born in Waynesburg, Green County, Pennsylvania. The obit also stated that their family moved to Guernsey County, Ohio.
  iii. Oliver.
  iv. Jeremiah Craig (1850-1934) who married Martha Jane Brittany.
  v.   Delockly (1855-1881) who married William Henry.
  vi. Barnes (1852-1895). Jeremiah Jr next married (2) Susan Todd on March 22, 1864.

The three sons of Jeremiah and Jerusha Boyce, Francis B., Albert, and Jeremiah Jr purchased land jointly in Morgan County, Ohio, in April 1840. The next month Jeremiah and Jerusha also purchased a tract of land there. In 1843 Jeremiah and Jerusha split their property and sold half to Francis B. and Jeremiah Jr and half to Jerusha Ann and Francena. In 1845 Francis B. sold his part of the land back to his mother, Jerusha. Francena Gallatin Wiley visited her father in Missouri shortly before his death and took a grandson, John Quincy Adams Gallatin, back to Ohio to raise.[2]

Jeremiah Gallatin Jr bought 53 acres in Greene Township, Greene County, Pennsylvania. The warrant was dated February 12, 1823. It was surveyed on March 10, 1823, patented on June 24, 1827, to Thomas Miller, and recorded in the Greene County Patent Book H24, page 454. He also bought an additional ten acres of land in Greene County and had it surveyed on February 12, 1823.[3]

Patent #3052 was granted on April 15, 1843, to Jeremiah Gallatin, Manchester Township, Morgan County, Ohio, for an improvement in plows, but no improved plows were produced.[4]

Jeremiah Jr and Tabitha Winfrey Gallatin were listed in the 1860 Census of Livingston County, Missouri, as family #228.

[1] Crumrine, Boyd. *History of Washington County, Pennsylvania with Biographical Sketches of Many of Its Pioneers and Prominent Men*, (L. H. Leverts & Co., Philadelphia: 1882).
[2] Evans, Lydia Gallatin. *The descendants of Jeremiah Gallatin and Tabitha Winfrey Gallatin, 1850-1980, 1901,* (L. G. Evans Chillicothe, Missouri, 1980).
[3] Pennsylvania Archives, Series 3, Volume XXVI, Warrantees of Land In the County of Greene 1795-1894.
[4] http://www.datamp.org/patents/search/advance.php?pn=3052&id=39725&set=1.

Nancy Ann Lynn Corbly died in 1826. She was buried next to her husband, John Corbly, in the Garard's Fort Cemetery. Her plot was on the south side of John; Betsey's plot was on the north side of John.

Corbly Memorial Baptist Church

Site of massacre

Garard Fort cemetery

Corbly home one mile north in the Big Whiteley Creek Valley.

INDEX

,

Made in the USA
Middletown, DE
16 December 2014